# THE EXTRACTIVE ZONE

**DISSIDENT ACTS**

*A series edited by Macarena Gómez-Barris and Diana Taylor*

# THE EXTRACTIVE
# ZONE

—

*Social Ecologies and*
*Decolonial Perspectives*

## MACARENA GÓMEZ-BARRIS

—

DUKE UNIVERSITY PRESS
*Durham and London*
2017

© 2017 Duke University Press
All rights reserved
Printed in the United States of America on acid-free paper ∞
Designed by Amy Ruth Buchanan
Typeset in Minion Pro by Tseng Information Systems, Inc.

Library of Congress Cataloging-in-Publication Data
Names: Gómez-Barris, Macarena, [date] author.
Title: The extractive zone : social ecologies and decolonial
perspectives / Macarena Gómez-Barris.
Description: Durham : Duke University Press, 2017. | Series:
Dissident acts | Includes bibliographical references and index.
Identifiers: LCCN 2017016488 (print)
LCCN 2017022944 (ebook)
ISBN 9780822372561 (ebook)
ISBN 9780822368755 (hardcover : alk. paper)
ISBN 9780822368977 (pbk. : alk. paper)
Subjects: LCSH: South America—Civilization—21st century. |
Imperialism. | Postcolonialism—South America. | Economic
development—Environmental Aspects—South America. | Human
ecology—South America. | Indians of South America.
Classification: LCC F2210 (ebook) | LCC F2210 .G66 2017 (print) |
DDC 980.04—dc23
LC record available at https://lccn.loc.gov/2017016488

Cover art: Carolina Caycedo, *Yuma Estancada* (detail), 2015.
Courtesy of the artist.

A MÍ MAMA, VIVIANNE RENEE DUFOUR,

QUE ME HA DADO TANTO.

# CONTENTS

ACKNOWLEDGMENTS ix

PREFACE
Below the Surface xiii

INTRODUCTION
Submerged Perspectives 1

**1** The Intangibility of the Yasuní 17

**2** Andean Phenomenology
and New Age Settler Colonialism 39

**3** An Archive for the Future:
Seeing through Occupation 66

**4** A Fish-Eye Episteme:
Seeing Below the River's Colonization 91

**5** Decolonial Gestures:
Anarcho-Feminist Indigenous Critique 110

CONCLUSION
The View from Below 133

NOTES 139

BIBLIOGRAPHY 165

INDEX 179

## ACKNOWLEDGMENTS

This project has been shaped by the many conversations and experiences I have had over the past several years. My view has been altered by my fortunate engagement with the Américas peoples and geographies I write about, but also by dialoguing with scholars, artists, and activists in Beirut, Europe, and South Africa. This work considers how to think comparatively, and about the important, if vexed, role of site work, perspective, and experience in decolonial knowledge production. It is also about how to survive and make anew within zones of extractive capitalism.

My research has developed in sustained dialogue with the Indigenous and Decolonization Research Cluster (IDRC) at University of Southern California, a group of faculty members and graduate students whom I have worked with through the Department of American Studies and Ethnicity since 2011. These include Crystal Baik, Jih-Fei Cheng, Athia Choudhury, Rebekah Fong, Sarah Fong, Rebekah Garrison, Floridalma Boj Lopez, Ho'esta Mo'hahne, Chris Finley, John Carlos Rowe, and Alex Young. In the IDRC, we formed critical bonds and intellectual affinities that I am grateful for. I also want to thank my graduate student seminar on social and cultural theory in fall 2016 for wonderful conversations, including Sarah Fong, Rebekah Park, Nicole Richards, Emmett Drager, Alexis Montes, Cristina Faiver, Athia Choudhury, Daniel Alonso, Sophia Serrano, Huan Hsing, Racquel Bernard, and Rosanne Sia. I want to especially thank Crystal Baik and Sophia Li for research and image support.

I have valued the friendship and example of so many, including Emma Pérez, Nicole Hayward, Paul Amar, Jose Quiroga, Jody Vallejo, Mel Chen, Julia Bryan Wilson, Kara Keeling, Gil Hochberg, Keri Kanetsky, Maria Elena Martinez, Ira Livingston, Iona Man-Cheong, Gabriela Fischer, Sarah Gualtieri, Licia Fiol-Matta, Lena Burgos-Lafuente, Neetu Khanna, Ana Paulina Lee, Ondine Chavoya, Joseph Pierce, Josh Kun, Ceci Bastida, Chandan Reddy, Lisa Lowe, Gayatri Gopinath, Rod Ferguson, Juan de Lara,

Wendy Chen, Michelle Rahejas, Sarita See, Kandice Chuh, Jodi Byrd, Jill Lane, Josie Saldaña-Portillo, Dean Saranillo, Mike Messner, Lanita Jacobs, Leland Saito, Shana Redmond, Chris Finley, Judith Jackson Fossett, Edwin Hill, Manuel Pastor, Ruthie Gilmore, George Sanchez, Fred Moten, Laura Harris, Jane Iwamura, Janelle Wong, Ricardo Ramirez, Lupe Ramirez, Roberto Lint-Sagrena, Alexandra and Jason Marchetsky, Policarpo Chaj, Sarah Banet-Weiser, Dorinne Kondo, Mishuana Goeman, Panivong Norinder, Viet Nguyen.

New colleagues at Pratt Institute and the Department of Social Science and Cultural Studies have generously welcomed me. Andrew Barnes has been an exceptional mentor and friend. Sincere Brooks and Sophia Babb make daily life better. Thank you Eric Godoy, Maya Seetharam, Zhivka Valiavicharska, Francis Bradley, Lisabeth During, Ann Holder, Uzma Rizvi, Liz Knauer, Caitlin Cahill, May Joseph, Carl Zimring, Sameetah Agha, Luka Lucic, Jennifer Telesca, Iván Zatz-Diaz, Ric Brown, Kumru Toktamis, Josiah Brownell, Darini Nicholas, Jennifer Pipitone, Svetlana Jovic, Hannes Charen, Kathleen Campbell Kelley, Michelle Standley, Jonathan Beller, Rachel Levitsky, Ellery Washington and so many others. My co-teacher Erum Naqui for "The Art of Protest" has been an invaluable resource and dedicated colleague during troubled times. I have treasured conversations amongst colleagues at our newly formed Global South Center.

Special thanks to friends and allies John Carlos Rowe, Avery Gordon, Lisa Duggan, Pierrette Hondagneu-Sotelo, Herman Gray, Rosa Linda Fregoso, David Lloyd, Marcial Godoy-Anativia, Nayan Shah, Jayna Brown, Amelia Jones, Sonia Rodriguez, Kitty Lai, Jujuana Preston, and Tim Biblarz for supporting my intellectual and personal growth from the incipient idea to the publication of this project. Cathy Davidson has many superpowers, and I am grateful she has shared them with me. Laura Pulido has been an extraordinary friend, mentor, sister, and ally. Nicole Hayward traveled with me to Bolivia during an intense and memorable research experience.

At Duke University Press, Ken Wissoker has been unwavering in his support and mentorship, and has expertly guided me. Sara Leone went far beyond the call of duty. Maryam Arain and Olivia Polk were invaluable comrades at key stages toward completion. I would also like to give much appreciation to J. Kēhaulani Kauanui and Nelson Maldonado-Torres for carefully reading the manuscript, and for superb suggestions that deepened my approach to the extractive zone, though I fully accept responsibilities for any errors. Thank you also to Diana Taylor as my co-editor of "Dissident Acts."

A group of brilliant scholars and friends sustained me intellectually during a period of intense writing and research in Ecuador in 2015, including Diana Coryat, Amanda Concha, Christian León, Claudia Sophia Garrigas Lopez, Maria Amelia Viteri, and Santiago Castellanos. Funding for the site-based research parts of this volume came from the Fulbright Research Fellowship, Facultad Latinoamericanos Ciencias Sociales, FLACSO-Ecuador, Department of Sociology and Gender Studies. Susana Wappenstein and Sara Hidalgo were especially supportive, and I thank all of the participants of a workshop and lecture there. David Harvey's think tank CENECET provided an additional forum for parts of this book. I presented an early chapter at the University of Zurich, and I thank Jens Anderson and the memory studies scholars for their engagement with it. I want to also thank the Radical Americas group at the University College London, where discussion on feminist anarchist history in the Global South helped me sharpen chapter 5. I also appreciate the insights from discussions with a group of scholars at American University in Beirut on the concept of decolonial gesture, including Anjali Nath, Manu Vimalassery, Kency Cornejo, Kuan-Hsing Chen, Anaheed Al-Hardan, Samhita Sunya, Adam Waterman, and Samer Frangie. Chapter 2 owes much to conversations with Juana and Francisco that helped me perceive anew. This project would not have understood perception otherwise if not for the future oriented vision, grounded artistic production, and friendship of Francisco Huichaqueo Perez and Carolina Caycedo. Thanks also goes to the University of Arizona Institute for LGBT Studies, and especially Adela Licona for hosting me for the Miranda Joseph Endowed Lecture precisely as new extractivisms have led to greater forms of intersectional pressure and oppression, but also to intense and hope filled activisms. Paul Amar and Jesilyn Faust's invitation to keynote on the "Rise of the Global Right" at the University of California, Santa Barbara came at the end of writing this book and allowed me to fine tune its concepts. I have been honored to share work at the University of Redmond with the Latino and Latin American Studies faculty and especially thank Mariela Mendez de Coudriet for hosting me. Thank you also to Chandan Reddy and Sebastian López Vergara for influencing this project through sustained dialogue at the University of Washington.

My mother, Vivianne Renee Dufour, is an incredible gift, interlocuter, and closest friend. Thank you, mamá, for all your generosity and love. As a single immigrant mother raising Lorena and me in the belly of the beast you displayed utter grace and dignity. I am truly honored to dedicate this book to you. To my honorary step-father Arnold Bauer, may you rest in peace. You gave me so much at a crucial time. Thank you to my sister, in human form and spirit, Lorena Gómez-Barris for your unwavering witness to the ebbs and flow of academic life. You make it all seem possible. Thank you too, Eric and Ethan Rocher and Roberto Leni for your solid support. Ixchel and Renato, you are amazing, flexible, and patient, especially while we were in Quito. I sincerely hope that the hours clocked on Minecraft will somehow be outweighed by the time we spent together in the biosphere. Thank you to the incredible generosity and inspired fox that is my lovely partner, Jack Halberstam — a model of public intellectual work and political commitment. Finally, gracias pachita mamita. Sín tí no hay vida.

*Below the Surface*

Through a fortuitous set of events about ten years ago, I spent a semester at the Marin Headlands Center for the Arts in California. I met May Stevens there, a socialist and landscape painter important within the 1960s American experimental movement, and someone I can only describe as a visual poet. In the decade before I met her, May made a series of blue-green oil paintings whose subject matter focused on the rivers and lakes of North America. *The Confluence of Two Rivers* (2002–3) depicts the merger of dark matter into gooey flows, cracked open by threads of earth. During her three-week residency at the Headlands, May painted the Pacific Ocean, swirling silvery words into the contoured waves on the canvas. Though this book is not about Northern California per se, and instead focuses on South America and how we perceive its social ecologies, artists such as May have allowed me to better see what lies below the surface of liquid, beyond normative modes of apprehending landscape, and toward a perception of the complexity within smaller scales of being and imagining.

As we walked together in the nearby hills, May turned to me, unprompted, and offered something I still ponder regarding the realm of perception. She had recently visited Sausalito and had found herself lingering over the yellowish green-brown muck that gathered within the ocean at the wooden base of the city's piers. For her, the biomatter that accumulated around the piers represented the "origin stuff" of creativity. This primal mix demanded a different form of attention and care, one that blends the way that each of us perceive ourselves with how we perceive the natural world, a cognitive and embodied mode of seeing. Incorporating that muck's color palette in her art led her back to what she called her original creative impulse, forcing her to reckon with a viewpoint that came from within—rather than from above, in relation to, or near—the thick water, and from within that "origin stuff." May referred to this as her "caca" story of creative origins.

Since that walk with May, I have thought a lot about a submerged viewpoint, about ways to see what lies within the ecologies all around us, and about how to perceive those things that are not usually available to the naked eye. After our conversation, I turned my attention to microbe worlds, to imagine the tadpoles and the amoebas that have swum within murky waters for millennia, to ponder what it means to see from below, to become mindful of what Maurice Merleau-Ponty refers to as "the space of vision that both surrounds us and passes through us."[1] Through subsequent walks and conversations, May continued to impart the importance of perceiving the natural elements as a source of unfolding—to expand perception by looking at the water, at muck, and at the submerged environment around me, the intermixing of caca as glistening life within the grasp of perception.

Recently, inspired muck came up again, this time in a conversation with Mapuche filmmaker Francisco Huichaqueo whose experimental films about the Chilean monocultural forest plantations I explore in chapter 3. Through spending time with Huichaqueo, another visual and sensual thinker, I began to understand his modes of perceiving, particularly in terms of seeing to the other side of colonial occupation. Mapuche peoples, he told me, place great importance on the dream world, including exchanging their content with each other each morning. Over the previous decade his own objective had been to embed his art with that long-standing practice, an effort to see within and beyond the world of materiality to the parallel dream world of ancestors. This is the realm that the Mapundungun language describes as the *perrimunton*. Francisco has intimated how, as a director of experimental films that visually communicate other ways of seeing and sensing the world, he plays with perception by dipping his camera below the water's surface, documenting the submerged worlds of Southern Chile's rivers as they wind through Mapuche territories, making visible air bubbles, bits of wood, and the greenish-brown moss of the riverbank's floor. Like the dreamscape he travels through to blend old and new viewpoints, his camera views the liquid planet in microform.

Such tangible artistic efforts to shift how we see, specifically by reckoning with the thick opacity of what lies below the water's surface, have been essential to crafting this book and its decolonial methodology.[2] In my research across five regions within South America, these artists have prodded

Francisco Huichaqueo, *Kalül Trawün—Reunión del Cuerpo*, video
still, 2012. Image courtesy of Francisco Huichaqueo.

me to see differently and to question what lies beneath the visible world of
*the extractive zone* and to seek out less perceivable worlds, life forms, and
the organization of relations within them, while creating new methods that
allow for this tracking.

My objective in *The Extractive Zone* is to document geographies where
coordinated forms of capitalist power advance, while also analyzing the
complexity of social ecologies and material alternatives proposed and proliferated by artists, activists, movements, submerged theorists, and cultural
producers. Second, I explicitly challenge the frames of disciplinary knowledge that would bury the subtlety and complexity of the life force of the
worlds that lie within the extractive zone. I address the importance of epistemological autonomy and embodied knowledge as necessary to pushing
away from a paradigm of mere resistance into the more layered terrain of
potential, moving within and beyond the extractive zone. Through detailed

studies of local spaces, Indigenous worlds, and natural ecologies in peril, I work to better conceptualize histories of conquest and dissent, especially those emergent in South America's resource-rich Indigenous territories.

Throughout this book, I deploy a decolonial femme methodology, or a mode of porous and undisciplined analysis shaped by the perspectives and critical genealogies that emerge within these spaces as a mode of doing research. My engagement with Andean phenomenology and the intersectionality of Indigenous anarcho-feminist critique, as queer decolonial options that lead us out of the deadening impasse that is extractive capitalism, is not bound to the disciplinary drive to claim or master the images or formations I study.[3] These submerged perspectives are anchored within social ecologies that reorganize and refute the monocultural imperative, as do I in my encounter with these other worlds. Submerged modes flurry in their activity, random, complex, and coordinated systems that are often illegible to those with state and financial power that assume simplicity where complexity actually dwells.

Here, I must explain how concept work allows me to simultaneously attend to the life-and-death dialectics that are operative within these geographies: by using the term *extractive zone* I refer to the colonial paradigm, worldview, and technologies that mark out regions of "high biodiversity" in order to reduce life to capitalist resource conversion. My book examines social ecologies, or networked potential, within the extractive global economy, the system that was installed by colonial capitalism in the 1500s and that converted natural resources such as silver, water, timber, rubber, and petroleum into global commodities. In its longue durée, extractivism references colonial capitalism and its afterlives: extending from its sixteenth-century emergence until the present day, and including the recent forty-year neoliberal privatization and deregulation process, as well as the rise and fall of the progressive states called the Pink Tide in Latin American nations.[4] This also refers to the global intensification of new forms of extractivism, or what Saskia Sassen describes as the expulsion by advanced political economies which accumulates wealth off of resource rich territories for a few, while permanently squeezing the many.[5]

In other words, we might think of a successive march of colonial and neocolonial actors operating in relation to South America as if it were an extractible continent; Uruguayan writer Eduardo Galeano long ago named this process "the open veins of Latin America," as these territories continue to provide sustenance for the global economy.[6]

*Extractivismo*, as extractive capitalism is known in the Américas, indicates an economic system that engages in thefts, borrowings, and forced removals, violently reorganizing social life as well as the land by thieving resources from Indigenous and Afro-descendent territories. As I attend to in the introduction, a burgeoning literature on *extractivismo* has emerged in South America that describes the claim to resources by global capital in the face of increased protests about the importance of local resource sovereignty. Since dense genetic plant life and natural resource regions often overlap with Indigenous territories, then we must work to analyze how Native peoples are both constructed by the state and corporate entities as obstructions to the expansion of extractive capitalism and literally block its reach. The Sioux and trans-confederation struggle contesting the Dakota pipeline is only one example of continual Indigenous land defense in the Américas. Therefore, throughout this book I show how the embodied activities that reject colonialism continue to alter and expand how we see and what we know about Indigenous spaces especially within the extractive zone.

While racial capitalism refers to the processes that historically subordinated African and Indigenous populations, extractivism references the dramatic material change to social and ecological life that underpin this arrangement.[7] Furthermore, the racial logics of South American states are expanded through new forms of extractive capitalism.[8] Even as new progressive states such as those in Ecuador and Bolivia propose policies to legalize Native peoples' rights, they enable and normalize resource exploitation that ends up perpetuating anti-Indigenous and anti-Black racism. Further, as The Feminist Constitution that I examine in chapter five makes apparent, redistributive states that do not broadly consider intersectional histories fail to address the needs and perspectives of female, gender-nonconforming, working class, and "cuir" populations even despite new legislative gains.[9] I address how extractive capitalism dramatically divides nature and culture through new forms of race, gender, and sexual exclusions.[10]

One of today's central modes of perpetuating racial capitalism in the Global South, in addition to expanding prisons and security regimes, is in fact mega-extractive projects, such as large dams and mines, which require huge technological and resource feats as well as what Enrique Dussel refers to as the "developmentalist fallacy," or the imposition of modernity as a universalized mode of governance.[11] State and corporate-designed mega-development projects operate through an economic rationale without calibrating for the life forms that exist beneath the gaze of such grand schemes. Extractivism functions within what Anibal Quijano first coined as the colonial matrix of power,[12] where corporate entities and states are indistinguishable in their economic interests and activities; states act on behalf of corporations, and corporate entities hire security forces to control and suppress anti-extractivist organizing.

Extractive capitalism, then, violently reorganizes territories as well as continually perpetuates dramatic social and economic inequalities that delimit Indigenous sovereignty and national autonomy. As the Uruguayan economist and executive secretary of the Latin American Center for Social Ecology, Eduardo Gudynas, explains, "Under neo-extractivism, the objective of national development, as 'endogenous development,' is lost; autonomy in relation to global markets vanishes. National industries do not recover, in some cases they are reduced."[13] Gudynas rightly identifies how developmentalism continues to set the agenda and structure conditions of South America's place within a colonial world system, further diminishing the possibility of state independence in relation to the global economy. Yet we must also critique the world system that reproduces nationalism at the expense of the sovereignty of Indigenous territories.

Genealogies of critical theories from the South (including dependency theory and decolonial theory) have importantly attended to the persistence of this colonial condition that produces regional asymmetries and an uneven distribution of resource control. My project builds on these insights to unpack a dual analysis of power: I analyze extractive capitalism's techniques of domination, showing how it expands through a series of legal, rhetorical, economic, and political contortions that both draw from and erase Indigenous peoples in their territories. The material and affective production of extractive capitalism crushes vernacular life and its embodiment, enclosing it within the leveling technologies of globalization. In relation to schemes of mega-development, large-scale extractivism assaults peripheral spaces, inflicting uneven pain upon regions where Indigenous majority communities continue to organize life and proliferate it, even in sites of extreme pressure and violence. This book lifts and names these submerged social ecologies. And the "extractive zone" names the violence that capitalism does to reduce, constrain, and convert life into commodities, as well as the epistemological violence of training our academic vision to reduce life to systems.

Nonindigenous scholars have cautioned against "romanticizing native peoples,"[14] however, some of that work does not centrally engage with the current dangers in the reduction of biodiversity and the genocidal practices that Native peoples face. In the case studies that I elaborate upon, all take place in the so-called peripheries of late capitalist activity, and Indigenous peoples are directly affected by neoliberal, economic, and cultural conditions that predetermine these spaces as colonial contact zones.[15] It is often in the heart of resource-rich territories that Indigenous peoples exist in complex tension with extractive capitalism and land defense. In these geographies, Indigenous peoples often multiply rather than reduce life possibilities, protecting land and each other at often extremely high personal and communal cost. For instance, a global map of recent ecocides, or the murder of land defenders, shows an acute rise in Latin America and the Asian Pacific, geographies that overlap with new social movements that organize against extractive encroachment.[16] The organization Global Witness documents a three hundred percent increase in the murders of ordinary people defending natural resources from mining, hydroelectric dams, conservation, and pollution.

Throughout the world, Indigenous peoples are also often at the forefront of defending lands in regions that are continually extracted for their biodiversity.[17] In the Américas, we see the complicity among state, police, and corporate actors in their attempts to violently shut down these land defenders, such as the case of attack dogs and pepper spray used against Indigenous protestors and their allies as they blocked the Dakota oil pipe. In resource-rich Ecuador, anti-extractive activists report that their emails are regularly hacked, that they are followed and intimidated, and, most notably, that the police and military rove Indigenous territories, facilitating the work of national and multinational capitalist enterprises.[18] Lenca activist Berta Cáceres, who was murdered in 2014, founded the Council of Indigenous peoples in part to oppose mega-projects and resource extraction in Honduras.[19]

As critical Indigenous studies have shown, colonial capitalism often expands its control over Native territories by legitimizing the neoliberal multicultural state.[20] And it is here that the exercise of autonomy matters. In each chapter, I ask, how can we differently apprehend not only the experience of and resistance to extractive colonialism, but also its generative capacity to see and activate beyond the colonial divide? As I elaborate, Indigenous territories often overlap with the geographies that constitute the Earth's highest biodiversity, and which extractive capitalism continually earmarks and occupies for commodity conversion, mapped through increasingly fine-tuned technologies.

In zones of continual extractivism, what responses, engagements, and viewpoints emerge that do not exhaust difference but instead proliferate it?[21] How do Native and African-descendent populations have perspectives on the natural world that engage it, rather than just take from it? And, to reach further into the work of decolonization, can feminist and queer interventions pose a challenge to patriarchal logics, monoculture, and extractive capitalism? Can we differently attend to Andean, Amazonian, Native life and the complex of senses never fully subsumed within the European colonial order? What cultural and intellectual production makes us see, hear, and intimate the land differently? What do we really know about the invisible, the inanimate, and the nonhuman forms that creatively reside as afterlives of the colonial encounter?

The map I produce is not connected through linear histories or Eurocentric expeditions, nor do I enter the colonial archive to read alongside it, even while I have learned much from some of these methodologies.[22] Instead, the map I draw is one of Indigenous and Afro-Indigenous spaces across the Andes, Southern Chile, and into the Andean Amazonia as continually occupied, either by colonists, settlers, or multinational corporations, where histories of decolonization arise within the violent condition of extractive capitalism. A disciplinary rationale inevitably fails for all the sites, texts, and geographies that I transverse with epistemological excess. In other words, rather than pursue one disciplinary frame, I engage standpoint and decolonial theory, regional histories, and relational critique to attend to several scenes of extractivism within South America. A decolonial entry into the extractive zone, then, reveals a differently perceivable world, an intangible space of emergence, where rivers converge into the flow and the muck of life otherwise.

# Submerged Perspectives

Let us never forget: that the poem was entombed in a collapse of the
earth. By habit, rather than commodity, the singularity and multiplicity of things were presented as divided couples and dualities,
before the genres and species were discovered. This cadence allowed
for a better distinction between things (we still think and react in this
dual manner, and often take surprising pleasure from it). But we're
also waiting for the renewed perception of differences to reveal themselves as such, and for the poem to reemerge once more.

**Édouard Glissant,** *Poetics of Relation*

*The Extractive Zone* attends to the regions of extractive capitalism by foregrounding submerged perspectives; it also engages the possibility of renewed perception. Throughout, I ask us to consider realms of differently
organized reality that are linked to, yet move outside of, colonial boundaries. Unlike the extractive view, I lift submerged perspectives that perceive local terrains as sources of knowledge, vitality, and livability. My
work is situated in five specific spatial geographies of study within South
America—the Bío Bío in Chile, the Sacred Valley in Peru, Potosí (and La
Paz) in Bolivia, Eastern Ecuador, and Southwestern Colombia. These areas
represent "other Américas," or regions whose marginal status remains central to the global economy and gives us clues as to how we might understand a range of decolonizing efforts in the hemisphere.[1]

In this study, I am attentive to shifting borderlands, queer and non-
reproductive worlds of horizontal and anarcho affiliation, experimental

film and vernacular performances as sites of potential, not only through social movements, but also through modes of seeing, living, and finding sources of exchange as alternatives to the destructive path that is extractive capitalism.[2] *The Extractive Zone* works across spaces that might not otherwise be organized together in one study, delinking from the naturalization of national histories and from the heteronormativity of the nation-state. Instead, I uncover what is submerged within local geographies that have been traversed by colonialism and extractive capitalism to show the ongoing force of the colonial encounter. This book also analyzes and engages majority Indigenous territories often constituted as *terra nullius*, despite palimpsest histories of social life that do not divide nature from culture, land into private property, or ecology from the vernacular.

Édouard Glissant's theory of relationality has become one touchstone for perceiving the modes of difference that emerge within the spaces of potential of other Américas, where a certain sensibility and attention to the oceanic is embedded in Glissant's poetics.[3] In the epigraph, Édouard Glissant refers to the "renewed perception of differences to reveal themselves as such, and for the poem to reemerge once more." The poem in Glissant's elegant line is a metaphor for seeing beyond the colonial divide, into "a relation between different people, places, animate and inanimate objects, visible and invisible forces, the air, the water, the fire, the vegetation, animals and humans."[4] To name the visible and invisible forces between the human and nonhuman, between animate and inanimate life, is to perceive a too-often-ignored network of relationality, or social ecologies, as I term them throughout.

In *Poetics of Relation*, Glissant makes reference to the rhizomatic networks that operate as the hidden worlds of opacity, where renewed perception takes refuge from enclosure and containment.[5] Similarly, to be able to see beyond the capitalist divide, renewed perception does not simply represent a structure of visibility. It instead refers to an enlivened sense of the relationships that inhabit autonomous and uncharted spaces within capitalism and those that exist between the tracking of colonial and disciplinary power.[6] By making visible microspaces of interaction and encounter within geographies where coloniality has left and continues to leave a deep imprint, I show how renewed perception offers a method for decolonized study.

If we take as our starting point that many spaces within the Américas have never been fully inserted into Western capitalism, then we might also consider vernacular colonialities as the site of renewed perception.[7] These are sites of differentiated and inexhaustible potential, complex Afro-Indigenous spaces of coexistence with the nonhuman world that have been formed in relation to the colonial Encounter.[8] In terms of perceiving otherwise, Indigenous perspectives have long apprehended what Eduardo Viveiros de Castro refers to as "reality from distinct points of view."[9] In studying Amazonian worldviews and creating a new Brazilian Anthropology, Viveiros de Castro illustrates how an Indigenous perception of nature does not divide itself from other realms of reality; instead, it apprehends from "an original state of undifferentiation."

Decolonial thinkers put into motion a range of methods and epistemologies that give primacy to renewed perception. Walter Mignolo describes how decoloniality delinks from the Western project of civilization where being and language have been inscribed through the structures of coloniality.[10] Furthermore, decoloniality moves away from singularity and the reduction imposed by the European gaze toward the proliferation of epistemological possibility. Rather than presenting one mode of seeing otherwise, a range of generative authors that include Sylvia Wynter, Enrique Dussel, and Lewis Gordon offer us diasporic knowledge formations that name and theorize the effects of heterogeneous colonial histories. Key architects of decolonial scholarship such as Walter Mignolo, Maria Lugones, Emma Pérez, Nelson Maldonado-Torres, Laura Pérez, Chela Sandoval, Catherine Walsh, Arturo Escobar, Sylvia Rivera-Cusicanqui, and Ramón Grosfoguel attend to the weight of the European continental tradition, while sorting through hemispheric sites of enunciation that renarrate colonial histories from the position of subjugated knowledges.[11]

Decolonial theorizations allow me to identify how new/old forms of colonialism, such as extractive capitalism, the digital surveillance of territories, the criminalization of Indigenous peoples as a weapon of neoliberal expansion, and the extraction of Native and Afro-descendent knowledges, all depend on prior civilizational projects, in which the Global South has long been constructed as a region of plunder, discovery, raw resources, taming, classification, and racist adventure.[12] However, if we only track the purview of power's destruction and death force, we are forever analytically imprisoned to reproducing a totalizing viewpoint that ignores life that is unbridled and finds forms of resisting and living alternatively. Therefore, I seek new approaches by analyzing submerged and emergent perspectives within the extractive zone, or the potential for forms of life that cannot be easily reduced, divided, or representationally conquered or evacuated.

Like any system of domination, extractive capitalism is not totalizing in its destructive effects. The term "Anthropocene," which has been used by Western geologists and climatologists to term the period of human intervention from 1610 forward, now popularly identifies the crisis of future life on the planet. Scientists and scholars in the last ten years have written their visions of a planet in crisis, a spate of literature that addresses a "no future" paradigm and how life on the planet will soon be destroyed.[13] The broad adoption of the term "Anthropocene" is a key shift in our willingness to acknowledge the impact the human has had on the planet. Yet we use the term too generally, addressing "humanity" as a whole without understanding histories of racial thought and settler colonialism that are imposed upon categorizations of biodiversity, spaces where the biotechnologies of capitalism accelerate.

In reality, the problem is far more specific: colonial capitalism has been the main catastrophic event that has gobbled up the planet's resources, discursively constructing racialized bodies within geographies of difference, systematically destroying through dispossession, enslavement, and then producing the planet as a corporate bio-territory. The Anthropocene, like the militarized production of the extractive zone, demarcates the temporalities and spatial catastrophe of the planetary through a universalizing idiom and viewpoint that hides the political geographies embedded within the conversion of complex life. Thus, naming the Anthropocene as such without grounding its impact is what Vandana Shiva refers to as a monoculture of the mind.[14]

My objective is to decolonize the Anthropocene by cataloguing life otherwise, or the emergent and heterogeneous forms of living that are not about destruction or mere survival within the extractive zone, but about the creation of emergent alternatives. Unlike these doomsday approaches that play with destruction scenarios on the scale of the planetary, I study at the level of submerged life worlds within Indigenous territories, while pointing to African-descended territories and ontologies, modes of living that, even if not often perceivable, exist alongside extractive capitalism. For the spaces, movements, artwork, and intellectual and activist genealogies I study, the paradigm of "no future" has already taken place and we are now on the other side of colonial catastrophe.[15]

Within wide-ranging, critical, and interlinked social ecologies lies the potential for what Anibal Quijano cites as "liberation from all power organized as inequality, discrimination, exploitation, and domination."[16] When coupled with Laura Perez's important caution that decolonization must necessarily be anchored within feminist-of-color queer thought and praxis,[17] we begin to enter into the terrains of emergent potential at the center of my study. As I detail in chapter 1, Andean and Amazonian spaces that contain what is often dubbed the highest biodiversity on the planet cannot be managed under the management state's incorporative logic of *el buen vivir*, or good living practices, that have become the institutional reduction of Indigenous knowledge formations. The locales and visual texts I examine in this book, therefore, proliferate with difference as alternatives, through strategies that inverse, reverse, or stretch the gaze; they elongate time, linger within third spaces, imagine ecologies of rupture, and see with a fish's eye into the flow of the river and away from the dam's blockage.

In my study, attention to the dynamics and operations of race and racisms, feminist critique, queer potential, and anticapitalist struggle organizes the chapters that follow. Shifting entry points into the microspaces of the local, experimental, and phenomenological allows for attention to the embodied and vernacular experience of what is contained within the extractive zone. My first objective, then, is to move decolonial theory into further engagement with scholarship on race, sexuality, and Indigenous studies, providing methods to see the encounter of coloniality through these multiple frames of analysis.

### The Extractive View

Before the colonial project could prosper, it had to render territories and peoples extractible, and it did so through a matrix of symbolic, physical, and representational violence.[18] Therefore, the extractive view sees territories as commodities, rendering land as for the taking, while also devalorizing the hidden worlds that form the nexus of human and nonhuman multiplicity. This viewpoint, similar to the colonial gaze, facilitates the reorganization of territories, populations, and plant and animal life into extractible data and natural resources for material and immaterial accumulation.

The power of the visual has been explored by theorists in great detail over the last half century. But these mostly Eurocentric visual theories ignore the weight of colonial seeing, neglecting its earlier forms of power. For instance, Michel Foucault's panopticon stands in for the state's ever-watchful eye,[19] a theory of power that is formulated with modernity rather than with colonialism in mind. Gilles Deleuze in his short but influential essay "Postscript on Societies of Control" picks up on Foucault's theory of modern visual power by naming and, to a certain extent, predicting a new configuration that he called the "control society."[20] While these theories are often cited as classic sources of visual studies, by starting with modernity they render invisible the enclosure, the plantation, the ship, and the reservation, quintessential colonial spaces where power was consolidated through visual regimes.

In particular, what forms of power can be located by naming the extractive view? How might a focus on extractive capitalism and its vertical model of seeing change how we understand the history of visuality and the way we name forms of power in the past and in the present? What if we, alongside Nicholas Mirzoeff's concept of countervisuality, consider a longer arc of visual regimes and disobediences that situated colonial rule over territories and the countervisual resistances of racialized populations?[21]

Historically, the extractive view rendered Native populations invisible, which legally rendered the settlement of foreign populations onto communal properties, and facilitated the taking of those territories' resources. European colonization throughout the world cast nature as the other and, through the gaze of *terra nullius*, represented Indigenous peoples as non-existent. If settler colonialism and extractive capitalism reorganized space and time, then vertical seeing normalized violent removal. By continuing to rupture Indigenous cosmological relationships to land, the state and corporations expand their control and purview over nature in new forms of settler colonialism. While none of this is particularly news, my point is to emphasize that colonial visual regimes normalized an extractive planetary view that continues to facilitate capitalist expansion, especially upon resource-rich Indigenous territories.

In widening a discussion of how we might think about visuality in the regions I study, extractive capitalism literally "sees like the state," the term James C. Scott deploys to describe high modernist developmental visions that require great scientific and administrative feats.[22] With specific relevance to the Américas, Scott connects the application of high modernist designs to the history and rise of authoritarianism. Indeed, colonial and state violence historically facilitated territorial oversight, where seeing like the state meant violently asserting its rule over human and nonhuman populations. Applying this to the specific condition of South American occupation, during the Jesuit restructuring of land in Paraguay throughout the seventeenth and eighteenth centuries, Guarani dwellings were organized to keep maximum control over the forcibly settled population, as well as expand monocultural production. These *reducciones*, or land enclosures, represent some of the earliest forms of extractive reorganization in the Américas.

If colonial seeing first appeared as administrative rule over peoples and land, then in the digital phase, extractive states currently dispossess through new technologies. Modernized states coordinate with multinational corporations, using reconnaissance systems to collect large data sets, acquire surface readings of the Earth, and produce high-resolution maps that are deployed to build extractive infrastructure on the ground. Since the US-led global war on terror, "Five Eyes" states (United States, Canada, United Kingdom, Australia, and New Zealand) have increasingly invested in satellite technologies that support the planet's mapping for military and surveillance purposes, as well as for the conversion of natural resources into commodities. For instance, the US government has spent billions of dollars to fund the Center for the Study of National Reconnaissance, contracting with specialized tech firms to develop high-resolution resource maps and produce military intelligence used by shadow states to expand global control.

Based on Eurocentric theories of the visual a growing field of new media studies describes electronic colonialism theory, the concept of digital colonialism, and technological colonialism, warning about an increasing planetary system of control. Yet, many of these approaches continue to devalue the differential ways that this power is experienced, in particular global regions and upon certain bodies, as a digital colony.

In the new digital era, surveillance, data mining, and the mapping of resource-rich territories work together as complexly interlinked, rather than discrete, manifestations of hegemony that extinguish Indigenous and rural communities, such as in the regions in South America that I study. These highly coordinated forms of dominance function by mapping resource-rich areas of the world (in Afghanistan, Iraq, South America, and so forth), and serve as visual gateways for multinational and international state investment in extractive industries.[23] Lisa Parks's research is exemplary in this regard in that it shows how mapping territories for resources does not function by remote means only but is instead intimately linked to capitalism, military technologies, and the parallel expansion of dispossession on the ground.[24] Digital technologies contribute to the diminishment of regional national sovereignty over natural resources by enabling a grand-scale view from above; satellites photograph large areas of the planet to convert them into commodities for utilitarian market ends. Remote sensing and satellite operating systems chart and quantify the amount of raw materials contained within a given territory, making predictions about the profit margins that can be actualized within areas with abundant resources.[25]

In extractive sites, we must pay close attention to the material changes born from late capitalism's digital frameworks, which proliferate new forms of colonial theft. For instance, information, confidentiality, and corporate oversight function in ways that occlude, turning nonrenewable natural resources into opaque nodes of digital information that are hidden away from public debate. In contrast to Glissant's definition of "opacity," in which difference proliferates in a positive form, this oblique apparatus of extractivism renders invisible the activities of the corporate state. At the same time, geospatial technology requires the opposite form of visuality, rendering natural deposits of human and nonhuman life transparent, mapping to accumulate, convert, and expand the global economy.

In terms of shifting the gaze of this planetary scale, we might return to the importance of perceiving otherwise that engages citations and research produced out of observations grounded in the experience of South America.[26] Three decades ago, Humberto Maturana and Francisco Varela theorized alternative modes of human and biological perception. Their interdisciplinary collaborative work, *El árbol del conocimiento* ("The Tree of Knowledge") first published in 1984, deals complexly with the human and nonhuman predicament of "no future" presented to us by extractive capitalism. Maturana and Varela's study subtly originates and learns from the forests of the Bío Bío; where the ancient *pehuen* tree, sacred to the Mapuche, serves as a model for how they map human hermeneutics and perception. Of many aspects of this work that could be highlighted here, a signature insight is the concern for all organisms as constitutively and autonomously reproducing circuits of living systems, where there is a cognitive blurring between perception and actual experience. By focusing on perception as the crucial nexus point, the work offers "an invitation to reflection by opening a space of awareness."[27]

## Decolonial Queer Epistemes

In the chapters that follow, to understand ways of perceiving otherwise, I engage what I refer to throughout the book as a decolonial queer and femme episteme and methodology.[28] My perceptual method is indebted to women of color feminisms, and specifically Chicana feminisms and Native feminist scholarship, and also builds from the insights of queer of color critique.[29] Like women of color feminisms that analyze through a relational field of multiplicity, I situate the theory and praxis of de-linking from the colonial as refusing to see from a singular frame of analysis, standpoint, interpretation, or experience. What I am calling a "decolonial queer femme" method valorizes nonnormative embodied femininity as sources of knowing and perceiving.

A decolonial queer femme method perceives otherwise by attending to the resonances of lived embodiment as world-shaping activities.[30] In this I draw from the work of Jacqueline M. Martinez, who proposes a phenomenology of Chicana experience and identity as an orientation that both ruptures the distinction between self and other and also methodologically offers embodied knowing as a research technology. Martinez argues for a mode of perception that is an "open-ended inquiry that interrogates both its theoretical and its experiential conditions of possibility." Based upon models created by Richard Lanigan (1988), Martinez engages Chicana feminisms as a means of reorienting perception away from the static "object of study" toward a deep "engagement with it," where lesbian identity offers a generative nexus of insight. In this phenomenology, Martinez takes seriously daily life, and believes that conscious experience becomes the foundation for personal and social transformation.[31] Such transformative readings that allow for subject position in relation "to the field" allow me to deepen my analysis and interpretations of what resides within the extractive zone in South America, especially through a nonnormative femme position that allows the field and cultural texts I engage to make its impressions upon and through me.

Emma Pérez's concept of the decolonial as a temporal imaginary also helps me perceive in these directions. To pursue the dynamism of thinking within interstitial spaces, Pérez turns to the poetics of seeing, where the decolonial imaginary "acts much like a shadow in the dark. The figure between the subject and the object on which it is cast." The shadow is a space in which the visible and invisible mix together, where potential exists in a decolonial imaginary that is not rendered through transparent language or representations. Queer decolonial methods and epistemes bring together nonnormative modes of engaging the social world as submerged and emergent perspectives.

If Martinez and Pérez offer language for seeing that affirms queer epistemes and embodiment as a source of theorizing power from submerged perspectives, then Linda Tuhiwai Smith offers a model for the stakes of my research. Within US Native studies, Tuhiwai Smith identifies the need for decolonizing academic research about Indigenous communities, whom she frames as the most studied population in the world.[32] Tuhiwai Smith emphasizes the importance of an ethical perspective that mutually respects and engages Indigenous knowledge without extracting from these communities, but rather carefully attends to the construction of otherness, especially given the overdetermination of categories such as observer and observed, civilized and savage, anthropologist and Indigenous other. Smith's focus on knowledge formations and ethicality is essential to a decolonized academy, as is the consideration of Native worldviews that meaningfully shift the terrain of encounter, interpretation, and analysis to decenter the colonizing power of disciplinary knowledge.

Furthermore, Smith's work reminds us that extraction operates through material and immaterial forms of converting Indigeneity into exchange value, where intellectual and spiritual resources are taken to produce new forms of colonial currency. I take these insights with me into the extractive zone as an important methodological and epistemological baseline of what I am calling a "decolonial femme method"—the nexus where experience, perception, and decolonization meet. This is the space for much of the analysis of the extractive zone that aims to explode unilinear and unilateral procedures by transiting in the murky epistemic and sensuous space of uncertainty. Situated and affective forms of knowledge production can provide new ways to analyze the colonial trace in ways that hopefully do not reproduce, tame, or obfuscate an intimate and intricate web of power relations.[33]

Decolonial queer epistemes, analyses, or methods also work in opposition to conventional training on how to understand the lushness of social life rather than seeing through any single frame. Furthermore, in a refusal to address the partiality of knowledge, normative methodologies often reproduce an episteme and representation of marginality.[34] My method abandons the epistemology of measure for something much more tenuous, reaching toward addressing the complexity and entanglements of potential within extractive zones of institutional knowledge. A queer decolonial femme method recognizes a plurality of meaning systems, interpretations, and selections to reconsider what we thought we had known by challenging its disciplinary foundation.[35] Untraining the social by engaging decolonial theory and an analysis of colonialism allows for histories of dispossession, enslavement, and appropriation to be put at the center of social theory, emphasizing submerged perspectives as those that must be learned from rather than suppressed.[36]

For US academics, South America in particular has been the object of scrutiny under what Ricardo D. Salvatore addresses as "disciplinary conquest." Making reliable visibility out of the peripheries was essential to how South America has been positioned in the US university since the nineteenth century.[37] If knowledge is a site of conquest, and therefore the extension of coloniality, a decolonial femme modus challenges a normative "American" disciplinary vision. It also challenges an area studies approach, or the subsuming of global processes under the category of the European modern.[38] A decolonial femme standpoint does not universalize or dehistoricize the specificity of global spaces or material formations, but instead offers micro and submerged entry points into spaces saturated in coloniality. Decolonial thought inflected by critical race, feminist, and queer scholarship, then, allows me to show the making of extractive zones as a dominant objective of the colonial condition.

### Submerged Perspectives

Central to how I analyze colonial capitalism and the possibilities of the future is the critical task of perceiving life otherwise, or what I refer to as "submerged perspectives" that allow us to see local knowledge that resides within what power has constituted as extractive zones. In each of these places, *submerged perspectives* pierce through the entanglements of power to differently organize the meanings of social and political life. In other words, the possibility of decolonization moves within the landscape of multiplicity that is submerged perspectives. Extractive zones contain within them the submerged perspectives that challenge obliteration. I describe these transitional and intangible spaces as geographies that cannot be fully contained by the ethnocentricism of speciesism, scientific objectification, or by extractive technocracies that advance oil fields, construct pipelines, divert and diminish rivers, or cave-in mountains through mining. Seeing and listening to these worlds present nonpath dependent alternatives to capitalist and extractive valuation.

Studying multiply to decenter a singular eye has long been a modality of decolonial perception, both as observation and as critique.[39] W. E. B. Du Bois's episteme of double consciousness, for instance, is multivalent, rather than solely Marxist, pushing against the grain of canonical knowledge and threatening always to disturb its carefully concealed boundaries. The irruptive potential of the terrain of multiplicity is enlivened in Du Bois's method that analyzes the Fugitive Slave Act of 1865 against the Eurocentric and normative subjects of sociology and its complicity with the postslavery racial state. Decolonial hemispheric studies can learn from Du Bois's form of multidirectional critique that both undoes and reworks unilinear historical narratives that erase its subjects. Further, we might consider how Du Bois's sociological imagination raised the submerged perspectives of Black social and economic life, rather than subsume them into existing disciplinary epistemes. Part of my work in this book, then, is to bring into conversation a variety of radical traditions in the Américas.

By raising submerged perspectives, I am often blurring the boundaries of the nation-state and Area Studies, reconsidering the operations of the disciplinary, conversing and dialoguing in scholarly and regional idioms that are my own and not my own, and stepping into the multiply defined and often overdetermined territory of the other's other. How can we confuse the normative boundaries of academic study by wading into what lies below the surface of late capitalism?

### Chapters

This book connects the destructive force of capitalism in extractive zones to expressive and emergent alternatives; as these forms emerge, we find lesser-known, but powerful genealogies of thought, praxis, and connection. In each chapter, I read the specificity and unpredictability of the *de-colonial gesture*, or the smaller spaces and moments of decolonization, in relation to racial and settler colonial projects.[40] In the chapters that follow, I consider regions that have all experienced massive transformation and upheaval under colonialism; in each of these places, neoliberal extractive capitalism has only accelerated these consequences.

Chapter 1, "The Intangibility of the Yasuní," analyzes the "most bio-diverse region on the planet" in an area of Eastern Ecuador where oil drill-ing has threatened the delicate ecologies of Indigenous territories. Since 1998, when the Yasuní-ITT treaty was first proposed, the Yasuní region offered the tangible possibility for radical conservation protection. Today, that project has been endangered by the expansion of the oil industry and the forces of multinational capital that fold Ecuador into the matrix of petro dependency. I meditate on the term intangibility as a decolonial con-cept of multiplicity, since the region is referred to as "the intangible zone" for Western science's incapacity to fully catalogue the plethora of life that exists even within one square mile of a 933-mile Amazonian territory.

While the Ecuadoran state promotes *el buen vivir*, or the idea of "good living" according to sustainable ecological principles, it continues to facili-tate oil extraction in the region as a violent act against Indigenous sover-eignty. The intangible zones, according to the Ecuadoran Law, are "pro-tected spaces of great cultural and biological importance in which no extractive activity can occur because of the region's high value for the Ama-zon, Ecuador, the world, and present and future generations."[41]

However, despite the constant rehearsal of the phrase "protected spaces" within the new Ecuadoran Constitution and the legislation of *el buen vivir* as protection of the Yasuní, the politics of greed continues to en-danger the Eastern Ecuadoran Indigenous peoples, their territories, and the complex systems of land management, resistance, and alternative anti-capitalist economies found there. I analyze alternative renderings that are the social ecologies of Indigenous communities, especially the Quichua within the Yasuní region, as another possibility for imagining the social from within and beyond the intangible zone. However, I situate such alter-natives as accompanied by the constant and necessary political pressure exerted by YASunidos, a cross-generational, urban and rural, transborder, queer, feminist, Afro-Indigenous coalition that works solidly to defend the

Yasuní region. Spontaneously formed in 2013 to confront the pressures of exogenous petro development, this multidirectional coalition proliferates alternatives to the "no future" model of the extractive zone.

Chapter 2, "Andean Phenomenology and New Age Settler Colonialism," considers a less obvious but equally perilous form of extractive capitalism by thinking about spiritual tourism as an extractive zone. By working through histories of "spiritual" taking, such as the colonial church and its control over Indigenous girls' bodies, and later the new age traffic of Andean cultural formats, particularly in relation to Q'ero peoples, I attend to the problem of the colonial divide through ongoing forms of settler colonialism that justify occupation and the speculation of sacred territories through new age rhetoric. I show how neoliberal tourist economies expand the paradigm of "playing Indian,"[42] especially in a transnational setting where Andean masculinity is commodified by sex and spiritual tourist economies. I also draw upon an important literature within US Native studies to show the commonality of extracting from Indigenous embodiment and worldviews throughout the hemisphere. Rather than foreclose upon the possibility of decolonization in this space, I engage local knowledge production, such as Andean phenomenology, as an experience of land and territoriality that does not pass through neoliberalism or its colonial projections.

Moreover, I navigate sticky realities through a decolonial queer femme method that is open to the less tangible perspectives, sounds, and experiences that are available by moving beyond the colonial divide. In other words, despite the raucous noise of neoliberal commodification and appropriation, what are the more silent spaces that refuse these terms and instead allow for a less determined set of interactions and pedagogies between Native peoples and nonnative foreigners?

Chapter 3, "An Archive for the Future," analyzes settler colonialism in Mapuche, Pehuenche, and Huilliche territories within Southern Chile, demonstrating the ongoing colonial state effort to "eliminate the Native."[43] Like the Chiapas conflict over Mayan territories, the ongoing violence and dispossession of Mapuche territories only increased with neoliberal governmentality in the 1990s. The resulting and very current crisis has terrorized thousands of Indigenous people through the massive deployment of the police state in the Bío-Bío region. Resistance through hunger strikes and political imprisonment, poignantly by Indigenous women, has been an important and highly visible mode of embodying dissent within the extractive zone.[44] Mapuche filmmaker Francisco Huichaqueo produces an archive of the future about the present-day violence of pine and eucalyptus export production, monoculture development that has displaced and reduced daily life for Native peoples within the Bio-Bio regions of the Southern Wallmapu territories.

In highly symbolic renderings of occupation, Huichaqueo refuses to follow documentary conventions. He also decenters representations of the human figure, instead making nature—particularly the omnipresent pine tree, the ancestral *pehuen*, and the giant native *Auracaria* trees—the narrative center of his films. With the director, the viewer laments the extinction of the sacred *pehuen* seeing beyond colonial occupation into the invisible Mapuche worlds he visualizes. Moreover, Huichaqueo incorporates experimental filmmaking language as a way out of constrained developmental visions. Through his use of opacity, namely as an obscuring perspective, we find a complex aesthetic challenge to the normative settler colonial gaze that renders territories as landscape and Indigenous bodies as criminal.

Having moved through the extractive scenes of spiritual tourism and forest and petroleum extraction, I turn to chapter 4, "A Fish-Eye Episteme," a title that refers to a submerged perspective that I discuss in the chapter. In particular, I address the commodification of water, where I analyze hydroelectricity as submerging lives and perspectives that waterpower attempts to drown. Attending to a body of work by Colombian mestiza artist Carolina Caycedo, I examine how an inverted view offers us a different order of perception than the empirical sight lines that peer below, above, and through the extractive divide. The "fish-eye episteme" that I refer to displaces the ocular centricity of human development and instead reveals a submerged, below-the-surface, blurry countervisuality.

Documenting the ontologies and textures of rural life in her videomaking, Caycedo shows how the Spanish company Endesa's land invasion upon biodiverse territories produces a virtual catastrophe for local river communities in the Cauca Valley of southwestern Colombia. In a long still take of the lush and verdant river, Caycedo inverts the camera so that the Magdalena flows at the top of the frame. This inverted view estranges and detaches from the colonial extractive gaze by seeing the river as a place of subtle yet staggering social and ecological sustenance rather than merely as moving water to be harnessed for electricity. I elaborate how Caycedo's aesthetic praxis also inverts the normative model of colonial development and its extractive technologies by resignifying satellite and drone technologies to instead represent local sources of knowledge and trans-generational communal relations.

In chapter 5, "Decolonial Gestures," I propose that Indigenous feminist anarchist critique offers another submerged perspective from within the extractive zone. Anarcho-feminist critique offers an important set of historical examples and modes of refusing global capitalism that range from intellectual and cultural production to embodied activities of dissent. For instance, Indigenous Aymara female hunger strikers, slag-pile workers, and *chola* market women share a history of an anticapitalist ethics that dismantle and remake the condition of possibility outside of mining that has determined Bolivia's position within the global economy since the fifteenth century.

Silvia Rivera Cusicanqui's decolonizing theories emerge from her fieldwork within the cultural modes of Bolivian anarchic-feminist history and help outline this chapter's theoretical work, which threads a genealogy of female figures that are often hidden by Left radical history. Furthermore, I address the decolonizing imaginaries of Mujeres Creando artists, performers, and activists, whose split into two organizations, Mujeres Creando and Mujeres Creando Comunidad, with two distinct visions, only multiplies the potentiality of its critical perspective. This chapter brings gender and sexuality to the foreground to address the utopic potential that has been enlivened within Andean politics and cultural spheres, especially over the past decade.[45]

Through five extractive scenes in South America, I return to and conclude with the submerged perspectives of social movements, artistic efforts, and intellectual formations that challenge the monocultural view of developmentalism and colonial capitalism. Whether through shadow play, by seeing from below, or listening to the water, these porous modalities expand the condition of possibility against Eurocentric, high modernist, and totalizing visions of differentiated planetary life.

# CHAPTER 1

# The Intangibility of the Yasuní

In Eastern Ecuador's Intangible Zone, the Napo River headwater tributary blends with the *aguas negras*, a small river that flows away from the apocalyptic movement of extractive capitalism. Where the vegetation thickens and the temperature of the water cools, the humming of the oil barges and motorized canoes ceases. Along the fifty-kilometer stretch of river from the oil boomtown Coca en route to the Yasuní, one transits on the Napo through intense industrial activity. Bright orange flames from oil refineries spike above the horizon; a myriad of floating riverboats that house petroleum company workers sit empty along the riverbank, while barges travel up and down the river carrying petroleum. Though invisible from the river, dozens of oil workers hack through long swaths of rain forest with machetes to make way for petroleum extraction.

Ten miles past the houseboats, the river divides again. Turning toward *los ríos negros*, or "the black waters," and away from the Napo River, the accelerated pace of extractivism disappears into protected Indigenous Shuar, Huaronani, Quichua, Tagaeri and Taromame territories marked only by a tiny sign that reads "Yasuní National Park." Unlike the raucous commotion that moves oil up and down the main part of the Napo River, on this smaller artery a single leaf falling into the water from the canopy above becomes a major event. Here, perception slows down where the frenetic timescape of extraction is not the sole temporality, and where the elongated sense of geological time enables a different perception to the intricate unfolding of the natural world. In the two meters of murky water that lap against our motored canoe, a million years of evolution is contained. As we sit silently in the boat, someone spots a river caiman, an animal that glides effortlessly through the water. The caiman is a useful guide for the multiplicity of seeing that we need in such a space: with its eyes positioned just above the line of water, its sight hovers above as easily as it dips below the shadowy, fertile waters.

In 1998, UNESCO declared the Yasuní region, located between the Napo and Curacay rivers in the southern provinces of Napo and Pastaza and encompassing 982,000 total hectares, a world heritage site worthy of international patrimony. Long considered the most bio-diverse region in the world, Yasuní National Park harbors millions of insect species, hundreds of bird species, and the greatest variety of tree species anywhere on the planet. Spaces of high biodiversity such as the Yasuní swirl away from full capture, despite the fact that teams of Western and Ecuadoran scientists constantly enter the forest to classify its plant and animal species and Indigenous populations.[1] Given the contrast between the expanding extractive activity I describe above and the patches of forest that contain immense biodiversity, is it possible to imagine an alternative future to the elimination of planetary biodiversity? If the extractive matrix engulfs resource-rich spaces into global capitalism, what exists beyond the reduction of heterogeneity into sheer destruction? I follow biologist William Sacher to ask "what life forms will exist in the future if we continue to devalue and eliminate?"[2] As the visible flames of oil toxicity burn outside its perimeter, what alternatives support another relation to the multiplicity of life that resides within the territories of the Yasuní?

To pursue these questions, and against late capitalism's absorption of language, intangibility names for me the capacity of life otherwise to reroute commodification and scientific classification. The intangibility of the forest metabolizes, grows, multiplies, and escapes the condition of monoculture, whose complexity forces consideration, as Eduardo Kohn asks, can forests think?[3] What do they remember? And, as Deleuze and Guattari explore in *A Thousand Plateaus*, engagement with molecular biology allows for a model of radical ecological agency that describes the coproduction of living systems with adaptive potential.[4] Their idea of novel becomings is another way to conceptualize emergence. Indeed, Deleuze and Guattari's ecophilosophy builds upon Southern theorists Humberto Maturana and Francisco Varela's notion of "autopoesis," or the ability of a biological system to sustain and reproduce itself.[5] In line with these concepts, intangibility reaches beyond reductionist models of representation toward enlivened social ecologies that shift, adapt, and extend normative categories of biological life.

In this chapter, I attend to intangible and autonomous life through an analysis of the Andean-Amazonian geography, its representation, and the modes of land and water defense that take place in relation to the Yasuní region of Eastern Ecuador. Specifically, I address the Yasuní-ITT Treaty, the radical conservation plan for the biosphere known as the Yasuní Ishpingo-Tambococha-Tiputini (ITT), as an important and profound, if contradictory, alternative to the exigencies of extractive capitalism. Like other alternative forms of representing the forest and land that emerge from within the Yasuní, the treaty contains within it the surprising acknowledgment of Indigenous sovereignty, the imperative to reverse the extractive view, and the practice of *el buen vivir* that gives primacy to Afro-based and Indigenous worldviews. Even as the Yasuní-ITT Treaty has recently come under grave threat by national and multinational oil companies, Indigenous, Afro-Ecuadoran, LGBT, eco-feminist, and labor union assemblages challenge its dissolution by enacting social ecologies that live beyond the colonial divide.

Intangibility counters the representational apparatus of the Yasuní as a pure Amazonian space, a territory of undifferentiated wildness, vastness, and untameability. In a surreal portrayal of colonial adventure, German director Werner Herzog's film *Fitzcarraldo* (1982) epitomizes this view of the Amazonian basin, where nature and "untamable" Natives are dangerous and threaten Man's domination of them. In a well-known monologue in *Burden of Dreams* (1982), the extraordinary documentary by Les Blank that chronicles the making of *Fitzcarraldo*, Herzog describes his frustration with the jungle, and suggests that the Amazon is a place of menace; a savage, fecund space where God has punished its inhabitants: "Of course we are challenging nature itself. . . . I see it full of obscenity, the nature here is violent, base. I wouldn't see anything erotical here, I would see fornication and asphyxiation, and choking, and fighting for survival, and growing and just dropping away. Of course there is a lot of misery, but it is the same misery that is all around us, the trees here are in misery and the birds are in misery. I don't think they sing, they just screech in pain."[6]

Herzog's rhetorical flair here, and the cinematic spectacle of the failure of modern utopian development, reproduces the colonial tropes of eighteenth- and nineteenth-century European travel writing that rehearses the language of Spanish discovery chronicles. The Amazon has a long representation as a chaotic landscape that is constantly under threat by civilizational impulses, a central tenet of the colonial paradigm.[7] A focus on the dangers of nature, its violence, and its presumed obscenity situates Indigenous territories in racialized and species-centric terms that imagines progress as its own end game.

In contrast to this spectacular and extractive view of the forest, a range of relational forms live with rather than "objectively" observe the Amazon. The Yasuní is not a pure space of untamed wildness, as Herzog would have it, but has maintained its biodiversity precisely because of the ingenuity of Indigenous seed selection, interplanting, and the meticulous cultivation and maintenance of biodiversity over a thousand years of systematic care; forest dwellers that live in the region, including the Huaorani, Kichwa, Shuar, and "no contact" populations, have carefully protected and cultivated plant life in ways that support its proliferation.[8] Intangible geographies function as entropic spaces that cannot be contained by the extractive view, Western science, the commodity logic of late capitalism, or racial governmentality, but instead are managed by Indigenous peoples, cooperatives, and "no contact" populations to amplify the multiplicity of the forest's life forms.

### The Yasuní Treaty

Biodiversity is not all that is found within the Yasuní region; the territory is also cursed with an estimated 920 million barrels of below-the-surface oil reserves, which represents twenty percent of Ecuador's total fossil fuel deposits. In 1967, Texaco discovered oil in the region, leading to the practice of *manos pintados*, or painting one's hands with oil from the open pits to celebrate the presumed riches that would come from its exploitation. By the lost decade of the 1980s, it was clear that Ecuador's increasing foreign debt and overreliance upon a single commodity further subsumed the nation into the global economy of petroleum dependency.

The Yasuní-ITT agreement, originally proposed in 1996, stated that the Ecuadoran state would refuse extractivist bidding to protect Indigenous territories and the "natural state" of nature for the relatively small sliver of land that had not been divided up by the oil economy. During his campaign for presidency, Rafael Correa promised to protect the Rights of Nature by diversifying the nation's economic portfolio. In 2005, Correa raised the possibility that the Yasuní-ITT agreement would garner funds from global entities, a plan that was touted as central to Correa's program for economic distribution. Newly sworn in president Correa asked the international community to pay 350 million dollars over ten years to the Ecuadoran state to leave the underground oil reserves alone.

Correa positioned the Yasuní-ITT proposal as a Global North responsibility that would ameliorate Ecuador's increasing position as resource and extractive dependent. The Treaty offered an opportunity from outside of Ecuador to prevent the exploitation of oil territories from within, a symbol of how the wealthier nations could right their historical culpability. However, by August 2013 Correa announced that the state's effort to attract international funding for the Yasuní had come up short, and the treaty would be terminated, recusing the Ecuadoran government from any further responsibility as protectorate of the region. Given that the Yasuní is comprised of incalculable and intangible genetic and species variation upon Indigenous territories, such news illustrated the failure of legal and political options to protect intangible zones from the calculations of global capitalism.

Though Rafael Correa was not the first president to defend the Yasuní region, the formalization of the 2008 Ecuadoran Constitution in Montecristi and the 2010 launch of the Yasuní-ITT proposal for protected territories were both actualized under his watch. In a press release on April 1, 2007, the day the ITT agreement was adopted, President Rafael Correa's Ministry of Energy and Mines made the following statement:

> Se aceptó como primera opción la de dejar el crudo represado en tierra, a fin de no afectar un area de extraordinaria biodiversided y no poner en riesgo la existencia de varios pueblos en aislamiento voluntario o pueblos no contactados. Esta medida será considerada siempre y cuando la comunidad internacional entregue al menos la mitad de los recursos que se generarían si se opta por la explotación del petroleo; recursos que require la economía ecuatoriana para su desarollo.

> [The government] has agreed to the first option, which is to leave the oil reserves within the earth, a result that does not affect the extraordinary biodiversity and doesn't put at risk the existence of various communities that live in the region with no contact. This policy will be considered

as long as the international community gives half of the resources that would have been generated had the option been for petroleum exploitation. The Ecuadoran economy requires these resources for its development.[9]

The "no contact" Indigenous peoples referred to here are the Tagaeri and Taromenane that live within the Yasuní region, who tellingly returned to the forest in the 1970s to avoid oil companies, the Ecuadoran state, missionaries, and other agents of coloniality. As Esperanza Martínez writes of the particularly strange phrasing of Correa's statement, "one can deduce from the declaration that from the President's perspective there was always a second option: to extract oil."[10]

Correa's petitioning of the ecological conscience of the world to make an investment in biodiversity offered a new alternative for Global South governments, resolving the burden of preservation costs by externalizing them to wealthier nations. Yet, the wording of the proposal obfuscates the fact that the surrounding territories had long been sold off to more than a dozen petroleum corporations. Maps show how the region had been carved up into "oil blocks" as early as 2009, and leaked documents reveal secret negotiations between the Ecuadoran state and Chinese petroleum companies over "Bloque 31," designating the territory of Yasuní National Park for oil extraction.[11] In other words, the state pursued an extractive agenda even while using the rhetoric of *el buen vivir* to promote international support for conservation efforts.

In Correa's statement above, the Yasuní is discursively positioned in a paternalistic fashion. The development fallacy embedded within Correa's statement is conservation as a binary choice: either protect resource-rich territories, or give in to extractive capitalism as usual. Both formulations operate within the logics of colonial seeing that depict land and territory as an extractive zone: as if it is there for the taking, to be owned, and ultimately to be protected by the state with little understanding of the intangible complexity practiced by the vibrant social ecologies that reside within the forest.

Despite the obvious disjuncture between state rhetoric and action, proponents continue to argue that the Ecuadoran Constitution of 2008 and the Yasuní-ITT Treaty of 2009 produced a giant leap forward as legal protections for the natural world. Scholar Freddy Javier Álvarez Gonzalez shows that the constitutional revisions were led by an important process that re-sulted in a wider social consensus, and made visible a new way to relate to the natural world.[12] Another way to read these processes, in hindsight, is that the state management of Indigenous concepts such as land protection and *el buen vivir*, a term I elaborate upon below, has worked to facilitate the expansion of extractive capitalism. Can the law, the very instrument of colonization, actually guide us about how to protect biodiversity in In-digenous territories? What are the alternatives to using the master's tools?

### El Buen Vivir

At its most fundamental level, *el buen vivir* refers to the organization of so-cial and ecological life based on Afro-Indigenous principles and the trans-mission of vernacular practices that maintain a deep and respectful rela-tionship to land, place, and the natural world.

> La idea del "buen vivir" se está difundiendo en toda América Latina. Es un concepto en construcción que aspira ir más allá del desarrollo con-vencional, y se basa en una sociedad donde conviven los seres humanos entre sí y con la naturaleza. Se nutre desde ámbitos muy diversos, desde la reflexión intelectual a las prácticas ciudadanas, desde las tradiciones indígenas a la academia alternativa.[13]

> The idea of "good living" is being diffused throughout Latin America. It's a concept that is under creation and that aspires beyond conven-tional development, while based within a society where human beings live well among themselves and with nature. It is nourished by very di-verse sectors, from spaces of intellectual reflection to citizenship prac-tices, and from indigenous traditions to the alternative academy.

The idea of *el buen vivir*, translated as good living, decenters the impor-tance of "the human" by focusing instead upon how the natural world pos-sesses its own sets of rights, logics, and capacities that cannot be solely ap-prehended, managed, or narrated through human language or scientific technique.[14] Rather than assume knowledge over, or exert a hierarchical re-lationship to, nature, *el buen vivir* pursues what Atawallpa Oviedo Freire terms "dynamic equilibrium" and "harmony with reciprocity" as ways of relating to the vast planetary life all around us.[15] As an active consciousness, *el buen vivir* surpasses the confined vision of the developmental paradigm toward an integrated form of living in the forest.

As Alfredo Pérez Bermúdez beautifully writes in the introduction to the volume *Bifurcación del buen vivir y el Sumak Kawasay* (edited by Atawallpa Oviedo Freire), good living is not a zero-sum game about material progress or "the American way of life," but instead incorporates the potential to live in consonance with the Earth.[16] This is set in sharp contrast to the individualizing logic of the American dream that is a resource-intensive enterprise. In other words, "good living" offers a different paradigm from the materialist impulse of the neoliberal discourse of "the good life" (*vivir bien*) that imagines endless personal expansion, a view in which the comforts of modern capitalist development fulfills one's individual material expansion.

Amid the failures of neoliberalism over the last forty years, the increased visibility of Indigenous peoples and ecological governance promised new formal political spaces for the protection of Indigenous territories in the Américas. The greatest hope for change came within the processes of social consultation that culminated in regime transition in both Ecuador and Bolivia. After Rafael Correa was elected president of Ecuador through a broad-based Indigenous confederation that passed through a process of constituent assemblies, in 2006 Evo Morales was elected president in Bolivia, an event that represented the apex of Indigenous visibility and the culmination of progressive social movements. Both presidents promoted Indigenous agendas and arrived at the presidential office by consultative and participatory means. They also both revisited and rewrote legal mandates, most notably by revising their respective national constitutions through consultative processes that visibly incorporated democratic participation. In the formal political sphere, constituent assemblies produced new configurations that broke with elite politics as usual.[17] Such broad-based incorporation of *el buen vivir* policies also created ruptures, or so it appeared, with the legacies of colonial racism that had long favored European modes of political, economic, and social organization.

Yet, two forms of *el buen vivir* have become increasingly confused. The first form refers to the sustainability of heterogeneous life forms based on Afro-centered and Indigenous "cosmo-visions," and the second is concerned with the rhetorical and instrumental use of *el buen vivir* as a form of governmentality, or what Michel Foucault defined as the organized practice of state rationality.[18] In the new extractive capitalism, the state's policies of hegemony over nature convert territories into extractible commodities by using the rhetorical cover of *el buen vivir*. As we shall see, however suggestive the concept of *el buen vivir* may be, it has increasingly become the rhetorical justification of a state that prioritizes capitalist agendas while diminishing the reach of actual decolonization.

### Distorting Vitality

*El buen vivir* is increasingly compromised by Andean socialism, or the new Ecuadoran state that continues to invest in extractive capitalist advancement even after the end of the Washington Consensus. Contrary to most predictions, over the last ten years progressive Latin American states expanded rather than reduced their ecological predicament and dependent global relations. At the January 2015 Caribbean and Community Summit meeting in Beijing, for instance, the Chinese government proposed $500 billion in trade, and $250 billion in investment, marking new configurations of geopolitical power within the region. In this new global economy that extends coloniality, Ecuador has acquired loans at cumulatively higher interest rates that make the prior system of World Bank lending and US-led development policies look relatively mild.

As Yasuní lawyer Pablo Piedra conveyed to me, "Some of us look nostalgically back at the earlier Washington Consensus model where you at least had a system of checks and balances in place. At that time, you could go to the International Monetary Fund overseer and file petitions against the excesses and terms of extractivist contracts."[19] The kinds of checks and balances that existed in the earlier paradigm, such as oversight commissions where advocates could petition for rights, are virtually nonexistent today. Perhaps more damaging, at a time of a precipitous drop in global market oil prices, the Ecuadoran government has increasingly become entangled within a matrix of high-interest loans, further indebting itself to foreign powers through the payment of nonrenewable natural resources. Such payment in arrears threatens regions and unique conservation initiatives such as the Yasuní-ITT Treaty.

To meet the logic of debt while expanding its authoritarian reach, the Ecuadoran state has either reissued or granted new contracts for development projects throughout the nation's five ecosystems. Thus, mining, hydroelectricity, industrial fishing, and oil drilling have become regions of intense extractive activities and areas of acute resistance over territory and resources. For instance, the communities of the northern Intag region of Imbabura Province have contended with mining extractivism through high-stakes tactics, violent face-offs between communities and the military that have only intensified with new megamining projects. By extracting resources from Indigenous territories while contradicting the foundational precepts of *el buen vivir*, the state seems ultimately unable to arbitrate, protect, or uphold the rights of nature, as I discuss below.

President Rafael Correa's three-year plan, "El Buen Vivir: Plan Nacional, 2013–2017," illustrates the distance between rhetoric and the implementation of state social and economic policy that protects the "rights of nature." In the document, the commitment to pursue *el buen vivir* serves as a measure against "infinite development and expansion" and takes economic redistribution into consideration while also extending third-generation social, economic, cultural, and environmental rights.[20] Even though Objective 11 of the state plan argues that Ecuador should consider converting its economic and industrial sectors to align with *el buen vivir* approaches, subsequent parts of the document detail how the model would be incomplete without increasing the capacity for resource extraction. As the plan makes transparent:

> El Ecuador tiene una oportunidad histórica para ejercer soberanamente la gestión económica, industrial y científica, de sus sectores estratégicos. Esto permitirá generar riqueza y elevar en forma general el nivel de visa de nuestra población. Para el Gobierno de la Revolución Ciudadana, convertir la gestión de los sectores estratégicos en la punta de lanza de la transformación tecnológica e industrial del país, constituye un elemento central de ruptura con el pasado.[21]

> Ecuador has the historic opportunity to exercise sovereignty in the economic, industrial, and scientific development of its most strategic sectors. This permits the generation of wealth and an elevation of wealth for the general population. For the government of the Citizen's Revolution, converting the management of strategic sectors is the point of technological and industrial transformation. This is central to rupturing with the past.

While parts of this document are infused with the will to protect nature, namely the need to rupture with dependent sectors of the economy through promotion of what Correa's administration has referred to as the "Citizen's Revolution," the real emphasis in these passages is on the "technological and industrial transformation of the country" that has paved the way for extractive expansion. Furthermore, there is little indication regarding how the state would accomplish the gigantic task of decolonization, and still less analysis about what sovereignty for Ecuador means given shifting geopolitical configurations.

Extractive corporate concessions have increasingly been granted to multinational companies, leading to the expansion of coloniality. Beyond the economic and social implications, there are severe environmental consequences as well: state and national companies are some of the worst offenders of polluting industries.[22] Given these material contradictions, the rhetoric of good living has not found a way out of the bind of developmentalism. More succinctly, "good living" has provided rhetorical cover for extractive ends. The distance between the Indigenous Amazonian-Andean principle of *el buen vivir* and the expansion of extractivist governance throughout the continent increases with every concession granted to a foreign state or company.

### Ecology and the Law

As a reaction against the extreme ecological and social devastation brought on by the hegemony of the neoliberal model, over the latter part of the twentieth century South American states increasingly incorporated environmental rights into processes of constitutional change. The Ecuadoran Constitution's originality was its ability to go beyond the 1980s and 1990s legal frameworks that had already been altered with the propulsion of third-generation rights, or protection of cultural, economic, and human rights in South American nations, especially following Colombia (1991) and Brazil (1998), that granted rights to future generations based on the conservation of nature preserves over the past several decades. Ecuador suffered considerable environmental degradation and persistent economic dependency, which emboldened social movements to intertwine a growing awareness of environmental rights with the ongoing quest for justice. At the same time, global climate change captured world attention that led, in 1996, to the inauguration of the Ministry of Global Climate Change in Ecuador. This ministry was charged with securing the future of biodiversity within the nation, a laudable objective that has been backtracked upon over the last five years.

From the opening article, the language of the Ecuadoran Constitution makes important overtures about the connection between national sovereignty and the rights of the natural world:

> Article 1. Ecuador is a Constitutional State of rights and justice, a social, democratic, sovereign, independent, unitary, intercultural, multinational and secular State. It is organized as a republic and is governed using a decentralized approach.
>
> Sovereignty lies with the people, whose will is the basis of all authority, and it is exercised through public bodies using direct participatory forms of government as provided for by the Constitution. Nonrenewable natural resources of the State's territory belong to its inalienable and absolute assets, which are not subject to a statute of limitations.[23]

While the language of sovereignty describes the protections by the law, it does not prevent extractive corporations from entering into protected terrains. Even though Laws 71 through 74 of the Constitution were drafted to prohibit the extraction of resources, loopholes have allowed corporate incursion into the areas defined as conservation zones. Thus, given that "nonhuman life" cannot speak for itself and has to pass through human advocacy and juridical representation, the law is perhaps wrongly assumed to be the appropriate site for the natural world's liberation from human authority.

In this sense, the 2008 Ecuadoran Constitution seemingly shifted the potential of the law, creating an apparatus for nature's representation. For instance, Article 71, called the "Rights of Nature" in Chapter 7 of the Constitution, considers the degree to which Pachamama "reproduces and makes life possible":

> La naturaleza o Pacha Mama, donde se reproduce y realiza la vida, tiene derecho a que se respete integralmente su existencia y el mantenimiento y regeneración de sus ciclos vitales, estructura, funciones y procesos evolutivos. Toda persona, comunidad, pueblo o nacionalidad podrá exigir a la autoridad pública el cumplimiento de los derechos de

la naturaleza. Para aplicar e interpretar estos derechos se observaran los principios establecidos en la Constitución, en lo que proceda. El Estado incentivará a las personas naturales y jurídicas, y a los colectivos, para que protejan la naturaleza, y promoverá el respeto a todos los elementos que forman un ecosistema.[24]

Nature or Pachamama, where life is reproduced and made possible, has the right to exist, persist, maintain, and regenerate its vital cycles, structure, functions, and evolutionary processes. Every person, people, community, or nationality will be able to demand the recognitions of rights for nature before the public authority. The application and interpretation of these rights will follow the related principles that are established in the Constitution. The State will incentivize natural rights and personal rights as well as collective rights to protect nature; it will promote respect toward the elements that form an ecosystem.

Pachamama's right to exist and thrive is at the center of Indigenous cosmologies within the Andean-Amazonian region, and a view of a positive relation to the natural world that must be considered with more depth. This form of recognition is not about a liberal appeal to the juridical apparatus or the state, but about an integrated and multidimensional recognition for the rights of nature or Pachamama.[25] If we place emphasis on the pervasiveness of this cosmological principle for Indigenous worldviews, then the crisis and reductive viewpoint of European juridical law becomes strikingly apparent. Within a Southern episteme, the colonial legal structures facilitate and accelerate the conversion of planetary geomatter into a capitalist catastrophe. Correa's governmental corporate concessions expose this contradiction.

Extractive governmentality shows that an ecological imaginary can never be fully actualized through the law. Even while legal channels can offset the plundering of the planet's resources, the Yasuní case serves as a cautionary tale that it cannot be the only route for conservation. Ultimately, the law is embedded within a global political economic and interstate system that does not serve as a steward to the natural world but sells it to the highest commodity market. In this sense, *el buen vivir* has become a tool of extractive states that reproduces the logics of neoliberal advancement. Ultimately, we need other modes of representation and action that exceed and surpass the legal systems that feed back into the matrix of coloniality.

## Yasuní Transitionality: YASunidos

Though its 2008 constitution mandated protection for environmental rights, Indigenous rights, and respect for biodiversity against "human-centric" development, the Ecuadoran plurinational state ultimately was not able to protect the intangible territories.

When in August 2013, Correa announced that the Yasuní-ITT treaty would not be upheld, activists expressed outrage at how Yasuní had been converted into an oil block tracked for petroleum extraction. In the days that followed, hundreds of people across the nation gathered in vigils, shattered by the announcement of this repeal. As Diana Coryat describes, such gatherings spawned the YASunidos movement, led by urban and rural youth who had come out of Indigenous social movements, ecological activisms, media collectives, and horizontal organizations that rejected the extractive model.[26] The spontaneous movement that began with Correa's announcement of the end of the Yasuní-ITT Treaty represents a cross-sectional coalition that has spawned a range of important challenges to the extractive zone.

YASunidos is a coalition composed of artists, Indigenous activists, journalists, middle-class ecologists, and land defenders. It draws upon the affective solidarity among activists who name the extractive complex, and who perceive the Yasuní as a powerful collective symbol of the global devaluing of Indigenous territories and biodiverse ecologies. For ecologically minded youth of Ecuador, the Yasuní region represents a psychological space of respite from a world increasingly defined by climate change, a place where "no contact" Indigenous populations reject colonization, and a region where biodiversity thrives amid the growing dystopia of mega-development projects. Thus, when a road was constructed as an extractive corridor through the Yasuní-ITT zone, the subsequent shock of finding out that Correa had ruptured the agreement produced an infuriated response by the YASunidos coalition, with effects that continue to reverberate.

In the following statement by YASunidos, worth quoting at length, we see how an alternative multidirectional vision organizes the coalition through a call that also specifies central principles of *el buen vivir*. YASunidos states:

> For us, the initiative to leave the oil underground indefinitely should not respond to the whims of the international community or those of a

government that has failed us by unidirectionally discarding the possibility of a serious public debate about alternatives for the conservation of the ITT.

We, YASunidos, demand respect for the human rights of the uncontacted peoples as guaranteed by Article 57 of the constitution. We demand that our ancestral, natural heritage not be sacrificed and opt for post-oil alternatives. We urge a truthful and transparent debate about our economic model and our energy base. Also, we demand that the government let us show our disagreement through the legitimate exercise of protest without repression or criminalization.

For us, the goal of leaving the ITT oil underground is more alive than ever, which is evident through the creativity and commitment demonstrated in the streets by citizens asking for their voices to be heard. We hope that the topic will be widely discussed and that various arguments will come forth rather than confusing information along with delegitimizing governmental propaganda.

It is essential to end poverty and improve education, but we do not believe that the exploitation of Yasuní is the way to do so. There are plenty of riches in our country, but they are poorly distributed, which is emphasized by the fact that the economic groups earning the most have increased their profits in recent years while at the same time there has been a decrease in the taxes that they must pay on their sales. If we increase the tax on their profits by 1.5 percent, we would get more than fifty billion dollars during the same period of twenty-two years that is being proposed for the exploitation of the ITT.

Just like the Yasuní-ITT Initiative, we propose a search for alternatives; we propose breaking away from the schemes with courage; in short, we propose a social revolution that challenges the values of energy consumption and that prioritizes the common good, defending the idea of the "good living."

We are aware that more than one person has attempted to use our platform to their own advantage, which is why it is necessary to clarify that we fight for life and an alternative to the extractivist model. We are citizens, not only urban citizens, and we are aware of the disasters that oil extraction generates for nature, humanity, and the economy. With a strong belief that this is the moment to take the debate to the streets, with the participation of everyone, we hope to overcome the oil dependency imposed on us, which, moreover, further aggravates global warming and environmental destruction, puts the lives of peoples in voluntary isolation at risk, and threatens not only the future of Ecuadorians but also that of humanity.[27]

The awareness of corruption and assimilation of coalitional principles are mentioned in passing here, but they are a constant referent in YASunidos' written materials, perhaps because of the loss of faith in formal politics that the breach with the Yasuní Treaty represents. More important is the expression of YASunidos' search for alternatives that break "away from the schemes with courage" and propose "a social revolution that challenges the values of energy consumption, and that prioritizes the common good, defending the idea of 'good living,'" principles that are at the core of the YASunidos movement and its search for ecological justice and futures. This impassioned statement by this coalition directly confronts how the petroleum dependency not only hyperexploits and toxifies the land and local peoples but also further entangles the Earth's inhabitants within a matrix of petro-coloniality that endangers the future of an inhabitable planet. Such multidirectional analysis and political action draw from the energies of assemblages with deep roots and experience within radical formations that include Indigenous activisms, ecofeminisms, transfeminist organizing and anarchic media and cultural production that searches for complex renderings of territories and viable alternatives to extractive thinking and its economies.[28]

At the end of the statement, YASunidos issues an invitation to all those "who love the country and who want to collaborate and contribute, to join the movement and walk with us in order to build a better future; as Ecuadorans we say, 'We can!'" While the appeal to nationalism is strong in this closing statement, the fusing of ecological living with postdevelopmental thinking as *el buen vivir* becomes the central tenet of a radical challenge to the assumed unquestionable logics that expand global extractive capitalism.

Threatened by YASunidos' energetic force and public rise to visibility, Correa's government initiated a strong-arm apparatus that criminalized ecological activists that defended Indigenous and protected territories, and anyone it deemed to be too critical of the state's policies.[29] With the rhetoric of democracy and the importance of the constituent assemblies as backdrop, Correa's government began deploying plainclothes police to constrain the activities of YASunidos.

YASunidos represents the "emergence" of the South American submerged perspectives that I theorized in the opening pages of this book. Its activities range from artistic expressions that emphasize the biodiversity of the Yasuní region to massive street protests aimed at denouncing Correa's breaking of the treaty. When the emergent becomes visible, then it must somehow be repressed. In weekly radio broadcasts, as Diana Coryat documents, President Correa began to methodically criminalize YASunidos' activities. Coryat writes, "As for members of YASunidos, Correa characterized them in different ways. They were either manipulated by politicians, 'the same stone-throwers as always' (associating them with a radical left political party that was frequently a subject of scorn on the *Enlaces*) or middle-class urbanites with full bellies that had never been to the Amazon, nor knew what it meant to live without basic services."[30] As the careful journalism of the bulletin "Plan V" carefully documented, Correa's trivializing of ecological activism and the accompanying criminalization and repression occurred precisely during the period when megaproject contracts in hydroelectric dams and mining expanded. The combination of an anti-extractive crackdown by Correa, and the rise of megadevelopment through concessions with Ecuadoran and Chinese companies in hydropower and water throughout the nation, made visible how extractive capitalism had always underpinned the promise of a "new" progressive state.

In fact, some believe the Yasuní-ITT agreement was tainted and constrained by extractive interests from the beginning. According to Acción Ecológica (Ecological Action), a radical independent environmental organization in Ecuador, the design of the ZITT was organized in "complicity with the big transnationals that have oil concessions in the Yasuní Biosphere Reserve. These companies have provided maps, information and infrastructure, as well as exerted considerable pressure."[31] That multinational and state interests emerged so forcefully to defend the treaty's rupture lends credence to the idea that the Yasuní ITT agreement was always bound to the model of economic dependency that has entangled the Ecuadoran nation in the global petro complex. In this gloomy scenario, what appeared to be broad-based, national, and democratic constituent processes that had given primacy to Indigenous politics actually functioned to expand the extractive state and its surveillance apparatus. In other words, rather than protecting biodiverse geographies, Correa's government has actually promoted and expanded extractive capitalism.

The coalitional efforts of the YASunidos movement, including direct action, grassroots media, and forms of autonomous participation, imagine biodiversity not as a rhetorical device but as a right. YASunidos continually finds new avenues to address the global configurations of extractive capitalism. For instance, by petitioning the case to the Inter-American Court of Human Rights, the movement aims to prosecute the government for breaking the protections that were written into the new Constitution and the Yasuní-ITT Treaty. One could argue that the global economy similarly taints the feasibility of the Inter-American Court. However, the real political gain of YASunidos is its ongoing demand for institutions of power to respond to ecological justice. This demand, whether heard or ignored, widens the space for a potential future alternative, away from the "no future" model that is extractive capitalism.

YASunidos has spawned new activist organizations that cannot be captured by the extractive view. Several smaller offshoots of YASunidos use both media and technology to turn the gaze of surveillance back onto the corporate state. For instance, the independent group GeoYasuni uses the technologies of surveillance and tracking to expose the new territories of extractivism. Rather than merely reject forms of digital mapping, such organizations expose power to better defend territories from oil interests. Counter-mapping technologies such as GeoYasuni reveal the extractive gaze for what it is, the new colonial mirror.

### Sustainable Futures?

In May 2015, I visited the Yasuní region, traveling from Quito to the eastern oil town of Coca through the Napo River and then up a small canal formed by the black waters I described earlier, before finally arriving at the Napo Wildlife Center. In the stretch from Eastern Ecuador's Coca, the once-booming oil town that overlooks the Tena tributary, fifty kilometers upriver to the Napo Wildlife Center, 22,000 hectares are collectively managed by Qichua communities whose canals and deep blue lagoons are accessible only by paddle canoe. Despite having been to Eastern Ecuador on prior occasions, which had already dispelled many of the myths that popular culture and European films had burnished into my mind about the Amazonian basin, I was still ill-prepared for how my preconceptions would be dramatically shifted along this route. In contrast to other Amazonian ecolodges along the Napo River that are foreign rather than Indigenous-owned, the Napo Wildlife Center addresses how to protect land while also producing alternative sources of wealth that benefit rather than extract from Indigenous communities.

The Napo Wildlife Center is a refuge and ecotourist destination, located in the middle of a pristine lagoon within legally protected territories of Ya-suní National Park; motorized boats are not allowed into the area, and new construction and fishing are strictly regulated. The center is run by the local Qichua community, an Indigenous group that reconstituted in the Ama-zon after fleeing from highland colonial terror in the sixteenth century. Some thirty families share ownership of the center, and manage hundreds of hectares of ecotourism. Each new child born into these families becomes the co-owners of an ecologically and socially minded model.

Ecotourism can be a passive enterprise, as Qichua guides float foreign visitors around on wooden-planked canoes to experience the sinuous turns of the rivers and the prolific life that resides within Amazonian black-water canals. Furthermore, my feeling about being floated around this pristine space was conflicted, as our guides were trained to help visitors see the action within the forest in order to photograph hard-to-spot animals. Yet Native guides also took care with the pedagogy of how to take in the mul-tiple sensual worlds and layers that existed in the forest. Traveling up these overgrown spaces where the forest turns into the lakes and rivers, with eco-tones living in the micro- and macrospaces of intertwined life forms, I can spot animal life only by following the green laser that Qichua guides point at the camouflaging branches. Whether distinguishing one of thirty tangier, one of three monkey species, one of five parrot varieties, the river otter, or the three-toed sloth, without Indigenous guides it is literally impossible to see the forest's multiplicity or understand the layered life worlds it con-tains. Could that small hairy ball really be a sloth? As I heard our guides say countless times throughout that trip, "We know how to see the forest. Do you see any Indigenous people here with eyeglasses?" While the scholar might react that this is a shallow and essentializing way to understand the differences in the contact zone between tourists and Indigenous peoples, this statement was repeatedly iterated by Qichua mediators to communicate the meaning of perception that operates within autonomous and co-extensive life systems.

Whether on night walks or on a path through the thirty-foot canopy filled with plant, insect, and animal life, a visitor, even an experienced botanist, cannot access the codes of the forest, neither in terms of its wildlife nor the kinds of creative capacities that emerge from the forest and the Qichua imagination within it. Walking under the canopy and hovering in a thirty-meter ceiba tree, for instance, our guides showed us how to play games with the fibers of palm trees, how to corral wild pigs, the importance of squinting to see animal life, and the thickness of insect life below the detritus of the forest.

One of the Quichua guides, Felipe, told our group about the sacred ceiba tree that often grows a 150-foot-tall canopy. When cut down, according to Quichua beliefs, the ceiba requires not only the physical labor of four large men, as he put it, but also several rituals to ask the tree's forest spirit for permission. The powerful ceiba has its own complex system of intelligibility. It sees above the other trees not to survey them, as in the extractive view, but as an enlivened force, an inhabited energy, as a being that can be perceived and felt as an *iman*, or magnetic center, of the forest's intangible vitality. Like the spiritual tourism I describe in the next chapter, mediation through Indigenous knowledge and an understanding of the forest enlist the deepening of one's attention, turning away from colonized vision toward a complex sensibility within the natural world, where the narration of cosmologies through story become the communicative texture of perception.

In the Yasuní, the focus on the rain forest and the ecological and redistributive material imaginaries of the Qichua is a refreshing counterpoint to the colonial logic of unrestrained dangers. As my guide at Napo Wildlife Center said, "The only way to protect such territories is through ecotourism. Nothing else will speak for the forest like our own communities, and those that travel here from other places learn from and engage the wildlife that can grow and evolve here."

Though ecological tourist sites such as the Napo Wildlife Center can be deemed as liberal efforts that work in tandem with state interests to assuage the monumentality of the capitalist assault on nature, after immersion and research into the site, I am persuaded by the statement that "nothing else can protect this forest" except those that know and live among its complexity—those who offer this mode of perceiving otherwise to curious and affluent ecologically minded foreigners. This form of Indigenous critique of coloniality and ecological praxis works within fractures of the extractive divide, seeks to defend through other routes that imagine alternative futures. Despite the fact that this model represents its own dynamics of coloniality, within the petro industry that surrounds the Yasuní, it may provide one of few remaining options for a present-future of ecological viability, especially for the intangible zone.

### Toward a Conclusion

To think about biodiverse futures, and in this geography in particular, it is impossible to ignore how, amid ecological destruction, Quichua and Shuar peoples and "no contact" populations mediate intangible geographies in close proximity to the global economy. The fight for the Yasuní illustrates many important operations about the extractive era, situated at the crossroads of ecological futures. More than a symbol, the Yasuní is a complex Amazonian basin system made up of multiplicity of life forms that constitute what is often described as the "lungs of the world." At the same time, the breaking of the Yasuní-ITT agreement is a very different, and unfortunate, event: a symbol of the desire for unquenchable revenue, and an emblem of national failure, especially in terms of economic and institutional arrangements that have reproduced old petro-dependent relations.

The intangible geographies of the Yasuní transforms themselves through the laws of entropy, as the random order of nature cannot be captured by the empirical imperative or by conventional scientific inquiry. As Western science concedes, it is literally impossible to catalogue the immense biodiversity of the forest and its constant change. Furthermore, the Yasuní represents fragile ecologies in need of conservation and a melancholic plea to the world about biodiversity, interculturality, and the potential planetary gains of radical ecological defense.

The work of YASunidos and other anti-extractive activisms, such as the geospatial mapping project, on the one hand, and direct contact with the forest through Indigenous-led ecotourism, on the other, provide new pathways to counteract the neocolonial condition. We might take a page from the "no contact" Indigenous groups that reject integration into colonial neoliberalism. The Tagaeri and Taromenane peoples have literally refused the extractive zone altogether by going back into the forest to live outside of the colonial divide. Though some may suggest that the centering of forest dwellers as romantic to planetary visions of the future, another way to frame the importance of this analysis is to consider the complex web of petroleum complicity that differentially toxifies racialized and gendered bodies of most of the world's geographies. The planetary extractive zone that is the petroleum matrix leaves few options for the future, even as complex and counter-intuitive refusals, creative extensions, and social ecologies continue to unravel its totalizing reach.

In terms of protecting "biodiversity," a nomenclature that could be applied to all social ecologies, the Quichua and Shuar present a second set of alternatives by operating at the edges of the extractive zones of the global economy, sometimes teaching foreigners how to see differently and to catalogue wildlife while also inviting a perception that sees the living world against reductionist viewing. Indigenous knowledge and cosmologies live alongside and within intangible geographies by cultivating rather than domesticating them. Such proposals offer a viable future for interacting with the natural world rather than merely ransacking it.

Ultimately, as I have argued throughout this chapter, the Yasuní cannot be apprehended through any instrument of the state or through the extractive gaze. Intangibility instead describes Amazonian life as evolutionary entropy and patterned complexity, where hard science and ecological rhetoric dissolve. In this landscape that escapes cataloguing, future alternatives show up as a radical coalition of transfeminists, ecologically minded, and urban dwellers that recognize how their activities function in concert with Afro and Indigenous peoples to defend and provide alternatives from within and beyond the extractive zone.

# CHAPTER 2

# Andean Phenomenology
# and New Age Settler Colonialism

In the hour after sunset and before moonrise there is very light in the Sacred Valley of Peru. Walking from the little town of Pisac a few miles back to where I was staying, I had no flashlight and only the night sounds as my guide. The sky hung in a shadowy thick black, pricked only by a dim arc of stars, making the path between danger and safety a narrow one, both physically and existentially. If I stepped to my right, I could have fallen into the muddy waters of the Urubamba River, disappearing without a trace into the tumbling currents brought on by the rainy season. To my left, wire fences demarcated the edges of fields that had been put up by a flurry of foreigners in a pattern that resembles rural gentrification. As I walked, I remembered that local cattle were occasionally mangled by the sharp barbwire, a thought that made me shudder as I imagined my own flesh torn like that of those massive animals. As I picked up my step, a sensation of utter powerlessness and intense solitude swept over me.

After a few minutes of total panic that left me breathless, I remembered the words of Don Francisco, a Q'ero highland elder, words that he had shared during a long workshop on Andean phenomenology earlier that day about the animation of the natural world. Locating the source of my embodied reaction as the fear of the unknown expanse, I forced myself to slow my steps and to breathe in the night air, clear and vast and moist because of the riverbed below. I became present to the surrounding four tall mountains, the rough rushing of the Urubamba River, and what in an Andean worldview is known as Pachamama, the Earth Being. Despite the unknown landscape, I was able to release the overwhelming sense of fear that had captured me. After several minutes, I made my way carefully, but more easily, on the last stretch of road, back to my little room in the Centro Paz y Luz, one center of Cuzco's spiritual tourism. Once there, lying on a small bed, I tried to come to terms with the feeling of falling apart I experienced on the dark road back. That overwhelming sensation, and my reckoning with it, has resulted in an exploration in this chapter of the submerged perception of Andean phenomenology.

The worldview of Andean phenomenology is, as I analyze in this chapter, always mediated and historically entangled through a colonial matrix. Therefore, the reader will note my cautious undertaking of Andean phenomenology through an analytical register that situates critical proximity with decolonial critique. For instance, narrating my overwhelming fear in this unknown setting is hopefully not to overindulge in anecdote but instead to work through a decolonial method that centers my own perception and embodied experience to perceive anew the complexity of the histories, entanglements, and colonial afterlives within the landscapes that I traverse. What I experienced alongside the Urubamba River and in relation to the road with so little light and my breaking apart in front of the unknown offers the possibility of a decolonized shift in the affective structure at the core of the late liberal self even as it could just as easily repel it. Losing control over my surroundings that night, unable to see two feet in front of me, I lost my composure and thus spun into an uncontrollable state of disorientation. This discomposure, I realized later, disturbed me profoundly, a lack of control that as a subject of US Empire I have come to instinctively, and deeply, avoid. But as I learned through my interactions with Q'ero elders, there was another possible path that transformed fragmentation, disorientation, and fear by instead dissolving into the surround. In other words, I had access to another way to experience, one in which dissolution of the self was distinct from and an alternative to the Western definition of psychological fragmentation.

If Kantian philosophy is built upon a discrete conception of the self, where the individual human mind structures experience and perception, and Freudian individuation places emphasis on developmental separation, then much of Western liberal society is built from the crucible of these two concepts of the self. As a Southern mode of thinking, being and living, Andean phenomenology, by contrast, starts from another vantage point: it locates the subject in multirelational terms and blurs the binary distinctions between the human and biomatter into porous interactivity. The self is not bifurcated between an inside and outside, and thus there is no simple divide into distinct formulations of the external other; instead, the self embraces (and is embraced by) a sensual and integrated relationality with the natural elements and everything that surrounds us. Unlike vitalism, Andean phenomenology is yet another iteration of land-based Indigenous ontologies, a way of being that disentangles from the discreteness of the "Global North" psyche and also from the artificial separation of life into organic, inorganic, mobile, immobile, animate and inanimate matter. While this unboundedness of being was not completely unfamiliar to me, because of my queer femininity and perhaps also because of my propensity to reach beyond the limits imposed by masculine, Western, and reason-oriented subjectivity, the reorientation of my encounter with existential fear made me realize the extent to which such an affective state is also a colonial and consumer capitalist imposition. It was only through the realization of an externally imposed relation to fear that I could usher in a different sensibility, one that extended into the unseen and unknown without the interruptions of the logics of separateness. As I describe in this chapter, Andean phenomenology, a perspective buried within the new age spiritual tourist economy, offers another way of knowing and feeling, one that alters and even shatters the self as a discrete entity that is transacted upon.

To understand this concept of the self, we must consider the Andean Indigenous relationality that Marisol de la Cadena has importantly written about in *Earth Beings*.[1] This is a relation to land, place, mountains, and the elements that assumes a profound sacred orientation and understanding of it that moves in registers that are not easily catalogued by the colonial project. For de la Cadena, the experience of interaction and friendship with the Q'ero elder Nazario Turpio and Mariano Turpio over many years allowed her to mediate between her world and knowledge base, and an Andean-centered belief system. De la Cadena presents how these interactions shifted her ways of knowing as mediated through these relations and Quechua speaking peoples' communication as Indigenous political strategies. On a few of my many site visits to the Sacred Valley, I too had the opportunity to meet Nazario and experience his *despacho* ceremony that he conducted to pay respects to Pachamama through ritualized offerings.

However, as I outline throughout this chapter, the spaces of mediation between Indigenous ways of knowing and outsider knowledge, within the region of the Sacred Valley, are often not organized by long encounters, strong friendships with Native peoples, or an intimate understanding of place. Instead, such interactions are fundamentally organized through asymmetrical power relations as they operate within the easy transactions of a commodified global tourist economy, where "Native-made" souvenirs are often imported to denote authenticity.[2] There are few spaces of engagement with Indigenous peoples, knowledge, and geographies that are not undone and remade through the vestiges of historical overdetermination. New age colonial fantasies are premised upon knowability, yet I show how there is nothing pure, unmixed, or directly accessible about Indigenous knowledge and technologies in the extractive zone. If the Sacred Valley geography and its inhabitants are constructed through taxonomies that racialize difference, then neoliberal extractivism comes with intense cultural and economic contradictions, which are the inevitable consequence of the vastly asymmetrical and historically mediated relations between Indigenous and non-Indigenous subjects.

Lisa Aldred addresses how white American consumption emerges from the loss of authenticity, a deep dissatisfaction and alienation, whereby the marketplace structures identities through Native appropriation. With her useful and expansive term "plastic shamans," Aldred takes up the consumer aspect of new age countercultural identification. She identifies the terrain of the new age as a wide assortment of practices that include "shamanism, goddess workshop, Eastern religions, crystals, pagan rituals, extraterrestrials and channeling spirit beings,"[3] estimating that anywhere between five and twenty million people could be considered new age spirituality practitioners. This astonishing prevalence of Native appropriation forces us to consider how US consumers are overwhelmingly complicit in appropriation with little economic payoff for Indigenous peoples. As I illustrate throughout this chapter, "plastic shamanism" and "playing Indian" perform empire in the international sphere, where mostly white and, to a much less degree, Black and Brown people of color transfer these structures of inequality from the United States and Europe to elsewhere, whether in the Américas or beyond.

Whereas in the last chapter I argued that thoughtfully conceived and Indigenous led ecotourism could be one of a range of solutions from the South for radical conservation, in this chapter I chart spiritual tourism as an often-unbalanced system that extracts from Indigenous bodies and knowledge with little positive result for local communities. In the Sacred Valley, the privileges of mobility and land ownership—what Cheryl Harris has referred to as "whiteness as property"[4]—structures the land into differentiated regions of gentrification and land dispossession that push Indigenous peoples even further up into the highlands. I examine how differential access to land becomes the basis for the expansion of new age spirituality, an expansion that promotes a racialized idea of individual human potential and expression while ignoring the historical debt of colonial dispossessions.

Furthermore, the spiritual tourist industry can easily fall prey to what I call Andeanism, whereby the region becomes a projection of romantic spatial imaginaries, an idyllic escape from the toxicities of the overdeveloped United States and Europe. Here, I reference Edward Said's concept of Orientalism as unidirectional representational hegemony over the object and subject of Western fascination.[5] I also refer to Mel Chen's invocation of the intimate relationship between the construction of racial difference, embodiment, and toxic environments within a differentiated global order.[6] The Andes has been reductively constructed, a place where the fantasy of leaving behind the stress, consumption, "eco-depression," and generalized dissatisfactions of late capitalism ends up exonerating the foreigner from local injustices and playing into new age settler colonialism. Against this overdetermined backdrop, can Andean phenomenology puncture these historical constructs toward producing another kind of relation? Even amid the fundamental asymmetries of colonial tourism, how do Indigenous technologies, instead of feeding racial extractivism, provide alternative forms of knowing, relations, and communication?

In this chapter, Andean phenomenology represents a submerged perspective, one that is difficult to access because of the fatal impact of religious colonial histories and extractive capitalism. Even so, it represents a way to diminish the fear and individuation that advance neoliberal capitalism, and offers another path on the road to a more integrated approximation to one another and to the nonhuman other. I explore this particular extractive zone to understand the potential that lies within it by first situating the rise of foreigner presence in a new age tourist economy. Given that spiritual tourism aims to interpret but cannot account for Q'ero knowledge, I analyze how Indigenous social ecologies such as Andean phenomenology often exceed the extractive zone, moving beyond capitalism's inevitable commodification, and beyond neoliberal noise, toward a sensibility of undivided states of being.

Over the course of six research trips between 2008 and 2013, I interviewed over sixty informants that were both Indigenous and non-Indigenous, accessed the materials of both the Cuzco municipal archive, and the library of Cuzco University, and spent countless hours within the spiritual tourist economy. In the Sacred Valley, I also visited a series of Incan religious sites, many of which are administered by the Peruvian Ministry of Culture, and other unmapped sites that are "off the national tourist grid." Part of the lure of spiritual tourism is to gain access to this set of interconnected geographies of Indigenous pasts that—invisible to the extractive gaze—configure an intricate sacred landscape for Q'ero peoples. Yet, the "spiritual gaze" has its own complicities and sets of problems that inhibit decolonial perspectives.

### Spiritual Enclosures

There were, of course, historical resonances that framed my experience on the road back from Pisac that night. My discomfort, disorientation, and existential fear carried a deeper register in a landscape shot through with the legacies of colonial fear that from the Spanish conquistador Francisco Pizarro's 1533 capture of Incan King Athualpa onward has been used to subjugate Native peoples and territories in the region. What was at first a relatively small army of Spanish soldiers used the combination of Christian religion and colonial violence to thoroughly dismantle the Incan Empire over the course of a few short decades. By transferring a durable racial order from peninsular monarchies to Nueva España, Spanish rulers worked to sediment Enlightenment worldviews on newly settled territories.[7] Nelson Maldonado-Torres describes how religious-ethical justifications were central to how Spanish colonialism was installed in the New World, with the consequence of subjugating Native and African peoples to a new order of being.[8] Furthermore, colonial capitalism gained traction through religious ideologies and hierarchies that depended on organizing and proliferating a racialized matrix of violence. In the face of the thriving Incan economies that took root in the Sacred Valley of Cuzco, which the colonial archive calls el Valle de Yucay, fear of how conquest might proceed must have been the colonizers' dominant affective response.

During the pre-Hispanic era, the Incan Empire centralized its governance, ruling throughout the Cuzco and Urubamba regions in part by consolidating religious traditions, and the notion of the sacred, over several centuries. The hierarchical Incan royal society organized the social, political, and economic dimensions of Incan life that included a highly developed agricultural economy and an extensive built environment. This system subsumed the heterogeneity of Indigenous groups within it, even prior to the arrival of the Spanish conquistadors. Many of these pre-colonial resentments continue to inform the sense that Q'ero peoples, as the "direct inheritors of Incans," are disproportionately privileged within the tourist economy.[9]

In 1542, Cuzco became the site of the Spanish viceroyalty and an epicenter of franchise colonialism in the New World. Here and throughout the Andes, Catholicism, alongside the Spanish crown and its military, played a powerful role in establishing a new social order against, but also syncretized with, the Incan sacred. As has been widely documented, the inheritance of *limpieza de sangre* (blood purity) ideologies brought from the Iberian Peninsula and imposed during the colonial period created a system of radical inequality for Indigenous peoples with taxonomies that represented a color/class/gender order.[10] More specific to Cuzco and the surrounding region, the religious order and colonial system of privilege formed the basis of the new land tenure system that granted land rights and legal titles to those with Spanish inheritance, dispossessing or leaving in limbo Indigenous landholdings.[11] The institutions of the Catholic religion, Spanish colonialism, and the military worked in concert to finance the landed *criollo* (Peruvian-born Spanish elite) and develop a regional economy through a complex tax and tributary system, all the while subjecting Indigenous peoples to debt peonage on latifundio properties where land holdings represented a structure of racial capitalism.

To emphasize the degree to which colonial religion has influenced the Cuzco region, one only has to note how the first South American convent was founded there in 1556. In *Colonial Habits*, a case study of three convents in Cuzco (Santa Clara, Santa Carolina, Santa Teresa), Kathryn Burns details the complex spiritual economy put into motion during the sixteenth and seventeenth centuries. This spiritual order extended into the republican and nation-building era wherein convents reshaped and newly defined the meaning of the colonial system.[12] Specifically, nuns legislated new forms of social exclusion by disciplining "unruly" Indigenous girls and educating them in Christian values. As nuns socialized young women into vows of poverty, they simultaneously grew to be one of the wealthiest sectors of the burgeoning colonial population, maintaining economic interests by acquiring property throughout the region, and becoming a major lender to local businesses and to the city government. As Burns's research evidences, spiritual interests and economic profit have been inextricably linked in Cuzco and the surrounding region since the colonial regime, often reproducing an extractive race, gender, and class economy that subjugated Native autonomy to expand the financial holdings of the Catholic Church.

Early forms of extractive capitalism also entangled religious and disciplinary violence against Indigenous peoples to consolidate the colonial order of being. Michael Taussig describes the colonial Andes as a space that was dialectically organized through a particular set of colonial narratives that insisted upon shamanistic magic as the site of Indigenous beliefs and that organized colonial fantasy production. From a European perspective, that Native peoples used magic provided evidence of their state of nature and incapacity for scientific reason, even while some forms of shamanism could not be read separately from technologies of resistance to the matrix of violence of the colonial order.[13]

As the extractive rubber economy in the south of Peru became insatiable during the sixteenth and seventeenth centuries, South American Indigenous peoples were increasingly represented as rebellious, untamable, animalistic, and irrational. Where violence was the main technique of labor coercion, magic differentiated the savage from the civilized, and was used to justify the torture and terrorization of Native peoples throughout the continent. Even though the rubber boom took place in a southern region of Peru, the effect of historical overdetermination was that colonial violence was installed through the production of fantasies about Andean Indigeneity that persist today. In particular, the "wild man" that Taussig describes is the shaman figure that served a number of colonial fantasies about taming native peoples while also extracting healing power from them. As Taussig writes, "Going to the Indians for their healing power and killing them for their wildness is not so far apart."[14]

While I would not want to claim that the current forms of neoliberal new age tourist economy form a straight pathway from these colonial tropes, I would suggest that we cannot understand the recent growth in a spiritual global economy without also attending to the fascination with and colonial investment in the Andean shaman. We must also look historically to understand the influence of the convent system in the region and the "retraining" and Christianizing of Indigenous girls and women on the part of the Catholic Church as a colonizing move to spiritually rule Native peoples. Furthermore, to truly undertake an analysis of what I discuss as the extractive zone in the region, namely the spiritual tourist economy, we must also consider the long production of fantasies about the other in relation to the colonial violence of extractive capitalism. Therefore, the legacies of the spiritual "wild man" are palpable and integral to the production of colonial fantasies about Andean shamans and their magical abilities to change the Western character.

A recent spate of cultural production, such as the video documentary *Q'ero Mystics of Peru* (2014) directed by Seti Gershberg, or literature that pokes fun at the tourist economy, rehearses some of these colonial tropes about the magical prowess of the Andean shaman.[15] In these representations, the Andean shaman is shrouded in the language of hyperbole, cast as either saving the planet from the effects of the Anthropocene or as a willing participant in commodifying the image of shamanistic magic. Attending to the histories of Spanish colonialism in this new era of tourist neocolonialism, perhaps we should reconsider how the colonial mirror reveals more about the observer than about the subject under observation. In relation to the fascination with the other's spirituality, Taussig concludes that if you seek hell, you should try looking inside.[16]

### Andean Phenomenology

Like African diasporic belief systems, in which ancestors (*orishas*), and animal spirits exert influence over the earthly realms, Andean cosmologies find their expression in the transitions between worlds and levels of experience that are not perceivable to the transparency of the extractive view. In Q'ero cosmologies, other forms of perception are available by attending to the invisible worlds that live within three overlapping planes: the upper sky realm (called Hanan Pacha); the middle, inner Earth realm (Uku Pacha); and the lower and outer Earth realm, which is the realm of human existence (Cay Pacha). Andean peoples call upon the *apus* (sacred mountains), the rivers, the rocks, the animal spirits, and the lineages of ancestors in all three realms to support ordinary activities and the business of healing humans. Furthermore, these invisible realms are vibrant with life to such a degree that the fear, anxiety, and melancholy of "loneliness" that describes the subjectification of living within advanced capitalism, is, according to Andean phenomenology, a figurative impossibility.

Josef Estermann calls the ecological potential of Andean philosophy "la Ecosofía Andina," an Andean ecophilosophy.[17] He describes a mestizx and Indigenous set of beliefs and practices based on ecological principles that rethink the catastrophe of late capitalism toward planetary rehabilitation. *La vida plena Andina*, the Andean notion of "full life," forms the basis of an intricate ecological worldview that does not disaggregate the material world from religious-spiritual dimensions. Furthermore, it considers the link between the two as a utopic imaginary based in the presence of the aliveness of being.[18] As I discussed earlier, this is not an anthropocentric or even an androcentric viewpoint, since the hierarchies of Western philosophy and its chain of being disappear into the "interconnected everything." Sustainability is, moreover, not a limited concept that leaves the structures of extractive capitalism intact but conceives of transgenerational stewardship that requires sustained attention in all human activities. The Earth's water, minerals, land, soil, and air are not thingified, or turned into commodities, but rather given due respect as part of an integral totality that must be taken care of by the human species, ideas that echo with Indigenous ontologies across the planet.

While constructivist theories emanating from Europe and the United Sates address the ecological predicament by pointing out dualisms between body and mind, and between matter and thought, much of this work ignores Indigenous perspectives, worldviews, and the concrete material struggles of land and water defense as historically antithetical to capitalism.[19] Furthermore, while new materialist theories often privilege technological innovation and scientific advancement, they often do so without consideration over the colonial condition and its consequences, even as they point to the vibrancy of material life.[20] Andean ecological notions of fuller life make animacy explicit as a set of Indigenous imaginaries that have long differently sensed and formed in connection to the natural world.

*Andean phenomenology*, as I use it here, describes the human relation to the natural world's sensual, intimate, and embodied dimensions that interlink the aliveness of material and immaterial realms. Though certain strains of feminist theory and praxis also consider embodied knowledge as co-extensive, new feminist materialisms tends to be contained by Western-only and Anglo-based discussions regarding the discreteness of the body and nature/culture binaries. For instance, Rosi Braidotti's nomadic philosophy argues for an embedded vision of embodied subjectivity that encompasses the body at all levels, especially, the biological body, referencing a Deleuzian philosophy of radical immanence.[21] Andean phenomenology, despite its mediation by coloniality, often places less emphasis on the making of individual subjectivity, since embodiment is defined as thoroughly sensitive, and as being in haptic touch with the surround. Different from feminist new materialisms, Andean phenomenology delinks from the individual biological body to reach out toward the body of mountains, rivers, stones, and the Earth body of Pachamama.

Reflecting again on the opening anecdote, my perceptual shift in relation to my experience on the road from Pisac that night occurred precisely by pulling away from the training of coloniality even if this occurred subconsciously and against my disciplinary training. Perhaps spirituality, narrowly defined, is too bound up with the religious colonial order to offer an alternate imagination of the world? Decolonial literature has raised this question for some time, particularly Enrique Dussel in his work on liberation ethics,[22] and Walter Mignolo's working through of Gloria Anzaldúa's border gnosis.[23] And Chicana and women of color feminisms have historically contended with precisely how to think beyond the colonial divide and place embodied knowledge as the source of a future-oriented imaginary of the planetary. Yet more work is needed to think through paradigms that elaborate worldviews that extend beyond the paradigm of the self, and that perceive Earth and the cosmos, through the means of perception offered through Andean phenomenology. How can we decolonize relations and the Anthropocene toward a nonextractive and anti-capitalist future? By thinking with Eve Tuck and K. Wayne Yang's important call that decolonization is not a metaphor, to answer this question we must also prioritize an understanding of Indigenous land dispossession, contending directly with settler dynamics and responsibility.[24]

## Owning the Sacred

Blue-green mountains surround the fertile landscape of the Sacred Valley, which is crossed through by the serpentine Urubamba River. Formed by the Urubamba River, the Sacred Valley is situated in the geographies between Calca and Cuzco, Piquillaqta and Ollantaytambo. Dotted with sacred Incan sites to recall the epicenter of preconquest Incan culture, the Sacred Valley has increasingly become a tourist destination, either as a stop en route to Machu Picchu or as the main destination. The river valley is frequented each year by tens of thousands of national and international visitors. A popular destination for spiritual tourism is Diane Dunn's Centro Paz y Luz, located between four sacred mountains that surround her property, and built in the shape of a *chakana* (Incan cross).

As the founder of Centro Paz y Luz, a center through which much of the Valley's spiritual tourist traffic passes, Dunn is a key figure in the region. As a white American "ex-patriot" who lived in Johannesburg and New York before moving near to the town of Pisac fifteen years ago, her story represents the larger phenomenon of new migrations from the United States to the Andes in search of a way out of the overdevelopment, consumption, stress, and alienation of everyday life.[25] However, unlike Cotacachi, Cuenca, and Villcabamba, where thousands of retired white Americans have relocated over the last decade, the Sacred Valley attracts younger tourists whose purported objective is to expand their spiritual consciousness, often through the programs that Dunn organizes. The center also attracts tourism based on ayahuasca, the Amazon hallucinogenic plant that is now circulated widely in the Sacred Valley and transits extensively within US cosmopolitan centers. In a period of three years, according to some estimates, ayahuasca tourism in the Sacred Valley spiked by 500 percent. Even though ayahuasca spiritual tourism originates in the Peruvian Amazon, it circulates with increasing frequency in the Sacred Valley, where travelers seek out a shift in perception, through hallucinogenic plants offered, sometimes by European "playing Indian" facilitators, as part of a spiritual tourist experience.

Dunn's notoriety increased after she published two locally best-selling memoirs about her experience in Cuzco. In *Cusco: The Gateway to Inner Wisdom: A Journey to the Energetic Center of the World*, Dunn describes how "visitors from all over the world now converge on Peru to take in its spiritual energy and learn the secrets of the Andean path."[26] In it, she details a life in the United States that, while creative, was filled with anxiety and a feeling of insufficiency. Her sense of absence led her on a search for something more meaningful, which brought her to what she describes as "the Andean path." As Dunn writes: "Still there was something missing, something pulling, something prodding. It always seemed to be just around the corner. If I could only get there I knew I would be happy. What was it, that illusive something? Was it a big theatrical hit? Was it fame and fortune? Was it a man to love me? Or something more?"[27] In the aspiration for something more, Dunn reveals an affective angst about her condition of belonging, an anxiety that opened the door to a spiritual search. The search for one's higher self, described as an arduous process that ultimately leads to more purposeful living, is a familiar trope of new age literature. While the trope of spiritual journeys promises fulfillment through a detachment from the ego that unveils universal connection,[28] Dunn's story offers a means to a different end. Namely, the journey's narrative permits her to establish herself as divinely preordained to build a healing center upon Andean sacred lands. The problem with this unexamined assumption is that it rehearses Christian settler colonial narratives that justify the taking of Indigenous territory for the expansion of a religious belief system.

After the 2006 publication of *Cusco*, many travelers began arriving on Dunn's doorstep, and the center became a well-known destination for those seeking mystical adventures in the region. Once she was attracting consistent numbers, Dunn began offering workshops to foreigners seeking training "along the Andean spiritual path." In this new workshop format, she included the participation of Native Q'ero elders, who taught a version of "ancient healing rites," called the Munay-ki rites.[29]

As a North American with Christian theological training, Dunn plays a central, if contentious, role within the Sacred Valley. Despite questions about Dunn's commitment to local land politics, and whether her interpretation of Native beliefs is readymade for foreign consumption, many of my informants credited her book, and her building of the center, as the single most important factor for increased tourism to the Pisac region, which they saw as having a central role in stimulating the local economy. In Dunn's account, she states very specific reasons for bringing international travelers to the Sacred Valley:

In the secret recesses of my being I knew, or rather had been reminded, that I had chosen (and been chosen) to be a healer and transformer at this wonderful time in history, to help bring about the *taripay pacha* described in the Inka prophecies . . . the vision Regis had was to create a large center where people from all over the world, from all different religions and faith traditions, could gather together for spiritual practice and social service. The Sacred Valley near Cuzco was an ideal location because of the strong energy vortex there, which would naturally attract people and assist in our efforts for unity and transformation. . . . Intention is everything, I reminded myself. I figured if I was being led to Peru to help develop the *Centro Espiritual*, then the ways and means would be provided.[30]

The Taripay Pacha that Dunn refers to is the future return to "meet ourselves again," or the suture back to wholeness after the colonial catastrophe. In Dunn's imaginary, the new age spiritual practice that she refers to in this passage requires her participation toward this wholeness, or Taripay Pacha, the Q'ero vision of a time of peace. Even while Dunn makes reference to Andean belief systems, the tropes that she uses are not removed from the assumptions made within the discourse of manifest destiny that allows settlers to fulfill their destined role, producing a settler worldview predicated upon erasing Native standpoints.

In earlier segments of her written narrative, Dunn had already positioned herself as someone who had found herself in the right place at the right time. For instance, in post-apartheid South Africa she worked as a spiritual counselor to aggrieved populations during the aftermath of the Truth Commission.[31] However, her potentially troubling position as a white North American within the transitional racial regime in South Africa was mentioned without comment or reflection, foreshadowing the binary split between spirituality and racial politics that undergirds much of the story of white and European settlement within the Indigenous Andes. More importantly, Dunn, both on paper and in interviews, eschews the question of historical land inequality or working to change the structures of colonialism for the betterment of Andean Native peoples, an issue broached by Andean intellectuals and activists throughout the postcolonial period. It is nearly impossible not to interpolate Dunn within the broader matrix that is new age settler colonialism.

If we consider Lorenzo Veracini's by now-familiar formulation of a global settler pattern that did not end with the colonial period but rather continues to expand into Indigenous territories, then we must also take seriously his theoretical framework that shows how migrants, arrivants, and settlers are all placed in relation to each other and against Indigenous peoples in a hierarchical stratum of territorial occupation.[32] New age settler colonialism is an even more pernicious formulation, as it describes a stark condition produced out of the interaction between foreign visitors and Indigenous peoples that reproduces the colonial condition in which the shaman is extracted from in order for subjects of late capitalism to become "whole again," remade away from consumer capitalism and its alienating force. However, the central concerns of occupation, gentrification, and appropriation remain completely absented from the consequences of new age settler colonialism.

In other chapters of this book, I describe the expansionist practices of states and corporations as a means of racial capitalism. In Peru, the extractive work of new age settler colonialism is actually much more straightforward. Given the histories of dispossessions in the Sacred Valley, in which Native peoples were increasingly pushed into the highlands during Spanish colonization, the territories that foreigners occupy for new age tourism reproduces the colonial dynamic of settler expansionism. Alongside Indigenous people's affective and physical labor, the land provides an extractible resource for the expansion of spiritual tourism, where the conversion of Indigenous territories to private property to farmland to new age retreats is embedded within the industry in the same way land occupation is essential to more conventional forms of extractive capitalism.

Private property forms the foundation for tourist infrastructure: whether for five-star hotels, ayahuasca huts, *residenciales*, or workshops, spiritual tourism depends on access to land ownership. In the Sacred Valley, this has meant that the extractive economy is not organized around discrete products, such as the oil within the Yasuní, or the pine, eucalyptus, oil, or copper that I discuss in later chapters. Instead, in a feedback loop, new age settler colonialism extracts from Indigenous bodies and lands to quell the anxieties and accelerated demands of consumer capitalism. As Joanna Drzewieniecki contends, Andean property structures changed with the arrival of European colonialism that inaugurated land privatization during the sixteenth century.[33] Indeed, the concentration of land access and tenure through the hacienda system has been a primary way that privatization has ruptured Andean systems of communal and customary law.

In his classic text *The Formation of a National Indo-American Culture*, José María Arguedas describes the irreconcilable difference between economic systems that are based, on the one hand, on a Western property ownership model, and, on the other, on an intimate sacred relationship to land and work that organized Andean life prior to Spanish colonialism.[34] During the 1920s and 1930s, an era of heightened modernization rhetoric, rural peasant unions and federations led Indigenous peoples to maneuver a radically stratified court system, with mixed legal results. As with other Latin American nations, the Peruvian agrarian reform process (1969–95) lasted for more than two decades during the crucial period of rural rights' recognition. More recently, neoliberalization has effectively led to the recent real estate system of speculation that dominates the Urubamba Valley today—led by new age settler colonialism, in which rural gentrification continuously dispossesses Native populations.

The land for Dunn's healing center was bought around 2000, at a time when Alberto Fujimori's neoliberal administration privileged the purchase of land by individuals and multinational corporations. Dunn built a home on a small piece of former farmland. While visiting a local restaurant frequented by foreign residents, Urika's Place, Dunn responded to an inquiry by a female travel writer from the *Lonely Planet* about possible new guidebook destinations in the surrounding area. Despite the fact that she had only one room to offer at the time, Dunn asked the *Lonely Planet* writer to visit the property. When the updated version of the guidebook came out, it included one line about Dunn and the center, referring to a "special place" run by a North American who conducted spiritual tours.

Using capital from a personal loan from her parents, Dunn's original land purchase near Pisac later doubled, and then tripled, over a few years.[35] Just as important, since Dunn bought the original property, a dozen or more European and North American new age entrepreneurs have followed her example, acquiring land in the area and settling there. Even a group of urban mestizxs that I encountered "returned to the land" and bought property elsewhere in the valley, and while they were more politically astute about the displacing effects upon Indigenous and local peoples in the region, they also contributed equally to increases in real estate prices. This form of settler colonialism imbricates with capitalist speculation to push

Indigenous peoples to the margin of the global economy. Even Dunn herself has had a hard time keeping up with the area's ever-rising property costs as she continually seeks to expand her center's infrastructure.

Dunn positions herself in her books and gatherings as an initiated Andean priestess, mediator of Indigenous knowledge, and teacher of energetic rites to a global audience. At the same time, she remains untroubled by her position as landowner in a region where the colonial construction of Indigenous difference historically permeates all social and economic relations. In a near self-critique, Dunn discussed how "a local taxi driver asked me to do a *despacho* in her house, but I felt awkward dressed up in my poncho and *chuyo*. There was something a little amiss here. When I started working on my own instead of me making the *despachos* I have the Q'ero come to make it, because I don't think it's appropriate for me to do it."[36] The appropriation of dress, embodied practices, and rituals by Dunn and others rehearses a form of Andeanism that extracts culture from Indigenous peoples while also occupying lands in ways that contribute to a racially stratified global economy. Michael Hill describes how religious seeking at the core of appropriating Indigenous cultural technologies is actually quintessentially about how neoliberalism produces new social identities.[37] These new social identities emerge as a new age "wild man" economy, which Taussig perhaps unwittingly also contributed to.[38]

Indeed, the figure of the Q'ero shaman is central to the appropriations and confusions that take place within the complex circuits of racialized globalization. When coupled with the patterns of rural gentrification as a technique of new age settler colonialism, there are few circumventions possible against the speculative fictions placed upon Indigenous bodies, land, and affective and material labor. Such conditions are subverted through a pedagogy of direct contact, by engaging within the tourist economy, and by passing along modes of perceiving that escape the logic of new age settler dynamics.

### Decolonizing the New Age

Anthropological narratives, the tourist industry, and non-Indigenous spiritual entrepreneurs all maintain a primary narrative about Q'ero peoples: namely, that they possess the unique distinction of being the direct inheritors of the Incan spiritual tradition. This lineage's "purity" attributes to Q'ero peoples a distinguished position within the local economy, which relies upon authenticity as the value added within extractive capitalism.

Talking to Pisac shopkeepers, townsfolk, and non-Q'ero Indigenous women across the valley, I learned that the problem with this dominant narrative is that it occludes the complexity of Native histories in Peru. "After all," said Julia, a Moche woman in the main plaza, "The Incan Empire absorbed dozens of previously autonomous native groups. We don't trust how dominant histories represent us." Julia described her own situation as highly precarious, working for a mestizx shop owner within Pisac selling crystals and peace pipes to tourists. "He is a bad man," she said of the shop owner, "and pretends to be spiritual when all he is interested in is commerce." Thus, the retelling of Q'ero purity within the tourist economy, combined with the consumer's eagerness to purchase authenticity, reproduces Andeanism, obscuring overlapping histories of empire as well as the production of commodified fantasies.

In fact, I would argue that fabulation, as in the colonial period, continues to form a central axis of exchange within neoliberal Peru, especially between foreign tourist and Indigenous peoples within neoliberal market structures. While fabulation in the Andes is nothing new, it does have contemporary valences and local specificities. Such a naming of the current condition resonates with critical Native studies in the United States, namely the notion that Indigenous communities have long been on the receiving end of white obsession.[39] As Phil Deloria demonstrates, in a historical moment of colonial complicity, and during dramatic urban and postindustrial transformations in the United States, playing Indian stabilized the meaning of Americanness. Deloria defines "white desire" as a particular version of Indianness that historically structures and formulates national identity as the affective project of American belonging. New age countercultures, he states, provide a coherent narrative to "Americans lost in a (post)modern free fall."[40]

One way to understand the troubled racial dynamics at play here is through the use of Jodi Byrd's concept of cacophony. By "cacophony" Byrd refers to a competitive racial paradigm that frames the "desire and fear of the colonizer who needs to continually and repeatedly articulate 'true' and 'real' representations." As Byrd states, settler societies "exist relationally and in collusion with the processes of racial, gendered, and sexual otherings that seek to make contesting histories and experiences resonate authochthonously through the lingering touch of the real."[41] The "lingering touch of the real" is an apt descriptive phrase for how spiritual tourists as non-Indigenous subjects desire personal transformation through contact with "authentic native spirituality." The spiritual tourist industry operates by transferring the cacophony of the US racial order to the site of empire. What emerges transnationally is the interaction of white foreigners, to a lesser extent foreigners of color, and national mestizxs all colluding to reach out to touch the authenticity of the Native shaman.

In contrast to some of the ecological tourist possibilities I discuss in chapter one, which are enlivened in places such as Ecuador, spiritual tourism in the Andes can be a highly mediated spectacle, where the violence of colonialism, the legacies of nation building, and neoliberal civil wars have led to increased Indigenous visibility routed through national markets that celebrate and potentially ossify Incan histories. The height of such events is perhaps the annual Inti-Raymi festival, a nine-day festival that worships the Incan sun god through costume, ritual, music, and banquets, a spectacle loosely based on the writings of the Inca Garcilaso de la Vega. Written during the *indigenismo* period that made Indigenous and mestizx subjects and cultural forms central to the building of national narratives, Inca-Raymi suffers from both the neoliberal tendencies of regional displays of "authenticity," or what might be termed neo-Incan cultural expression. How do submerged perspectives negotiate such overdetermined terrains?

### Andean Translations

In August 2008, a weeklong workshop gathered a group of thirty participants at the Centro Paz y Luz to learn from Q'ero shamans; the participants were mostly from the United States and Europe, and were mostly white, except for two Black women from the United States, and one mestizx each from Chile and Peru. The workshop was organized around nine Munay-ki healing rites, drawing on what was described by Diane Dunn as "ancient traditions of Q'ero healing." Opening the workshop, Dunn explained how former anthropologist turned spiritual guru Alberto Viollda, as a student of Andean cosmologies "first downloaded the rites from the universe." As Dunn put it, "Viollda was able to receive this information and share it with the world."[42] As I later found out, Four Winds, a new age company owned by white North American Alberto Viollda and based in Palo Alto, California, had circulated a pamphlet based on Munay-ki rites. As the workshop unfolded, through the narration of Diane Dunn it became increasingly apparent that the Munay-ki rites represented a new age version of Q'ero mysticism. Indeed, from the first day onward, it was difficult to understand exactly the relationship between Q'ero philosophies and the Munay-ki rites; however, it is important to note that Viollda was given primary credit for disseminating the rites, even as two Q'ero shamans stood behind Dunn during those same early remarks.

Francisco and Juanita, the two shamans, were present throughout the eight-day workshop and also played an important role in facilitating ceremonies, creating spaces for meditation, and contributing to the sense that we were learning something valuable. When given a chance on day two, Francisco told us that the rites were based on a lineage of Q'ero knowledge passed in a patrilineal fashion from father to son until he, in an unusual break with tradition, initiated Juana. The couple were presented to the group as shamans, healers, and the keepers of ancient traditions, though Dunn never told us exactly what highlands community they were from. Don Francisco and Doña Juana later told me that they came from one of the eight Q'ero *ayullus* in the Andean highlands, with about one thousand community members who lived at a fourteen-thousand-foot altitude in the Paucartambo region, a twelve-hour journey by foot to the Sacred Valley. Many Q'eros have integrated into Cuzco's capitalist tourist economy, or travel between the city, the upper highlands, and the Sacred Valley, working as weavers in the artisanal markets or in the spiritual tourist industry as guides and as shamans conducting rituals for foreigners and Peruvian visitors.

At Paz y Luz, Juana spoke only Quechua, while Francisco spoke Spanish and Quechua; neither spoke English. The obstacles to linguistic translation between workshop facilitators and its participants added to the complexity of cultural mediation, as well as to the inability to access a fuller rendition of Francisco and Juanita's lives in what otherwise appeared as decontextualized spiritual pedagogy. In fact, several times during the course of the week, I thought about the differences in context between the workshop and the book *Andean Lives*, the classic oral history of another Quechua-speaking, albeit Aymara, couple, Gregorio Condori Mamani and Asunta Quispe Huamán.[43] As a powerful testimony taken by Peruvian anthropologists Ricardo Valderrama Fernández and Carmen Escalante Gutiérrez during the 1970s, *Andean Lives* relays the exploitative conditions of Quechua-speaking peoples in the highlands, where Gregorio worked as a strapper (a human mover of materials) and an agricultural worker on a latifundio, while Asunta worked as a domestic servant, experiencing high degrees of physical and verbal abuse from her employer. The oral history details the colonial domination and ongoing violence embedded within the interactions between indigenous peoples and *misti* (white) landowners, priests, and state authorities, and inadvertently contextualized for me the experiences of Francisco and Juana, prodding me to ask more about their lives in side conversations, or during the times they were selling artisanal crafts from cooperatives to the workshop participants.

As translators, Paul H. Gelles and Gabriela Martinez Escobar suggest of *Andean Lives*, "The narratives vividly illustrate the discrimination and exploitation in which *runas* [Quechua] are subjected by local power holders."[44] Gelles and Martinez Escobar translated the original oral history multiple times, from Quechua into Spanish and then into English. Throughout, they insisted on linguistic and conceptual precision. Indeed, in one of many examples of their attention to detail, they point out the difficulty of translation by discussing how Quechua, unlike Spanish or English, attaches suffixes at the end of a sentence to clarify whether the information conveyed was learned "through direct experience or through hearsay."[45] Even while the book contains a detailed glossary that allows for an expanded translation of Quechua grammar, the subtlety of the position of speaker, participant, and witness within any sentence underscores what can be lost in the act of translation. Moreover, this example about positionality in relation to the experiential dimension of language shows the degree to which Quechua allows for multiple subject positions in relation to any given event.

I bring up this classic text to suggest how our six days together were shadowed by the complexity of language and cultural mediation. While most of the twenty workshop participants were monolingual English speakers, a few spoke German or French as well as English. They understood little, if any, Spanish, so the participants were often confused by the presentations or group activities. Furthermore, because of the lack of translation for the Quechua language, it was ultimately rendered as a mystical idiom rather than the representation of ordinary life that contains within it relational elements as well as the colonial afterlives as everyday oppression.

These many linguistic and epistemological problems of incommensurable communication added to the macronarrative of Andeanism; the retreat was yet another instance of a voyeuristic perception of Indigeneity—the extractive gaze in action. Neocolonial structures framed the experience of language, interactions, and property, and the mediations of empire hung in the shadowy background of these new age exchanges.

Even though these encounters between "foreigners" and Indigenous Q'ero elders were overdetermined by layers of coloniality, another form of perception emerged for me during my time in the Andes and with Juana and Francisco. In much the same way as I experienced through May Stevens, Francisco Huichaqueo, and Carolina Caycedo, as I describe in the introduction and in other chapters of the book, Don Francisco and Doña Juana's creative praxis facilitated access to other sensibilities. One morning, we woke early and walked down to the Urubamba River with the directive to simply slow down one's observation of the natural world. Our requirement was to spend two hours doing nothing but listening to how the water rushed over the pebbles, mapping its pathways, collecting bits of moss and bark. Over long days of engagement with the natural elements, without access to Internet and without the bombardment of catastrophic news from the outside world, participants reported perceptual shifts, including a sense of time that was not constantly interrupted by media or the incessant chatter of consumer capitalism. My own search to deepen my relation away from binary separation to a perception of more thorough-going relationality turned this simple exercise into a profound landscape of sensibilities.

By orienting toward the sonic landscape and the spatial surround that became available through Juana's and Francisco's directions, I turned away from the more unidimensional perception of the Western gaze and the experience of melancholic individuality. Even though I carried my earlier critical resonances with me, something else was made possible through sonic spatiality. In the rituals that Q'ero elders offered, Francisco and Juana often used the condition of silence, meaningful gestures, and small instruments, all while invoking Quechua as a symbolic ceremonial language to engage a sensorium of experience. Whether imbuing the surroundings with bells, or chanting words over and over again, the landscape filled with the reverberations of their sonic intimations.

While English and Spanish had dominated in the controlled space of Diane Dunn's center, in the sacred sites that we visited—by the Urubamba

River, near Machu Picchu, at the temple of Ollantaytambo, and at dawn in the Pisca ruins—Quechua was the only audible language, with little or no translation. These ceremonial experiences called forth the sacred elements of fire, water, earth, and air, and engaged the senses both prediscursively and, more importantly in terms of breaking down the Western perspective, in the space where language failed in translation. In such moments, the sensibility to Andean phenomenology opened a space for perception that perforated the colonial divide. In other words, indigenous landscapes that were not fully colonized by new age tourism, like the flowing river itself, allowed for a more direct experience of Andean phenomenology with Francisco and Juana's guidance.

Reflecting again on the opening anecdote, my own perceptual shift occurred precisely by pulling away from the symbolic and material weight of coloniality, even if this took place through a different order of understanding, and, again, against my sociological disciplinary training. Questions about my own political longings kept echoing during the experience with Francisco and Juana: Was it possible to decolonize the violence of colonial ideologies through an Andean ecological phenomenology? Or is spirituality too bound up with the religious colonial order to imagine an outside? Decolonial thinkers have addressed this second question (Maldonado-Torres, Dussel, and Mignolo, for instance), yet the need persists to find paradigms that acknowledge colonial legacies, elaborate upon contemporary notions of power, and insist on other realms of experience beyond the material.[46] If we understand the current economic rationale that reduces relationality to the legacies of colonialism, and that permeates the affective and relational deficit of the current period—what we can call the "melancholies of late capitalism"—then we might be able to move toward a more complex sense of what decolonized spirituality looks and feels like.

In contrast to the mass market of tourism in the region, whether amid a remote landscape, beside a waterfall, or within rock formations, Juana and Francisco offered an intimate space of exchange. While mediated, this space of interaction moved toward the transmission of Andean phenomenology and away from spectacularized Andeanism. Like the melting of fear that I described earlier, my faculties had been conditioned to be hyper-reactive, but in each of the rites that included being by the river, participating in *despachos*, and climbing sacred mountains, I found instead that I was perforated by sensations and possibilities. Other participants I spoke to described a similar melting away of their mistrust. These micro-encounters were ultimately unnameable to me in their affective density, yet something took flight and escaped the logic of capitalism, and could not be reduced to a remunerated exchange. Perhaps only these situated aporias, in which other kinds of knowledge were not touristically "on display" and instead occurred through interactions, could provide a way through the reductive spaces of overcommodification and new age settlement of Indigenous spaces in the Andes. The future on the other side of catastrophe was presented and perceived as unmediated relationality with the natural world, a sensual spatiality organized by Juana and Francisco that created the possibility for the unnameable to emerge. To my surprise, Juana rang bells around my ears and splashed me with the sacred water of the Urubamba until the encounter became a stirring flow with all that mediated it.

On the last day of the workshop, in a rare moment of direct address, Francisco spoke intently to the group, telling us how the knowledge he had transmitted to us had come directly from his Q'ero elders in the lineage from father to son. This paternal inheritance had been broken by Juana's training as a Q'ero shaman, indicating both a break in Andean patriarchy and in the reign of male Indigenous figures within the spiritual realm. Juana's inclusion in the lineage, like the dissemination of Q'ero principles more broadly at the Centro Paz y Luz, represented a time of opening, he said. As Francisco suggests, in the period of increased environmental degradation to the Earth, the elders had decided that it was time to "unlock these secret traditions and pass them on far beyond his own local communities."[47] Francisco's direct hailing of the changing practices of gender, and the initiation of female figures into the work of the tourist economy, can be read both as a decolonial gesture and as a way to secure more opportunities for Indigenous women within an uncertain and segmented global economy.

Don Francisco went on to discuss the evidence of environmental destruction in highland communities; for instance, they watched as water tables receded, observed changes in local climates, and mourned the fact that many from their own communities were leaving for the cities. For Francisco, all of these were signs of imminent catastrophic events. These signs, however, were not limited to the imminent future but also represented the legacies of Incan histories in relation to colonialism. Finally, the transfer of knowledge from Indigenous to non-Indigenous peoples that Francisco spoke of on our final day in the group laid the groundwork for situating Q'ero beliefs as one important solution to the pressing situation of the world's ills. Francisco suggested that the time had come to spread global awareness and increase consciousness about Pachamama through an ethics of care for the planet. Unlike the liberal environmental version of this call, however, Francisco's invocation of Andean phenomenology, in which Indigenous peoples were central, offers a multidimensional way of relating to the land that works to decolonize the Anthropocene by creating another relation to the planetary.

As a female entity that regulates the three levels of cosmological relationality, Pachamama is one way to think through a queer femme and decolonial episteme to the experiences that I have described. While queer methods are not new, the legacies of extractivism and racial capitalism as products of the colonial experience have often been underdeveloped. By decolonial queer episteme here I refer to allowing the field to speak rather than foreclosing on the conditions of possibility, or presuming that a disciplinary frame of analysis will unlock and straighten out the complexities of the colonial condition. The Andean landscape and those who have millennial relations to it cannot be straightened out. Furthermore, phenomenological mediations that imagine space, time, and cosmological being as interconnected realms of knowledge counter the reductive perspective of new age thinking, which primarily commodifies, usurps, and bends the Other into its own rendition of that which is either invisible or unknown. Juana and Francisco directed me to an experiential relationality to the natural world, which is governed through its own logic that pulses outside of catalogues of social and historical injustices and their colonial legacies. A decolonial queer femme positionality based in Southern knowledge allowed me to be open to the forms of relationality that unfolded before me.

Since Francisco had opened up these rites, after his pronouncement, I asked him about the role of Juana in this work and what spiritual role female counterparts had in Q'ero culture. Francisco suggested that this was part of opening up the Q'ero tradition so that everyone could be more involved in the kinds of practices that would be what he called "preservationist."[48] Unlike normative meanings of "preservation," Francisco's idea was based on an Andean ecophilosophy of vernacular practice. In this book's introduction, I claim that many constituencies—those with power, those without, Indigenous and non-Indigenous, the state, civil society, political parties, and state heads—all often resort to the rhetoric of Pachamama.

But, beyond the discursive realm of formal politics, Andean phenome-nology incorporates a fundamental praxis that demonstrates, rather than discursively diminishes, the aliveness of the natural world. In this narra-tive, Don Francisco and Doña Juana also demonstrate a kind of nonnorma-tive understanding of gender complementarity that shifts and changes rather than assumes each member within the heterosexual couple as having separate spheres of influence. The decolonial queer femme sensibility I de-scribe was available through multiple encounters, either through Juana's communication of the Q'ero sacred, or through a growing sensitivity to the surround, in relation to acknowledgment of microspaces of potential, and away from a unidimensional view of the spiritual tourist industry. This is an encounter with how to inhabit and be attuned to the multiplicity of life as an antidote to Western fear and melancholia through sensuous knowl-edge about Pachamama.

### The Not Yet Ending

In each of this chapter's scenes, it should be clear that I remain wary about the possibility of intercultural dialogue within the colonial matrix of spiri-tual tourism. Despite all of this, as the opening story suggests, the assump-tion that all exchange between the Global North and the Global South, between the Indigenous, mestizx and others must inevitably lead to asym-metrical power relations is not the takeaway here. Complex processes of cultural hegemony are ever present in what I have referred to in this chapter as a set of mediated relations between Q'ero shamans and non-Indigenous peoples. Land, and real estate speculation in rural places that are highly transited, is certainly one place where alliances toward decolonization might concentrate efforts. Even as agrarian unions have been dismantled throughout the Américas, finding ways to counter increasing rural gentri-fication is essential to the project of decolonization.

Though Andean phenomenology cannot be read outside of its long en-gagement with colonial mediation, as a sequence of narrative dissonances that never finds an origin, it is a mode of perception and embodied thought that cannot be fully subsumed into extractive capitalism. There is much to be learned from Andean Indigenous worldviews that infuse daily life with a planetary imaginary that animates rather than deadens. A decolonial queer episteme works to give porous attention to what Andean phenomenology sees, feels, touches, hears, and senses. If one can slow down and really listen to the bells, or the sound of the river, we might tread outside of the exigencies of colonial fear and the consumer logic of desire toward a more capacious sensitivity.

# CHAPTER 3

# An Archive for the Future

## *Seeing through Occupation*

In his thirty-two-minute independent film *Mencer: Ni Pewma* (2011), Mapuche filmmaker Francisco Huichaqueo draws attention to the current dystopic landscape of the southern territories in Chile.[1] This is a continuous nightmare that stretches back over five centuries, from the colonial endeavor to nation building through Pinochet's neoliberal experiment and into the current period of the ongoing invasion of pine and eucalyptus plantations; a nightmare that takes place within the extractive zone of the Bío Bío region. In Mapudungun, the term *ñi pewma* translates as "a bad dream," and one interpretation of Huichaqueo's use of the term in the film's title is that the Spanish colonial nightmare persists in the hands of the Chilean state. *Mencer*, on the other hand, is a word that "came to him in a dream" (and a term that we could not find a definition for), thereby adding to the nonlinear and experimental dimensions of its effect.

Unconcerned that his film has screened only once in public, Huichaqueo has deliberately created an archive "that will illuminate to Mapuche peoples living in the future the terrible conditions that we live through now."[2] The exceptional quality of the film's work, then, is to document the persistence of the colonial dystopic through experimental means: in the past three decades, Mapuche lands have been reduced to 510,000 hectares, or just 6.4 percent of their original territorial holdings.

As Huichaqueo says about his film, "I use the symbolic language of our ancestors to help us shape, live, and act in the world as if occupation did not ravage all of our existence."[3] Like the genre of Indigenous video art that has proliferated in the hemisphere, and the work of Native visual media more

Francisco Huichaqueo, *Mencer: Ni Pewma*, poster for Sala Juana
Eugenua, 2011. Image courtesy of Francisco Huichaqueo.

globally, *Mencer: Ni Pewma* documents the struggle for Indigenous life as
an ongoing conflict between two fundamentally distinct epistemes.[4] In this
chapter, I take the opportunity of this little known work to disentangle the
layers of complexity within the extractive zone, analyzing the symbolic,
representational, material, spatial, temporal, and epistemological dimensions of the permanent war against Indigenous peoples and their territories
in the Southern hemisphere.

Since the sixteenth century the colonial occupation of the original territories known as Wallmapu that span the Andes from Southern Chile to
Argentina is a permanent war against Indigenous populations. This war
advances on material and representational fronts, ranging from genocidal
atrocities, such as those that took place during the failed Spanish conquest
of the region, to the expropriation during the "Reducciones" and enclosure
period of the 1800s, to the neoliberal privatization of Indigenous territories
from 1973 forward, to the multicultural state's project of incorporation and
expulsion during the 1990s.

A financialized view that sees land as transparent exchange value is distinctly opposite from Huichaqueo's viewpoint, whose opening scene is an opaque landscape with blurry boundaries between land, sky and trees, offering a mode of perceiving beyond the neat delineations of the extractive zone. Mapuche embodied thought systems see past monocultural transaction to address the *perrimonton* dreamscape as a parallel plane of existence. *Mencer: Ni Pewma* follows this cosmology by rendering and making audible the worlds of ancestors, the elements, and erased anticolonial histories, challenging the dominant discourses that decontextualize the present-day conflict between Mapuche land and water defenders, on the one hand, and the colonial state and its military apparatus, on the other.

Rather than recur to the documentary paradigm of direct address and testimonials often used in human rights representation, or to a mode of cultural politics that appeals to the state as the main site of redress and recognition, Huichaqueo instead breaks open the matrix of representational confinement and evacuation.[5] And, unlike the sociological impulse of many other films in the documentary genre, in Huichaqueo's monochromatic palette and echo-chamber soundtrack, Mapuche worlds can be accessed through visual and sound bridges that invoke the supernatural; it is also conjured through the use of the elements of fire, earth, air, and water, all of which become the symbolic anchors for a visual imaginary that perceives life otherwise. As I address throughout the chapter, the cumulative effect of these experimental techniques is an assault upon colonial modes of representation. More specifically, Huichaqueo's experimental film plays with conventions, incorporating elements, such as repeated motifs and echoes, non sequitur edits, long takes of performance art, literary and theatrical references, and footage from other films, to make connections to similar landscapes of violent colonization throughout the Américas.

An experimental, and more radical proposition emerges in Huichaqueo's work, one that challenges what it means to witness and live with devastation and genocide by shifting the viewer's sense of time, space, and narrowly framed constructions of reality. In particular, Huichaqueo offers a fragmented, partial, and often confused view that disorients the viewer in order to insert Mapuche viewpoints into the frame. Thus, *Mencer: Ni Pewma* imagines the sensual and natural worlds not as fatally destroyed by colonial capitalism but as counternetworks of possibility enabled through dreamscapes and the invisible parallel worlds of cultural memory.

How does experimental film shift normative imaginaries of land and landscape through visuality that documents the already arrived apocalypse toward life after extinction? Can experimental film sort through the memories of Indigenous experience that work in opposition to the state, especially in the heightened conflict within the southern territories of Wallmapu? By giving us a filmic language based in Mapuche relations to the visible and invisible realms, how does Huichaqueo open up an aesthetic sensibility that perceives territory as a multidimensional space that curates an archive for the future? Can experimental film suggest what the land remembers?

## Retakes on Occupation

Huichaqueo's experimental film must be situated alongside a range of productions made by Indigenous filmmakers about violence, contestation, and increased militarization of Mapuche territories.[6] For instance, *Wallmapu* (2001), by Mapuche filmmaker Jeanette Paillán, and the story of Pehuenche activist Berta, as told in *El velo de Berta* (Berta's Veil, 2004), both begin from a Southern Indigenous point of view that documents how Mapuche, Pehuenche, and Huilliche peoples are differentially treated before the law through a developmentalist offensive upon territory and rural life. As we will see, such films carefully attend to the resource-dense Bío Bío region, illustrating the degree to which communal lands have been increasingly legislated as zones of state terror, displacement, and bare life; yet at the same time, this geography has become fertile ground for submerged perspectives, where sources of creativity and collective resistance multiply. When placed within this filmic genre, Huichaqueo's film is unique in that it considers colonial representation in order to eventually destroy it, working from the presumption that despite extinction, social ecologies continue to flourish.

The first image in *Mencer: Ni Pewma* is a colonial portrait of a young, bare-chested Mapuche man gazing directly into the camera, recalling the famed warrior figure Lautaro and the historical victory by Mapuche militias against the Spanish Crown from the 1520s to the 1540s. Lautaro is a complex figure for Mapuches and huincas (nonindigenous) alike, given that Republican literature recycles the undefeated warrior as a symbol of its national pride. In Pedro Subercaseaux's nineteenth-century paintings, Lautaro was idealized as a hero of war. He is also the protagonist of nationally celebrated novelist Alberto Blest Gana's *Mariluán* (1859), as well as a genre of nationalist writings that formed Chilean literature.[7] In the colonial transition to nation-state formation, constraining images of Mapuche peoples served to construct the "appropriate" place of the Native in the nation. By opening the film with an image of Mapuche portraiture, Huichaqueo immediately registers the entanglements of the colonial referent with the national history of European tropes of Indigenous representation.

Writing specifically on the Mapuche context, Patricia Richards discusses how, "like their counterparts elsewhere, Chilean revolutionary patriots symbolically incorporated the Mapuche to justify their war for independence from Spain (1810–18). For the patriot leaders, the rebel Indian represented love of the soil, of the fatherland and irrevocable liberty, high values that had impelled them to fight victoriously during long centuries against the Hispanic conquistadors and against the royal army."[8] As Richard carefully points out, this rhetoric of revolutionary struggle worked as nation-building discourse, and a way to celebrate the masculinity of the Native warrior figure as proper to the anticolonial project of nation building. Against the Spanish colonial regime, the Republic used the rhetorics of patriotism and specific portrayals to construct a controlling image of Native rebellion. Throughout *Mencer: Ni Pewma*, Huichaqueo returns to the image of the anticolonial Indigenous leader Lautaro, precisely to emphasize the figure that haunts the colonial imagination and who continues to be aggrandized within the state's modern media apparatus.

Huichaqueo's film dramatizes these tropes about Indigenous revolutionary protagonists to point out contemporary historical and media dissonances. For example, midway through the video, Huichaqueo stages his own version of the "angry Indian": we watch a bare-chested Mapuche teenage boy, who first stares at the camera—reminiscent of the colonial portrait that opens the film—and then begins to yell at the camera. "A for Anarchy" is spray-painted on the wall behind the young man to exaggerate the negative media stereotype of Mapuche masculinity, but also plausibly to make anarchist presence visible as an integral part of regional social movement histories.[9] During the course of this four-minute sequence, through a tight focus on the male Mapuche body, Huichaqueo visualizes how Indigenous anger and rebellion is portrayed across dominant media platforms as the defining trait of the Native.

Such ossified tropes of masculine rebellion give us an analytical register from which to understand the recent "fake news" videos that supposedly show Mapuches setting fires upon their own territories. Despite the fact that the footage was either staged or filmed ten years prior, the short video circulated relentlessly within dominant media representations, resonating with a longer genealogy of criminalized images of Indigenous masculinity. Joanna Crowe shows, for instance, how the conservative newspaper and state organ *El Mercurio* and other media sources have historically defined Mapuche peoples through discourses of marginality. Yet, she also tracks how this history rests upon criminalizing acts of self and collective land defense.[10]

As Indigenous media has documented, most headlines of the last twenty to thirty years describe Mapuche activism as terrorist activity while simultaneously celebrating particular Native poets as exempt from such narratives. In other words, representations of Indigenous masculine subjects oscillate between the criminalized Native and what Charles Hale calls the *indio permitido*, the civilized, whitened, and passable Indian who gains exceptional acceptance within the nation, perpetuating stereotypes for the majority Native population.[11] *Mapuches sospechos* (suspect Mapuches) and *Mapuches terroristas* are common terms that reveal how ancestral territorial land defense functions outside of the bounds of order, the law, and civility. These reiterative images use reductive understandings and mistake anticolonial rage, in Frantz Fanon's sense, for individualized expressions of anger and resentment. By repeatedly returning to the scene of the state's crimes, where communal lands are visualized as the backdrop for pine expansion, Huichaqueo asks the viewer to reconsider the source of anticolonial rage and mourning for dispossessed Indigenous peoples.

In the legal war against Mapuches, Indigenous land and water defense has been constituted as a problem of national terrorism. For instance, in 1998, the Chilean government passed the Anti-Terrorist Law, which deemed land defenders criminals. This law worked to suture the negative historical image of Mapuches in ways that have had devastating effects for those defending communal lands, as I discuss below. Furthermore, whereas Mapuches have been constituted as foreign and alien to the nation, land has also been rendered as needing taming, first by the civilizational paradigm, and later by the neoliberal economy. During the expansion of extractive capitalism, this discourse was made possible by Augusto Pinochet's legislation against political "subversives," and the Chicago Boys' transformation of Indigenous territories into privatized and increasingly concentrated land holdings.

In an early black-and-white sequence, Huichaqueo visualizes long stretches of dimly lit radiata pine and eucalyptus plantations, not native to the region, and which conjure the vastness of monocultural forest plantations in Southern Chile's Bío Bío. In a low pan, the camera tracks through row after row of foreign trees as a strange voice-over echoes in the background, a scene that sonically and visually bridges the colonial period with the neocolonial present. What follows is a startling poem delivered in voice-over, rife with Mapuche symbolism and the director's take on recent political events:

Y me barren mis hermanos, la cruz, esa maldición;
El fuego que se alimenta de todas nuestras muertes;
Tu tienes el miedo de mi morena conciencia porque tu riqueza es mi
 muerte.
Con pena del árbol secandose al sol nos afiebramos en el pasado,
Pasos marcados en las cenizas sobre las cenizas.
Llora tu sangre sobre tu sangre. Los ancianos mueren solos.
Roble huacho, laurel solitario. Pehuen extenguido.
Pinos, pinos, pinos, pinos, pinos, pinos.
Como llora el viento anacleto! Como cuentan sus millones!
Pinos, pinos, pinos, pinos, pinos, pinos. (from *Mencer: Ni Pewma*)

And they imprison my brothers, the cross, that curse;
The fire that feeds all of our dead;
You have the fear that is my Brown conscience, because your richness is
 my death.
With the fear of the tree, drying in the sun, we are interwoven with the
 past,
Steps that are marked by the ash layered with ash.
Your blood cries layered over blood,
The elders die alone.
*Roble huacho*, solitary laurel. Extinguished Pehuen.
Pine, pine, pine, pine, pine, pine.
How the burning plain wind cries! How they count their millions!

In these powerful stanzas, Huichaqueo conjures the histories of disputed territories, establishes the southern region as a frontier war zone, and hints at the long-term effects of the layered conflict between Mapuche peoples and the Chilean state.

In the last lines, the poem references the Pehuen or *Auracaria*, what is called the Monkey Puzzle tree in English because of its tangled branches that wrap to its tree top. In Mapudungun, the Pehuen is known as the "ancestor trees" as they can live more than two thousand years and are what botanists refer to as an archetypal tree whose ancestors date back 200 million years. Auracaria and Alerce trees comprise a unique southern temperate forest ecology that stretches from the central coast to the High Andes, even as the entire complex ecosystem has been endangered from Pedro de Valdivia's 1540 colonization forward. The Pehuen's decimation accelerated during the mid-1800s because of European settlement, and by the mid-1900s when land was cleared for livestock grazing and agriculture more than fifty percent of the original forest had been disappeared. After Pinochet's privatization agenda in 1973, Chile's forest industry was ultimately concentrated in the hands of a few large companies who continued the operations of extinction.[12]

Until the replacement by "commercially viable" tree monoculture, the Pehuen's seeds were harvested by Mapuche peoples for flour, historically providing the main staple of local diets. In the space of several frames, and through the metaphorical language of the poem, Huichaqueo condenses this history of colonial and modern occupation by focusing on the shadow presence of the aruacania ancestors, a ghostly presence only invisible through the omnipresence of pine and eucalyptus plantations.

In one particularly poignant line, we hear of "the fire that feeds all of our dead," which refers to fire's capacity to both destroy and rejuvenate as a memory symbolic of a Mapuche worldview. But the connotation of fire has a more layered meaning that turns on the prior line, "and they imprison my brothers, the cross, that curse," a reference not only to the advancement of the Catholic Church during colonialism, but also to antiterrorist legislation that has imprisoned Mapuche land defenders since the 1990s, accusing them of arson committed on state-owned and privatized lands. Currently, there are over 100 Mapuche political prisoners within Chilean jails, many of whom are members of a Mapuche organization called the Arauco-Malleco Coordinator (CAM) the most politically militant of the spectrum of diverse Mapuche organizations.[13] The line references the historical relationship between Eurocentric Chilean identity and the occupying force of Catholicism, implying its complicity in "that curse" that has condemned Indigenous peoples to second-class citizenry. By suturing the temporalities of the colonial wars and Mapuche militias to the occupations of the modern period, the poem suggests the ongoing criminalization and physical and symbolic imprisonment of Indigenous land defenders in their struggle against frontier colonialism.

Far from acceding to the accusation of "arson" that is imposed upon Mapuche peoples, land and water defenders instead reveal the criminality embedded in the corporate repossession of Mapuche lands. Fire, Huichaqueo notes, feeds the ancestors and forms a bridge between the living and the human, animal and plant life that has perished in an ongoing frontier war to advance capital. By interpreting the line of the poem "and they imprison my brothers, the cross, the curse" as the nexus of colonial occupation, we traverse deeper into the genocidal operations of representational evacuation.

### Representational Evacuation

Colonial capitalism's territorial expansion in the Américas has historically operated through the appendages of state violence, especially through a biopolitical strategy that converts original territories into extractive zones. As Thomas Miller Klubock's *La Frontera: Forests and Ecological Conflict in Chile's Frontier Territory* impressively charts, the recent conflict over Mapuche lands was born through technocratic designs that transformed the Bío Bío's rain forest into a North American conifer forest.[14] During the Pacification of the Auracania, Mapuche peoples' territories were reduced from 10 million hectares to 400,000 and 3,000 communal territories were legally given as "mercy titles." However, during the Pinochet years forward, neoliberal expansion within the Bío Bío region occurred precisely through the process of Indigenous land evictions that were codified into new legislation by repealing rights to communal property.[15]

During the next decade, Mapuche "counterinvasions," or a taking back of territories, heightened the material struggle over ancestral lands that had been occupied by plantation economies. Such counterinvasions offered one strategy among a host of symbolic reoccupations, which together formulated a collective response to the territorial formula of the monocultural paradigm. Within the Mapuche-led organization Consejo de Todas las Tierras, particular groups chose to tactically commit arson against pine plantations as a means to resist corporate and state privatization of Indigenous landholdings. These land burnings, or *quemadas*, as a strategy of reoccupation were aimed at symbolically refusing forest colonization rather than allow further expansion upon Indigenous territories.

In Francisco Huichaqueo's archive of the future, fire and burning are key technologies of visible resistance to the Chilean state's logics of extinction. Given fire's sensationalist potential and centrality in the film, primarily through interspersed scenes of burning tires in the streets, it is important to further explain the trope of fire. In particular, fire becomes a weapon against monocultural expansion. Under the legal architecture of Augusto Pinochet's authoritarian regime, neoliberalism legitimated its reduction of Mapuche territories that made Indigenous survivability impossible. The legal lynchpin of land-reduction policies pivoted around the implementation of the Decree Law 2.568 of 1979. As Timothy Clark details, the law's purpose was clearly spelled out in its name: "The Division and Liquidation of the Indigenous Community." Through the law, the legal infrastructure allowed for the dividing of territories through the "request by only one occupant, who need not be either indigenous nor a landowner in the community."[16]

In 1993, the post-Pinochet government ratified the Indigenous law, and then established the *Corporación Nacional de Desarrollo Indígena*, National Corporation for Indigenous Development (CONADI), the state arm that oversaw a massive transference of legal titles from Indigenous landholders to private corporations. In sum, a long and painful process of national and multinational property expropriation displaced thousands of Mapuches from their original communal territories, reducing livability in the region to bare life. As I discuss elsewhere about the complex issue of Mapuche hunger strikes, the act of burning lands can be understood only in the conditions of extreme scarcity and duress that many Mapuches must reckon with.

In terms of bare life, Giorgio Agamben's explanation of the figure of *homo sacer* in relation to the state of exception is useful, even as its Eurocentric bias of world history has rightly been critiqued by Scott Morgenson and Alexander Weheliye.[17] Agamben elaborates upon the figure of *homo sacer,* or the Roman legal subject, as a term describing a bare life first coined by Walter Benjamin in an essay on violence and the state. Accordingly, Agamben pursues this figure because it remains "undertheorized" by Benjamin, even as it is pivotal for how to conceptualize the state of exception, which reproduces sovereign power through the split between bare and sacred life. *Homo sacer* refers to the figure of bare life that is always consecrated to death through the legal apparatus, or "a life that may be killed but not sacrificed," whereby sovereign power discerns between life and death.[18] Bare life is the condition of the exceptional as it is applied to particular marginal subjects, which the law constitutes as unrecognizable through its granting and withholding of rights and protections. The reduction of land, the elimination of the *pehuen* tree, and the expropriation of communal lands has led to increased food scarcity and a crisis of livability that produced "bare life" responses. Yet, if we stayed solely with the model of Agamben's bare life we would not be able to perceive the continuous histories of colonial capitalism, and the active search for another future. Mapuche life uses *quemadas* and hunger strikes in addition to a range of technologies of resistance as declarations of autonomy within the extreme conditions produced by neoliberal colonialism.

Land-burning strategies, as founder and leader of the organization Consejos de Todos las Tierras (Council of All Lands), Aucán Huilcamán Paillama told me in 2004, worked to literally irradiate the acute affront upon Indigenous territories. More specifically, Huilcamán described *quemadas* as a method of land recovery in line with both an Indigenous praxis of Earth renewal and a "symbolic reoccupation," a term that reveals the degree to which material and discursive occupation function together to reproduce the colonial divide, which in turn must be doubly decolonized. "Reoccupation" is a counterstrategy that calls to mind Gil Hochberg's recent understanding of "visual occupation" as the operations by which oppression is first reproduced spatially through the extension of, in this case, the Israeli settlers that occupy Palestinian territories.[19] Burning the lands could offer a means to counter the vast armament of the state, which had long contracted with US and Israeli companies to expand its occupation of Indigenous territories.[20]

As a mechanism of power, the visual command of space has functioned as an important site/sight of colonization, in which occupied landscapes become semiotic geographies that contain metonyms of power. For in-

stance, the replacement of the ancestral *pehuen* tree, that had for generations been at the center of Mapuche daily life with pine plantations, transforms both the physical landscape and the practice of livability. In terms
of the biopolitical imperative to control Indigenous populations, it is important to remember that state and corporate power reorganized the Bío
Bío region by subsuming Mapuche territories into an extractive viewpoint
aimed at what Patrick Wolfe has described as "eliminating the native" by
first eliminating the forest.[21]

Within the colonized visual geography, fire does the important symbolic
work of reoccupation, as a symbol of unruliness, an expressive format of
dissent, a retaking of the land, and a method to visibly cleanse the occupied
territories. Indeed, fire both illuminates and burns through, the conditions
of coloniality.

### Dreaming, the Sonic, and Ancestral Mourning

As the reader might sense, the film is not a facile viewing experience.
*Mencer: Ni Pewma* performs what Jennifer Doyle has referred to as "difficult art," which mediates a range of complex emotions whereby viewers
may feel interpolated by the subject matter.[22] In this case, when coupled
with its aesthetic unconventionality, the work's affective charge produces a
sensation of fragmentation and unease. Poignantly, *Mencer: Ni Pewma* incorporates accessible elements, such as documentary footage, animation,
performative reenactments, still images, voice-over narratives, and footage
that spans from the early 1970s until 2011. Even with these more approach-
able elements, however, the film disorients the viewer with sharp, discon-
nected edits. The immersive view is unclear within a darkened landscape,
while a jolting narrative voice on the soundtrack calls out, creating a mnemonic echo to an ancestral world that reverberates as a colonial haunting.

As the camera tracks through the forest at ground level, our view is
mapped by the matrix of ubiquitous "pine, pine, pine" trees, the foreign
species that replaced the *pehuen*. As we travel quickly through the neatly
lined forest, the voice-over is loud and startling, as if to invoke the onto-
logical space between the visible and the immaterial realm. The state cannot perforate the invisible line between this world and the "one beside," as
Francisco Huichaqueo reminds us, because the invisible world of ancestors
is ungovernable and out of the reach of extractivist corporations, politi-

cians, and technocrats and the ideologies that all of these use to displace and dispossess.

With the *kultrün*, a sacred Mapuche drum, beating in the background, the ghostly voice of a man speaks for the nearly extinct *pehuen* tree: "Pehuen extinguido. . . . Como llora el viento ancleta. Como cuentan sus millones. Pinos, pinos, pinos. Eucaliptos. Eucaliptos. Eucaliptos" (Extinct *pehuen*. . . . How the wind cries. How we count your millions. Pines, pines, pines. Eucalyptus, Eucalyptus, Eucalyptus). With the mourning cry for the endangered *pehuen*, Huichaqueo returns us to the scene of ecology not simply to represent melancholic loss and separation but also to render how capitalist valuation depends upon Native territories for its profit and expansion, and how those territories bear their own traces of historical violence. Indeed, through the reverberation of the moans and the pounding of the drum,[23] Huichaqueo sonically renders late capitalism's effect of flattening the rich worlds of relationality with respects to the ancestors and the forest. Certainly, amid the state and corporate land invasions, the genealogical and cosmological dimension of Mapuche histories has not been considered on the balance sheet of accumulative profit, yet Huichaqueo offers another way to understand such past-present subjugation. In a montage that follows, a Mapuche elder points to the land and sky, even as in the background we still hear the resounding cry of "Pino, pino, pino. Eucalypto, eucalypto, eucalypto."

The echo in the film functions not only in the off-track voice that reverberates but also in the repetition in the poem, and finally as visual repetition. For instance, the sequence ends with a shot of a young woman in the city, a *machi* figure, the powerful female healer and spiritual center of Mapuche society. The *machi* stands in a warrior position with a laurel branch in her teeth, contrasting with the governmental coat of arms of the Republic with its motto, "Por la razón o la fuerza" (By reason or strength), that the camera pans to. The echoes both of sound and of image propose that, through the reverberations, Mapuche agency can be articulated against statecraft, whether through the sound of the sacred drum, the invocation of the ancestral realm, or the spiritual figure of the *machi*.[24] Huichaqueo seems to assert that the history of occupation on Mapuche territories cannot be reduced to extinction, colonial absorption, or violence. The Mapuche histories that echo through this film are sustained by a continuous process of resistance—through fire, song/mourning, and acknowledgment of the ancestral realm that dips into invisible realms beyond the extractive zone.

In the next scene, we see a second portrait, this time a *longko*, the head male figure of Mapuche culture. This figure, a tribal chief, is central to Mapuche social, economic, and political organization. The photograph of an Indigenous male authority figure reminds the viewer what is at stake in the visual realm, since South American Indigeneity was first captured within the colonial portrait studio.[25] In another scene, an establishing shot of a Native *cacique*'s (overseer) colonial portrait further illustrates how the paradigm of coloniality constrains representation, and recalls the period of Mapuche communal land, in contrast to the neoliberal corporate takeover that has stripped Indigenous legal claims to land.

The metaphor of slow-burning fire, the *quemada*, again makes an appearance as burning land, as burning tires in the street, and as the burnt-orange sky. By visualizing burning land as a recurrent symbol of Mapuche resistance, *Mencer: Ni Pewma* references and intervenes in the overdetermined symbols of colonial domination. In its deployment of fire, the film also interestingly echoes other texts that have historically worked to interrupt past state violence. Most vividly, the image of a lit-up landscape alludes to the literary and visual work of avant-garde poet and performance artist Raul Zurita. In 1979, Zurita published *Purgatorio*, with a cover image of the author's self-inflicted wound. The cover featured a close-up photograph of a scar that was the result of a performance in which, Zurita explains, "I locked myself in the bathroom, I put an iron in the flames of the hot water heater until it was red and I put it to my left cheek. At that—I don't know why, and maybe a psychiatrist could explain it well—I felt that that action reunited me a little. I was in a state of total dissociation. After a while I realized that if I were to write something, it had to start from this."[26]

In an essay that describes these acts, Matías Ayala reads Zurita's performative, and literal, self-infliction of a wound as the descent into purgatory, or Dante's inferno, and Zurita's quote suggests as much. However, the photograph of the scar is also a way of marking a collective body and showing how the self-inflected wound is, as Nelly Richard argues about the same performance, an act of "self-punishment that merges with an 'us' in that it is both redeemer and redeemed" within a "tradition of communal sacrifice or the ritual exorcism of violence."[27] Indeed, if Zurita's facial self-mutilation, an act that has important resonances as part of experimental aesthetic practice, enacts the resistance to modern state violence, then surely the collective immolation of Indigenous territories in Huichaqueo's film represents a longer arc of historical violence and refusal. The collective act of lighting fire to the land becomes the supreme example of communal sacrifice, and, to borrow Richard's phrase, its own "ritual exorcism" of settler violence. Invoking the nightmare (or *ñi pewma*, bad dream) as a descent into colonial and neocolonial hell, Huichaqueo's visual language experiments with the dystopic surreal as a way out of the trap of realist representation.

### Water and the Death of Ophelia

Whereas fire symbolizes the space of resistance and collective redemption in the film, water most often signifies the cycle of death and renewal. For instance, in the powerful recreation of a scene from Shakespeare's *Hamlet* that takes place in the last third of *Mencer*, the river contains a floating, and presumably lifeless and masked Ophelia.

Water is a protagonist, a living force, both in the film itself and at the center of Mapuche, Huilliche, and Pehuenche life. Water repeats, or echoes, at least a dozen times throughout the film. Steady shots of the Maule River reference the iconic body of water that was first diverted, and then blocked, by the Spanish company Endesa's building of the Ralco Dam in 1996, which, as we will see in the next chapter, was the blueprint for mega- and regional development in the region. Stopping the building of the hydroelectric dam's infrastructure was an international touchstone for Indigenous and environmental rights movements, since its construction reduced the local water table by half, meanwhile displacing dozens of Huilliche communities living or resettled in the upper Bío Bío region. The long takes of the Maule River and the lifeless figure of Ophelia serve to remind the viewer of these more recent and material and symbolic histories of colonization, but also link up to ecological crises wrought by state-corporate alliances within the new global order.

Huichaqueo most likely is not referring simply to Shakespeare's Ophelia here but to the famous Pre-Raphaelite nineteenth-century portrait by John Everett Millais from 1852. Millais's sumptuous image of the mad Ophelia floating down the river and singing to herself in her madness before she drowns captures not only the death of the maiden but also the abundance

Francisco Huichaqueo, *Mencer: Ni Pewma*, "Floating Ophelia,"
video still, 2011. Image courtesy of Francisco Huichaqueo.

of both growth and decay along the fertile banks of the river, which create a fecund backdrop for her passage from life to death. As in other Pre-
Raphaelite paintings, human life looks pale next to the abundance of flora
and fauna, and we are invited to see Ophelia's death alongside the continual
renewal of the natural world, beyond the damming and occupation of the
Maule River.

In the film, Ophelia emerges as a masked figure in a long white dress,
floating on screen and surrounded by wildflowers, as if in homage to the
Millais painting. Indeed, the video moves out of its monochromatic palette
into pastel coloration that mimics the rich Pre-Raphaelite colors. Huichaqueo adjusts the video with color enhancement, which enhances the sense
of surrealist time and space, and calls even more attention to the paint-

erly scene that the sequence brings to life. In a particularly slow sequence, Ophelia floats through a dreamtime state of suspension, embodying the figure of a chaste romantic heroine, that also merges colonial notions of life and death with Mapuche dreamscapes of a parallel surreal state.

With this poignant image, Huichaqueo gestures to other histories of Latin American surrealism that are neither confined to the commercial genre of magical realism nor completely separate from European aesthetic traditions. Instead, these new imaginaries offer different mappings of aesthetics that destabilize traditional art histories, and illustrate the mixing of Indigenous cultural production against, but also through, European codes. In a recent influential volume on Latin American surrealist art, editors Dawn Ades, Rita Eder, and Graciela Speranza suggest that the transits between the Américas and Europe regarding surrealism have been both poorly understood and contemporarily misconstrued.[28] The volume shows how the mutually constituting aesthetic formations that might cohere within the category of surrealism are too often separated out by national boundaries. Movements such as surrealism cannot be reduced to any prescribed or preset definition or given a European origin story, but instead must be understood as emanating from multiple points of diffusion and influence. The film illustrates and then dissociates from romanticism in order to show multiple trajectories of aesthetic influence that travel from north to south, from south to north, and south-south, and cannot be cast simply in terms of a European influence within South America. These transits remind the viewer of colonialism's tangled aesthetic and political legacies.

In Huichaqueo's restaging, Ophelia embodies a global preoccupation with water, the natural world, and land, and while the tragedy of Ophelia is often emphasized in European critical contexts, Huichaqueo uses her death to figure the tragedy of land loss and water reappropriation upon Indigenous territories. Given the Chilean nation's imbrication with not only Spanish colonialism but also British Empire and a fetishistic relationship to English culture, we can read the sudden insertion of the immobile Ophelia as both a metaphor for the death of Eurocentrism and a reminder that ecological degradation is the dystopic future everywhere and for everyone.

We can think about this film as an archive of the future that shows the centrality of the river to Indigenous life. *Mencer: Ni Pewma* also relies on images of the Maule River to show its flow and to activate a memory of the local and international efforts that fought against the Ralco hydroelectric dam. Huichaqueo weaves through several shots of the river in motion, visually suggesting its cosmological vitality, and imagining its life source. In these long shots, the river becomes another protagonist in the film. Like the unpredictability of fire, it too cannot be contained or tamed by human developmental designs, a view of natural world where memory animates against the river's erasure.

By distorting a linear sense of time and visualizing a sensual relation to place, Huichaqueo searches for a means to document the past-present, one that leaves a trace as an archive for the future. The choppy fragments of *Mencer: Ni Pewma* make most sense, therefore, when viewed not within the suffocating logics of colonial visual culture but rather within a larger Mapuche ecological relationality to land, water, air, and fire, and within the histories of occupation. By highlighting the struggle over representation, the viewer begins to understand the multidirectional sensorium of Indigenous experience that, because it lives on the other side of colonial catastrophe, is always at odds, and defends against ongoing destruction.

### Forest Recovery

Within the highly reorganized landscape of occupation, it is perhaps difficult to imagine a different future for Mapuche territories and the once resource-rich region. Yet, the work of Indigenous and international organizations throughout South America, and acutely in the Ralco conflict, illustrates the degree to which conservation and protection of lands is an important antidote to statecraft upon naturally resource rich lands. However, the question of conservation in relation to Indigenous territories is a more complex one as I addressed in the previous chapter, and, given the modes of decolonization that Huichaqueo attends to, I consider it central to the different imaginaries of the planetary at the heart of Mapuche praxis and cultural production.

An impactful and still relevant report from 1990 on South American conservation, *National Parks without People? The South American Experience*, suggests that state policy aimed to protect nature has historically been accompanied by a lack of consideration for the Indigenous presence on those same lands. As the report's preface indicates, one approach to the project of land conservation has been to "systematically close one's eyes to reality and refuse to recognize the fact that a large number of the national parks are not spaces without inhabitants. This has caused a sort of schizo-phrenic behavior in many officials: formally enforcing the laws and regu-lations, maintaining publicly that human populations do not, or should not, exist."[29]

What the report describes as "schizophrenic behavior" is actually an-other iteration of the history of colonial discovery that representationally evacuates Native peoples in order to produce an innocent account of Euro-pean settlement. The immigration policies of the nineteenth century in Chile would be the parallel instance, in which the Law of Selective Immigra-tion of 1845 accommodated several thousand German and Swiss families into the southern territories, and had as its consequence an impactful wave of "reduction" laws aimed at eliminating Indigenous land titles.[30] This legis-lation historically forced Mapuche communities onto poor lands, reducing viability for everyday activities, leaving lasting consequences in the region as the violent dispossession of Mapuche land and water rights. Contempo-rary conservation schemes, then, must be historicized within this context of "selective immigration" as forced removal and representational evacuation.

When I first visited Southern Chile in the early 1990s, a time of rapid forest decimation, I heard of the conservation plan that was put into place through the wealth and vision of Douglas Tompkins, the former co-founder of the US clothing company The North Face. His idea was to con-serve the rapidly decimated ancestral forests by "buying them up" and taking stewardship of the land. Local communities were wary about US corporate ownership, not because they did not see the validity of what might come from conservation practices, but because it put vital lands and resources into foreign hands. Tompkins's public statements have done little to disavow this local view of US paternalism, since he has often only super-ficially responded to the question of motives. For instance, he stated in an interview, "I bought the first piece of land almost whimsically, because it was so cheap and so beautiful . . . that's where it all started."[31] Tompkins has been situated as a global leader of ecophilanthropy, a movement that has gained momentum among elite liberal entrepreneurs invested in reducing global climate change. Yet, these unthinking statements ignore the weight and persistence of colonial control over Indigenous territories.

Conservation has deeper roots in a liberal imaginary about land and biodiversity that sees nonhuman life as its principal site of advocacy but that also often makes recourse to representational evacuation. With rare exceptions,[32] conservation initiatives usually perceive Native peoples as an obstacle to, rather than an imperative for, preservation.[33] Well-meaning reports by nongovernmental environmental organizations contribute to the representation of Southern Chile as an unpeopled landscape, what Martin Berger has referred to as a "racialized discourse of property."[34] Though Berger studies art history and US perception as the objects of an analysis about structured audience responses to cultural phenomenon, his interpretive methodology is useful in the context of the South American preservationist gaze. It demonstrates how whiteness reduces land to a representation of *terra nullius*. For Berger, whiteness fluctuates, but is unified in its "magisterial view," as a visual entitlement that symbolically appropriates land as patterns of racialization that reproduce material inequities. Here, Berger's model of whiteness may be applied to the extractive view that privileges empty "beautiful" land over seeing Indigenous territories.

Although the World Watch Institute report criticizes Tompkins and questions his interventionist, ecophilanthropist interests, it also reproduces the problematic assumption of Indigenous absence in the region, such as in this passage:

> It is easy to see why the place so enchanted them. Densely forested slopes plunge from snow-capped volcanic peaks into icy waters. The mist-shrouded old-growth rainforest receives 6,000 millimeters of rain per year and shelters giant *alerce* trees that were already a thousand years old when Jesus walked the Earth. Once a common species, similar to the California redwood, the *alerce* has almost been logged into extinction. To Doug Tompkins, this extinction crisis is the central problem facing the planet and humanity, and the struggle to preserve biodiversity is the primary concern, "the point upon which everything turns."[35]

Like the extensive regions of preservation that exist globally, Tompkins's land ownership forms part of the system of forest management and conservation, that functions within a colonial paradigm that privileges outsiders, erases Native peoples, and imagines saving the planet through "American philanthropy." In this missionizing project, forest management and conservation protect land that privilege a colonial viewpoint that contributes to the dispossession of Indigenous peoples.

As the Chilean state continued to expand its governance on the Bío Bío frontier, *La ley de bosques* 4.363, known as the 1931 Forest Law was put into place to protect lands with little acknowledgment of its Mapuche, Pe-huenche, and Huilliche inhabitants. As Gutierrez-Vilches explains:

> The Forest Law was the first to address how national parks should regu-late timber trading, guarantee the survival of certain tree species, and preserve scenic beauty. From a conservation perspective, the Forestry Law allowed for the creation of national parks in Chile that established certain criteria that served as the basis for the present protection system. Such criteria included the type of property on which national parks may be created, creation by presidential decree, and divestment by law; the objectives for which protected areas are created; the administration of such areas by a specialized agency; and the feasibility of their use by the public.[36]

In other words, the state organized forest protection without consideration for Indigenous peoples' claims on southern territories. In addition to rep-resentational evacuation, such laws, from their "magisterial perspective," overlook the expansive literature addressing how Native peoples contrib-ute to, rather than degrade, biodiversity.

Neoliberal governance links the law to administrative and technocratic nation making, what Fred Moten and Stefano Harney refer to by using the shorthand term "policy and planning."[37] As a technique of governmentality, policy and planning produce a complicated incentive system that results in the ubiquitous presence of forest industry within the Bío-Bío region. More specifically, Lucio Cuenca, national coordinator for the Latin American Observatory of Environmental Conflicts, explains the incentive conun-drum for Indigenous peoples this way: "The response by the State has been to provide favorable legal and social conditions to enable the forestry com-panies to fulfill their production goals and continue their expansion. On the one hand it does this through repression and criminalization [of Mapuche opposition], on the other it reroutes subsidies that were formerly aimed at large companies to small farmers and indigenous landowners. This obliges them to convert to forestry activities. Thus, the strategy for expansion be-comes more complex, operating through political and economic blackmail that leaves no alternatives."[38] In this quote, Cuenca describes a perverse legal and political model wherein subsidies are diverted to small farmers and Indigenous landowners to facilitate their participation in the monocul-tural forest industry. In this "no alternative" paradigm, Mapuche peoples either incorporate their lands into the extractive zone or become the target of state repression. In this logic, the state reinforces a system that produces criminals out of those it has dispossessed.

Mapuche peoples, as Cuenca indicates, are often locked within extractive schemes that dispossess them, either through privatization of lands or through conservation that produces expulsive migrations. In spaces where states offer no alternatives, survival must be tactile and practical. For instance, after the pine and eucalyptus trees have been harvested, Mapuche communities who stay move in to plant subsistence gardens between the scars left on the earth by large bulldozers. Reshaping the state paradigm that leaves no alternatives is at the core of a vernacular archive of the future. In this way communal gardens have become an important and seasonal means of subsistence, an imagination of the future out of reduction and bare life.

A Mapuche worldview reconstitutes the future by interpreting the processes of extractivism and conservation as two sides of the same developmentalist vision. In the poles between conservation and land defense, Huichaqueo decolonizes Western aesthetics and Chilean representations to make room for perceiving and making life otherwise.

### Beyond the Colonial Divide

I have discussed how dominant representations of Indigenous people in southern territories is, on the one hand, trapped within the hypervisible logics of racism and extractivism, and, on the other hand, rendered invisible by discourses of conservation and liberal multiculturalism. My own stake in addressing Huichaqueo's experimental generativity is to make visible and available the multiple strategies that challenge occupation toward moving beyond the colonial divide. Through a nonlinear sense of time, surrealism, and a critique of representational evacuation, we find decolonial alternatives.

As we have seen, Huichaqueo's multimedia experiments constitute an archive of the future; his subject matter and sensibilities very squarely consider the project of decolonizing perception—whether through the sonic, through dreamscapes, and through the undoing of romanticism, or by inverting dominant racial and colonizing tropes. An archive of the future documents occupation so as to see beyond its capitalist rationale. Through the use of surrealist techniques, Huichaqueo often swaps formal linearity for fragmented content, and he exchanges a liberal viewpoint that merely documents violence and destruction for a perspective that sees through and to the other side of occupation. Furthermore, through images and performances that symbolically make visible how racialized tropes differentiate to facilitate extractive capitalism, *Mencer: Ni Pewma* condenses the events of the last thirty years in the state war against Mapuches linking them to Spanish colonialism and settler colonization in earlier centuries.

By way of closing, I want to return to what the decolonial queer method can offer in the landscape of occupation. In conversations over a two year period with Francisco Huichaqueo in which we built trust and ultimately a close friendship, I slowly found out that the production of the film was coordinated to reflect a Mapuche cosmology through a symbolic idiom that was guided by the hands of a *machi*. If the *machi* is the powerful spiritual and ritual center of Mapuche culture, then it is through her embodied enactments, as mediated through Huichaqueo's filmic techniques, that we are able to conjure and see beyond the colonial condition.

In conceiving the film together, the *machi* Silvia Kallfüman guided Huichaqueo to include elements of Mapuche symbolic language, and to bring the mnemonic echoes of the ancestral realm forward into the sound and visual tracks. As Huichaqueo summed up to me, *Mencer: Ni Pewma* was "consciously and subconsciously made in fragments as an orchestrated memory for the future."[39] By leading the viewer through the symbolic realms of dreaming and the parallel sensibilities of the ancestral realm, Huichaqueo found other ways to perceive and film the images of occupation, often in ways that he has yet to decode for himself. A decolonial femme episteme that is porous to the possibility of multiple viewpoints avows the *machi*'s ability to render the language of dimensions, and to tread into unseen and unknown realities. Kallfüman guides Huichaqueo into unmapped terrains, and brings the viewer with him to the other side of the collapse of the extractive zone.

Rather than mediating the past-present occupation through a recognizable, conventional narration of political and collective experience, Huichaqueo chooses a more opaque, experimental, and irreducible form of contending with occupation's legacies and social traces. The *machi* whispers her secrets to Huichaqueo and into the wind, speaking her own dream and visions through the filmmaker mediator. Thus, the film's experimentation

Francisco Huichaqueo, *The Dreams of Machi Silvia Kallfüman*,
video still, 2015. Image courtesy of Francisco Huichaqueo.

enters us into the landscape of dreams, the archive for and of the future that
exists in parallel tension with a wounded landscape.

In a two-minute segment from *Dreams of Machi Silvia Kallfüman* (2015)
that was made for the Chilean archaeological museum, the first time in the
history of the museum that a Mapuche curator had organized an exhibit,
we see Huichaqueo's guide at the center of her cosmic world, the river. In
my estimation, this film is the most realized in its submerged perspective,
and allows me to stage the decolonial femme method explicitly. In this film
segment, the director uses the technique of temporal lag, as well as the inhabitance of the *machi*'s repetitious gestures, to entice us into the flowing
river water. This haptic sensual movement that flows alongside the river's
undulation opens the parallel *perrimonton* dream world. Once we enter the
dream, as an imaginary, an ancestral world, and a parallel real, we can perceive anew, outside of the duality that the visual has conventionally occu-

pied. This other world emerges in saturated tones of the filmic landscape as rich blue and green hues, where light plays on water, and where sound vibrates through the rush of the waterfalls. By using a decolonial femme method, we can perceive the *machi*'s immersion in the water, her repetition of gestures, the dancing of light on the river, and the undulating waves as guiding us toward a world before and beyond the extractive zone.

Through the *machi*'s view, Huichaqueo shows us submerged and emergent perspectives as parallel perception. This space otherwise flows like the river, a dream that escapes colonial duality, and that moves toward a state of undifferentiation. If we take this perception seriously, Huichaqueo and Kallfüman seem to intimate, then we can learn how to reoccupy through a full return of the senses.

# CHAPTER 4

# A Fish-Eye Episteme

## *Seeing Below the River's Colonization*

It takes many aesthetic strategies, modes of critique, engaged activisms, acts of land and water defense, and forms of perception to decolonize the dominant viewpoint that misrecognizes territorial relations for the extractive zone. One strategy that mestiza Colombian multimedia artist Carolina Caycedo employs is to repurpose the images taken by satellite technologies so as to visibly document how hydroelectric corporations block the flow of South American rivers.

In the installation *Dammed Landscapes* (2012), Caycedo works with digital imaging to document five stages of the El Quimbo Hydroelectric Project construction, a highly controversial plan that has led to widespread dispossession in the region.[1] In Caycedo's hands, satellite photographs become the source for enormous wall panels that illustrate how the Southwestern Colombian landscape has, since 2011, been thoroughly damaged by the onset of hydroelectric development. What time-sequenced images show over a four-year period is the trail of barren territory left in the wake of hydropower's advancement. The riverbed scar visibly reminds the viewer of the pathway where the powerful Magdalena River once flowed.

The sectional erasure of the river body, and the dispossession of communities that depend upon the Magdalena, is at the core of Caycedo's impressive body of work. *Dammed Landscapes* pursues how technocratic designs distort a multi-tiered perception of life through stark images that track a twenty-mile stretch of the disappearance of the Magdalena River. Caycedo inverts the extractive view to show how the Magdalena's confluence with the Páez River literally damns the river to extinction.

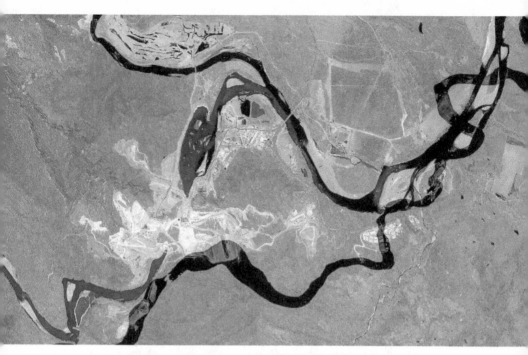

Carolina Caycedo, from *Dammed Landscapes*, Magdalena River
(Yuma) after Endesa river diversion, satellite image, 2012.
Image courtesy of Carolina Caycedo.

In *Yuma: Land of Friends* (2014), Caycedo offers important video work
that testifies to the process of literally submerging the rural mestizx and Indigenous communities that for generations lived intermixed with the flow
of the Magdalena River. In this chapter, I take a close look at *Yuma: Land
of Friends*, a video that blends the experiences of those most affected by
damming with long shots of the river's movement, its sound, and its voice.
That dams "silence rivers" has been an important way to perceive modernization's separation from the agency and life forms of the natural world.[2]
Caycedo's visual and sonic techniques are based in anti-dam counterlogics
and do not "silence the river," but instead allow for its rushing sound and
the gurgling voice of Yuma to emerge. Through edits that literally submerge
the camera into the mucky brown water below the surface, Caycedo lifts
submerged perspectives within the extractive zone.

Perceiving anew matters on a continent where small, medium-sized and large-scale dams are planned for much of its rivers, and where the pervasiveness of megaprojects in mining, petroleum, and hydroelectricity is hegemonic.[3] Almost one hundred new dams are currently under construction throughout South America, obscuring the promotion of energy alternatives that do not depend on life's extinction. Despite growing social movements that aim to protect territories and an accompanying vast political ecology literature that challenge the costs of hydroelectric power on human and nonhuman life,[4] mega dams are often constituted by state and corporate actors as the necessary means to continuing to pursue a retrogressive view of national and regional integration toward globalized modernity.

We might pause to consider how hydropower functions on a scale of extractive capitalism that demands exponential, if finite, social and ecological resources.[5] Large dams require expansive infrastructure and intensive capital investments, usurping thousands of acres of land. Whether it is the Itaipu Dam along the Paraná River, the Three Gorges Dam that spans the Yangtze River, or the projected "Master Plan" that imagines building seventeen dams along the Magdalena River, since their design in the nineteenth century, large dams have continually dispossessed millions of Indigenous and rural peoples.[6] What conceptual tools allow us to puncture the assumption of dispossession that is embedded in the logic of hydropower? How do local communities counter these colossal schemes and their cycloptic viewpoint? Because of its sheer size and potential for destruction, mega dam development often casts doubt about the potential for local responses, yet in this chapter I enumerate how visual and embodied resistance finds ways to fissure the dam walls, working to perforate the matrix of capitalist expansion.

By centering on hydropower, I analyze how plans to absorb and drown the proliferation of life are contested by local communities, specifically in the Cauca Valley of Colombia by the Asociación de Afectados por el Proyecto Hidroelectrico El Quimbo (Association of Affected Peoples of the Quimbo Hydroelectric Power, ASOQUIMBO). In tandem with this movement, the artwork and decolonial praxis of Carolina Caycedo inverts, refuses, and subtends the visual formats of the dam's view to instead support the experiences of local social and ecological movements that live and die within the extractive zone.

## Seeing Like They Do

Over the past decade, the Spanish hydroelectric company Endesa has threatened territories in the Department of Huila with the construction of the Quimbo Hydroelectric Project. In 2008, President Álvaro Uribe Vélez's neoliberal government (2002–10) sold ten thousand hectares to Endesa, legally handing over rights to land alongside the Magdalena River, territories that had been inhabited by Indigenous groups, mestizxs, and local fishing and agricultural communities for generations. Eschewing their responsibility for resettlement and ecological mandates, the state office of the National Authority of Environmental Licenses has become notorious for systematically ignoring the land rights of local communities. As the ASOQUIMBO activist Jose Avilá described it, "We lost everything, this land is what has supported my family for generations and all we demanded was to be relocated or compensated fairly as stated in the environmental license."[7]

Carolina Caycedo has worked both independently and alongside Descolonizando La Jagua (Decolonizing La Jagua, ASOQUIMBO), and Rios Vivos (Rivers Alive Colombia), anti-extractivist campaigns based on local membership that has spearheaded organizing against Endesa. The strategies of these local movements proliferate to include protests, marches, forums, press conferences, and legal pressure aimed at stopping both Endesa and the Chinese state-owned company Hydrochina from dredging and blocking the river. Overall, the objective has been to decolonize the river communities that have been flooded with state agents, corporate workers, the military, dam builders, bulldozers, cement, and so forth, that have made artisanal and low-resource ways of life nearly impossible.

Since 2011, ASOQUIMBO's work has focused upon Endesa's disregard for local communities, and taking back lands along the Magdalena River that were illegally granted to the extractive corporation. More recent efforts have placed emphasis not only on the river's destruction and dispossession but also on the resilient and vibrant aspects of river life, such as the intertwined living that takes place between riverbank communities and their interdependent relation to the Magdalena River. In this announcement, for instance, there is a palpable expression of a future-oriented desire to recuperate land and place: "On March 14, 2015 we will initiate a great mobilization for the defense of the Magdalena River and the territories of life. We take a journey through the country from Macizo Colombiano to Bocas de Ceniza to reject the Master Plan that takes advantage of the River Magdalena. We do this to recuperate memory, identity, and culture by an entire nation that has constructed its life, territory, and history alongside the river."[8] Taking long walks alongside the Magdalena River as a mnemonic experience of community identity allows for the acknowledgment of the imbricated relation with and deep respect for the Magdalena River.

Such acts as organizing collective walks not only signal the importance of local land memory as constitutive of regional and national identity; they also point to how the river itself is enlivened by human activity that does not merely extract from its ecological life. Taking this insight one step further, we might imagine how the river possesses its own form of memory, as a witness to the dialectic between life and death of damming, as weighing in on the contradictions between converting value and devaluing, and as a source of flow that energizes against its own erasure. Seeing, watching, knowing the histories of riverbank communities and being enlivened by their presence is a submerged perspective that one might imagine could emanate from the river. These submerged perspectives refuse to be limited by regional or national boundaries, as they are able to flow beyond the corporation's efforts at containment.

In the demand for legal accountability from Endesa, over the past decade transregional communities have compared and shared knowledge across national borders to support them in their legal battles. As I mentioned in chapter 3, the Mapuche struggle against Endesa in the Bío Bío region of Chile began in 1996 and continues until today, marking an earlier era of hydropower expansion in South America. When ASOQUIMBO in the Cauca Valley learned about the successes and failures of anti–Ralco Dam struggles, it used knowledge of what worked there to combat Endesa on its own territories. Furthermore, as in the struggle against Ralco, ASOQUIMBO also coordinated its actions with International Rivers and other international NGOs, in effect strengthening its vertical and lateral alliances. Like the Magdalena River that transits through multiple regional borders, the flow of knowledge between affected Indigenous and rural communities moves freely in ways that facilitate the positive deployment of resistance strategies.

To combat the violent disarticulations and dispossessions required by the presence of the hydropower corporation, over the past decade ASO-

QUIMBO has taken an increasingly militant stance. Violent escalation in the extractive zone occurs through a familiar sequence of events: militarized dispossession leads to confrontations between local organizations and the state, conflict that is then followed by the state's criminalization of land and river defenders. The ASOQUIMBO case is legendary in this respect, in that there are currently dozens of river defenders who have been imprisoned without trial or promise of release, in many ways replicating the violent scenes and media frenzies that have taken place in other sites around South America.

Through militarization of the extractive zone corporate control is able to advance its capitalist agenda, by dispossessing Indigenous and rural peoples of their territories. In Caycedo's visual and narrative work, she makes this link directly as she plays with the multiple meanings contained within the word "dam," using it alternatively as a verb, simile, noun, and metaphor. For instance, in Spanish the word *represa* is used for "to dam," and also for "to repress." A *represa* literally contains the river's natural flow as well as signifying the political repression against local land and river defenders. For Caycedo, then, extractivism cannot be separated from forms of violence and repression that are rendered invisible by current economic and political models. Attending to this colonial matrix, her work "explores the interrelations between social repression, and the planning and construction of water dams/reservoirs. Dams generally serve the primary purpose of retaining water by stopping the flow of a river. By analogy, we may think of repression as an instance of power that also interrupts the flow of social and community organization."[9]

Thus, Caycedo's visual work does a kind of relational mapping of power that uncovers the epistemological, material, and bodily violence that thwarts biological life. It also reveals how the river's diversion does not block submerged perspectives and movements that look to defend local autonomy.

### Damned Landscapes

Damned landscapes are extractive zones where military, corporate, and state technologies of resource surveillance convert Indigenous and rural territories into a digital colony. Caycedo's unique approach to the digital colony is to produce countervisualities that expose the extractive viewpoint by presenting the containing logic of damming. Nicholas Mirzoeff's *The Right to Look: A Counter History of Visuality* historicizes visuality within a Western genealogy, and outlines the contours of a countervisual methodology that moves against the organizing principle of colonial seeing. Though Mirzoeff's effort to produce "a comparative decolonial framework" is only suggestive and might require more sustained attention to the scholarly and cultural production of the Global South, his book generates an important set of proposals about the potentialities and constraints of the visual. Drawing upon the classic work of W. J. T. Mitchell, Mirzoeff imagines a range of medium theory as a venue "for the transmission and dissemination of authority, and a means for the mediation of the subject of that authority."[10] If we consider that the extractive viewpoint succeeds precisely by becoming the normative way we see and universalize the planetary, then in the regions I study countervisuality reveals extractive zones as corporate and state collusion over the destruction of life, refocusing our attention upon a smaller scale of experience.

Rather than condemn technology to its hegemonic use as surveillance, Caycedo's eye inverts the instrumental usage of colonial digitality, presenting the devastation of local communities and the landscape from multiple scales. In other works, Caycedo weaponizes digital technology to facilitate the visibility and vitality of communities that persist despite hydropower's extinguishing footprint. Overriding the viewpoint of the digital colony, her artistic production eschews the developmentalist fallacy that assumes that hydroelectricity is good for everyone.

In a video of a midrange satellite image, we see Caycedo's hand drawing over the white space where the emptied river once flowed. This movement of her pen renders the memory of the river's flow and offers a mapping of the Earth's rapid changes at the hands of human development. Rather than reproduce the extractive view that sees like a satellite from above to enable the management and diversion of the river's resources toward capitalist accumulation, Caycedo's pen instead works in the opposite direction: Tracing the flow of water reverses the flow of capital and its amnesic evacuation of what was once there, placing the river back in the frame and outside of the digital colony.

Drawing the connection between damming, violence, and the evacuation of localized territories was at the center of her solo exhibitions *The Headlong Stream Is Termed Violent, but the Riverbed Hemming Is Termed*

*Violence by No One* (2009) and *Beyond Control* (2010) that took place in Berlin. In them, Caycedo used multiple artistic formats to invert the gaze and rearrange the way we relate to the mutations imposed by hydroelectricity. Her photographs and sculptures illustrate the degree to which hydroelectricity in the Quimbo region has blocked the flow of long-term residents, rerouting and reconstituting the memory of the region's ecological biodiversity.

In *Represa/Repression* (2012), Caycedo depicts a fragmented and carved-up landscape that has been violated by the Endesa dam construction. She describes this work as a "research-based project that explores concepts of flow and containment, while investigating correlations between the mechanisms of social control and the unethical aspects of projects including large water dams and reservoirs."[11] This quote implies that regions are extracted by sending police and military personnel that first repress, then quell, and later displace local residents. Caycedo's work shows that these submerged perspectives and counternarratives require deep investigation into how peripheral spaces and community are repressed. Caycedo's viewpoint utilizes the same technologies of research and digital output that corporations use but she diverts and repurposes them to deauthorize the extractive view.

## Other Views: Fish-Eye Episteme

If satellite technologies, which identify high-resolution social and ecological activity, so completely map and commoditize the landscape from above, does any view reside outside of the society of control? The answer to this seems to depend on how we enter the colonial condition. In *Epistemologies of the South: Justice against Epistemicide*, Boaventura de Sousa Santos argues that what underlies grave social inequalities in the current global configuration is the persistence of cognitive injustice—what I refer to as forms of perception—that have reproduced asymmetries through colonial systems, modern states, and global capitalism's economic rationale.[12] Western modernity, as de Sousa Santos maintains, devalues heterogeneous knowledge formations and reduces diverse life forms into a modern scientific perspective, underscoring both the limits of disciplinary knowledge as well as the erasure of the multivalent ontologies that express themselves within the vernacular practices of peripherally constituted spaces.

I find De Sousa's naming of cognitive injustice a useful point of departure with respect to seeing otherwise. "Cognitive injustice" refers to the constraining paternalisms imposed on the Global South through colonizing discourses and practices that continue to perceive these regions as purveyors of natural materials, and undervalue the heterogeneity of life embedded within local epistemes. De Sousa's larger contention is that multifaceted knowledge formations already exist, and it is the task of scholar-activists, and, I would add, artists and performers, to lift up those submerged epistemes and juxtapose them within a Western canon that cannot apprehend its own limitations.[13]

Eduardo Viveiros de Castro, whose perspectivist insights have come out of a thirty-year ethnographic engagement, helps me to define such a point of view. His work both parallels and departs from subaltern genealogies and other Global South epistemes.[14] Moving beyond the object-subject divide, Viveiros de Castro's work increasingly poses a decolonizing challenge to Western anthropology, and to the reproduction of the human as a singular entity standing within a world of subordinate beings. Through ethnographic critique, Viveiros de Castro offers Indigenous thought as a philosophical challenge to the classic European distinction between Nature and Culture. Inverting the signifiers of "multiculturalism," which has been the center of colonial/modern thought, to "multinaturalism," Viveiros de Castro references how Indigenous peoples acknowledge the coexistence of multiple perspectives in the human and nonhuman world. The fundamental conceptual shift of perspectivist theory, then, is to reorder the nature-culture divides of primordial immanence: reversing the order of universalism to follow that of nature, and particularity to that of culture.

Indigenous thought, as Viveiros de Castro shows us, has long been engaged with apprehending "reality from distinct points of view,"[15] and ontologically has organized its societies and spiritual practices accordingly. A constantly shifting imagination of the Other is not constrained or delimited through the privileging of Homo sapiens.[16] For my purposes, Viveiros de Castro's work not only moves us into the realm of decolonial possibility, it also pursues and elaborates a rescripting of European thought. More importantly, it proposes that agency exists within a multiplicity of vantage points that are irreducible. As Viveiros de Castro puts it about Indigenous perspectivism, "We must remember, above all, that if there is a virtually universal Amerindian notion, it is that of an original state of undifferentiation or 'undifference' (don't mistake this for 'indifference' or 'sameness' between humans and animals)."[17] This state of undifferentiation does not propose a unifying viewpoint but instead shows how the act of viewing can itself contain an agency that is not uniquely human. Furthermore, by conceptually naming multinaturalism, perspectivisms locate agency within the realm of the animate as well as the inanimate. Thus, in opposition to the gaze that is merely about ocular extensions of centralized power, perspectivist thought escapes the view of dominant visuality to encompass the modes of seeing that emerge outside of the range of the human eye and its capture.

My insights here touch upon, and also depart from, the recent turn in the humanities to new materialisms. The work on posthumanisms and new materialisms has been important as shifting epistemes that function within European logocentricity and the human-centered approaches that much of European continental philosophy has labored upon. Through a philosophy of vibrant objects, in which materiality enlivens through its active shaping of human and nonhuman events, Jane Bennett gestures to a nonhuman something else.[18] The expanded vocabulary of new materialist analyses are provocative. How can we read such work through the realities of marginality and expulsion faced in the growing extractive zones around the globe and through the regions that already experience biomatter as not separate from the human? How can we understand the human as already inscribed within the logics of coloniality?

There may indeed be an emergent consciousness about how to think about the natural world through other knowledge formations. As Diana Coole and Samantha Frost explain about the new materialist turn, "We are finding our environment materially and conceptually reconstituted in ways that pose profound and unprecedented normative questions. In addressing them, we unavoidably find ourselves having to think in new ways about the nature of matter and the matter of nature; about the elements of life, the resilience of the planet, and the distinctiveness of the human."[19] Yet, Global South epistemologies and philosophies of race and racism, ranging from postcolonial and decolonial theories, to Indigenous critique, to Afro-based thought, to Black Studies to perspectivisms and relational models, have long anticipated the ways to differently imagine knowledge and perception as the foundation of planetary inhabitance. These other knowledge formations when grounded in the material relations of social ecologies form a sustained way to see and sense life otherwise. As Caycedo shows us, in the *Land of Friends* there is much to perceive anew.

## Other Views 2: *Land of Friends*

> Yo no tengo ningún idea romantica de como era el pasado. Las cosas no estaban perfectas. La tierra quizás no se uso de la major manera. Pero en sí eso de ninguna manera es raison ni logica de supultar todo el territorio.
>
> I don't have a romantic idea about the past. Things were not perfect. The land was perhaps not used in the best way, but that is not a reason or logic to drown a territory.
>
> Activist in *Land of Friends*

As a Latina, mestiza, and once resident of the Magdalena River communities, Carolina Caycedo's point of view draws from Indigenous relational understandings of land that imagine these geographies as enlivened and enchanted by its social ecologies. An artist skilled in multiple techniques and media, Caycedo is obsessed with the microlevel of gesture, social texture, and embodiment that contrasts the transparent logic of an extractive view that leaves no place "undiscovered." In *Yuma: Land of Friends* (2014), a thirty-eight-minute video that experiments with the genre's conventions, Caycedo focuses on seemingly small images and micromoments of everyday life to highlight the tensions and struggles between local fishing communities and Endesa's conversion of the Magdalena River into hydroelectric power.

Importantly, the river was called Yuma by the Musica confederation whose inhabitants intermixed with the Incan extended empire several centuries before the river's discovery by Spanish colonizers. In 1501, it was renamed after Mary Magdalene. As a symbol of these palimpsest histories, vernacular objects from the Musica confederation have recently been unearthed by the dozens during the drowning of territories by Endesa.

Panning across a dense view of highland Andean landscape, Caycedo expresses great affection for the Yuma River. Indeed, the fertile landscape at the center of *Yuma: Land of Friends* is an important way to feel the perceptual shift we are making against the extractive viewpoint and into a hybrid river nexus. Yuma territories are where Afro-Caribbean cultures meet

Carolina Caycedo, *Yuma: Land of Friends*, mosquito on hands,
video still, 2014. Image courtesy of Carolina Caycedo.

the Andean region, and then one thousand miles further downstream find confluence with the Amazonian basin. By tracking these trans-regional spaces through long pans, Caycedo makes the river the flowing center of Huila residents' living.

Using her own photographs as intertextual stills, Caycedo opens the film with a satellite photograph of ongoing dam construction that has already blocked and diverted long stretches of the Magdalena. In the next scene, a large mosquito sits on a pair of folded hands. "I have no nostalgia about the past," an activist from Entre Aguas says. As he continues to talk, the soundtrack gets quieter to the point that his words are inaudible. In this way, human voices are decentered and minimized so that visual ontologies that frame the river become the subject of emphasis within the film. About the Magdalena River, Caycedo narrates in a whisper, "It's also the golden thread, a sacred place where the ancestors and spirits dwell. Yuma's strait is especially magic. We all have our own quotidian rituals, our own goddesses and gods. They are among us."[20]

In the scene that follows, the director returns us to the satellite view of El Quimbo; her hand traces over the shadow terrain, the absent river, filling in the place where the river used to run before Endesa's construction in the Cauca Valley. The camera cuts to midlevel views of the river before holding for a full minute on a thick and squat waterfall that settles into a brown shadowy pool of rock and ferns below. Then we are taken under the falls, into the beige then blue-gray space of moving water. We wait, holding our breath, acclimating, and we begin to see both clear spaces and those that are more opaque. We move with the ribbons of currents and the circling movements of oxygen below the water. We accept the fact that our sight is obstructed by the cloudy water, with pieces of leaves blocking the view, fleeting away, as small and then larger bubbles force us to try to find something familiar in the visual muck. In long takes that submerge the camera completely in the muddy water, the field of vision hovers in that transitional zone between the translucent and opaque, between oxygen bubbles and swirling currents.

The effect is remarkable: I felt as if I were seeing what a fish sees, perhaps itself an anthropocentric viewpoint. By dipping into the muck, Caycedo produced a fish-eye epistemology that changes how we might relate to Yuma as a sentient being, rather than as an extractible commodity. Coincidentally, the term "fish-eye" also refers to an extreme wide-angle lens shot in which the edges of the frame are distorted to a near circle, with the center of the image forming a pregnant bubble. Both meanings work for the kind of material and philosophical shift in perspective or "fish-eye episteme": an underwater perspective that sees into the muck of what has usually been rendered in linear and transparent visualities.

In *Yuma: Land of Friends*, Caycedo's camera often dwells on the movement of the brownish-green water, the moss-covered stones surrounding it. The river in Caycedo's perspective, inhabits a generative if turbulent landscape where the human, animal, and plant life that surrounds it lives off of its provisions. However, there is no illusion that the Magdalena River is an unspoiled utopia; its cold waters make swimming for long periods difficult; its small fish do not fetch a very good price in local markets; and overall the terrain is rough and untamed, and its currents dangerous to untrained swimmers and nonhuman animals alike. Yet, without lament, local knowledge accustoms to and becomes flexible with what the river offers. Submerged, from below, seeing out from underwater, how do we think about the complexity of ecology, humanity, and the conditions of other beings from the fish-eye point of view? And, as I elaborate upon throughout the book, how do nonnormative viewpoints from within social ecologies decenter the logocentric perspective of the human?

In a significant moment in the film, Caycedo's camera lingers on the

Carolina Caycedo, *Yuma: Land of Friends*, inverted view,
video still, 2014. Image courtesy of Carolina Caycedo.

verdant green space. We are in the river's brown flow, surrounded by loud insects and birds and immersed within a roaring river's soundscape. The camera holds this still shot for three minutes; we breathe with the river's flow. Suddenly, and with the disorientation that comes from unexpected inversion, the camera is turned upside down, our view flips 180 degrees. From the top of the screen the river continues to flow, and this is the moment that fabrication breaks down, the instant we know that Caycedo has constructed the river world as the protagonist. The flow of gravity shifts, and the safety of our distant viewing is finally pierced. Caycedo's viewpoint is not only off-kilter but completely inverted, fundamentally reordering the river before us. What is this mirrored being that flows continuously from the top of the screen, the triangulated ferns that signal some kind of other worldly divinity? The gasping river, the inverted gaze we cannot move forward as we did before, now that we know of this place teeming, flowing, diverting our visions. The extractive view dissolves.

Earlier in the film, Colombian senator and opposition leader Jorge Robledo conjectures about the colonial and hydroelectric presence in the region. Offscreen, he states,

> The key question is why did they come here? There are two theories. The theory for idiots is that they came to save us from underdevelopment,

un-civilization, and poverty. They came for one thing. The profit margins are higher here. Not that they can't use their capital and gain profits over there. The fact is that they gain more here, and under globalization policies they can move that money easily without the risk of it getting stuck so there is more motivation to come here, because in the current time there is not even the risk of a strike or a revolution.[21]

As he speaks, the camera remains focused on a still shot of the flow of the river. And then, when the interviewee begins to raise his voice and talk about something else, we no longer see him on camera, and instead the view returns to the river to become completely submerged within the brown water, as more foam streams to the surface. Robledo continues,

> Y en la medida que han ido logrando, con la globalización que esa plata pueda entrar y salir libremente, sin los riesgos de quedar atrancada, con mayor razón intentan a venir más.[22]

> And, to the degree that they have been able to, with globalization that money can enter and exit freely, without risks to forestall profit, giving more reasons for them to come and try the same thing again.

In the background track, the water echoes and finally drowns out the voice of technocracy, the flattening speech of a man-splainer; and, despite his solid analysis of the prevailing situation, what seems more important now, and again, is the river's voice. That is, Caycedo authorizes cognitive justice for the river itself, drowning out the global economy and its rationalized logic, and instead offers us the fish-eye point of view that sees below the surface.

In the scene that immediately follows, Caycedo introduces us to Zoila, an artisanal fisherwoman, who stands knee-deep within the Magdalena River. By moving from a fish-eye episteme to a local fisher, Caycedo emphasizes the web of local economies and perspectives. Behind the woman, the water flows at a surprising rate compared to her stillness. Zoila repeatedly throws out her net, casting it farther each time and gathering a few fish with each catch, the protein for the soup that she will later make for her children, grandchildren, and adoptive kids: "If there is nothing else to feed the kids, then you take these little catfish home, you make a cut here and take out the entrails, you cook them with onion and salt. Many times this makes for a nutritious broth; boil them for ten minutes and they are ready to eat."[23] The camera focuses on the small fish that Zoila catches, whereby the repetitive close-up of hands becomes the local perspective that resides within the extractive zone. This is not a stranger's land but a territory of friends.

## Embodied Geographies

So far, I have addressed visualities and countervisualities within Caycedo's oeuvre as doing important work to decolonize the extractive view. However, at a certain point, visuality can only take us so far into the realm of the senses and daily life experiences from within the extractive zone. In 2014, Caycedo, in conjunction with the local collective Descolonizando La Jagua (Decolonizing La Jagua) began a project that took into consideration the question of embodiment through a set of performances called "geo-choreographies." These Earth-based performances are collectively authored to expose the dispossession of damming, as well as to show how kinesthetic movement by affected communities works to redirect the deadening logic of developmentalism. This work began through a series of choreographic workshops organized in partnership with Descolonizando La Jagua that engaged local communities in the towns of La Jagua, El Agrado, Oporapa, and Gigante. In recent years, Caycedo's work has extended this project throughout the Américas, using a hemispheric framework that considers embodiment in relation to rivers throughout the continent. More specifically, Caycedo has performed and made work in collaboration with the ecological organization Friends of the LA River and with Indigenous networks and river defense projects throughout the United States, Canada, and Latin America.

Geo-choreographies theorize how water functions as connective tissue, wherein rivers express the microlevel of human embodiment. In this view, rivers form the arteries of liquid, as Caycedo puts it, "for the river is to water as the veins that carry our blood." While I am not convinced by all of this project's analogies, in that they sometimes reach into generalities about human bodies and rivers that leave little room for textured analysis, the aesthetic and performative work of these comparisons seem important. And though the colonizing move of Eurocentric thought and exploration first sutured Indigenous peoples and the female body to land and nature, Caycedo differently names these historical lineages, avoiding the trap of essentialism through an artistic practice in which many angles and takes avoid a unidimensional view. While one might point to how this work could easily reassert the binaries of female/nature, indigenous/land, and human body/planet; ultimately, Caycedo's geo-choreographies seek out forms of human kinesthetic movement that mimic or work alongside the motion of the river in an expression of collaboration with it.

Caycedo's performance work in particular links to a genealogy of feminist performance praxis in the Américas that finds new ways to express the old questions of embodiment as it relates to land, ecology, and politics. For instance, the recent video piece by Guatemalan artist Regina Galindo, *Earth* (2011), expresses the dangers of extractivism as she stands in what's left of a piece of land that has been cut through by a giant yellow bulldozer that digs out all around her. Though the reference to collective burials such as Ayotzinapa in which young Indigenous students have become fodder for the corrupt state is evident in Galindo's piece, the video could just as easily reference more conventional forms of extractive capitalism that bulldoze the earth to reap capital from it. Whether in the violence and poetry of Ana Mendieta's images and performances, or Laura Aguilar's land-based photographs or the Earth performance by Regina Galindo, the dimensions within Caycedo's work clearly link her to a feminist hemispheric genealogy of producing work about embodiment, disappearance, visibility, and against a normative and extractive view of landscape. In particular, the body of work shows us how to see from the perspective of the fish, or the inhuman, or even the local river communities to appreciate the transits between these bodies as fluid encounters of perception, engagement, and vernacular meaning. Through the performative mediations of community knowledge we learn how to move and be in relation to land and water otherwise.

Caycedo's particular vision is multidimensional, integrating the formats of visuality, whether it be satellite images, still photographs, documentary video, installation, or the embodied collaborative performance work with communities that blurs the distinction between human and water bodies. Caycedo multiply sources formats and materials to communicate the alienated conditions that extractive capitalism produces, foregrounding the issue of scale to directly respond to the question I initially posed: How does the micro matter anyway?

While much of "geo-choreographies" is a work in progress, these performative iterations are key to producing spaces of communal meaning

Carolina Caycedo, ASOQUIMBO, Rios Vivos, "We are not just the defenders of the river; we are the river," 2015. Photo courtesy of Carolina Caycedo.

that avow the expression of territorial loss, and toward finding communal forms that abate the melancholia of ecocide or the sadness of experiencing the river's death. This anti-damming intersectional and coalitional work finds its resources in producing embodied art that intervenes in the normalized view of the extractive zone.

## Toward a Conclusion

I have been tracking social and knowledge formations that exist alongside the colonial developmental paradigm, showing how the extractive zone has not managed to fully colonize life, but reduces, eliminates, and destroys its heterogeneity. In this chapter, we returned to the river to analyze its submerged perspectives that exceed where the corporate management and technological domination over La Jagua, Colombia. I showed how life along the Yuma River in Colombia, which stretches from the Caribbean basin through the length of the entire country, depends upon a vast and interconnected river system that hangs in balance as it is organized into an extractive zone. If the extractive view naturalizes hydropower as the inevitable solution to the voracious energy demands of global urbanization, then the art and performance work of Carolina Caycedo renders visible a range of submerged perspectives that see from below and beyond its viewpoint.

I have illustrated how regimes of visual power are both used toward extractive ends and find their inversion through the viewpoint of artists such as Caycedo. Fundamentally, Caycedo's visuality gives us tools for analyzing complex modes of power toward the decolonization of mestizx and Indigenous territories. She provides the texture and context for how to think differently about visual power as a digital colony of the extractive zone. The networked society from below counters extractive regimes that control, silence, and extinguish the rivers. Such decolonial viewpoints emerge from the struggles of local populations in relation to their own subsistence economies, and also in relation to what it means to be under surveillance within the extractive zone. In this vein, ASOQUIMBO and Rios Vivos activism and the moving artistic practice of Carolina Caycedo insist that the future is now or there will be no future. Despite the fact that new extractivisms and megaprojects leave little room for the subtlety of riverbed knowledge, but what the fish eye sees is precisely the muck of the neoliberal and colonial condition.

# CHAPTER 5

# Decolonial Gestures

## *Anarcho-Feminist Indigenous Critique*

In the Casa del Museo de la Moneda (House of the Coin Museum) in Potosí, Bolivia, large glass exhibits display the first coins produced from silver extracted from within the nearby Cerro Rico (Rich Mountain) mine. First made in 1536, before switching to tin in 1576, these rough-edged coins circulated within the local and global economy until they became odd-shaped pieces that had to be taken out of circulation when bits of silver were picked off each of the *monedas*. By early in the seventeenth century, Potosí, Bolivia, was a bustling cosmopolitan center. Dubbed "the richest city on the planet," Potosí became the epicenter of a colonial global economy based on extracting silver from Cerro Rico, a mountain sacred to Aymara Indigenous people, and originally named Sumaj Orco. The extreme conditions of the mine diminished the Indigenous labor force that worked there, and after a request made in 1608 to the Spanish Crown, African slaves were imported to the Andes to supplement the arduous death work of silver extraction, fundamentally reshaping the character of colonialism, slavery and the racial caste system.[1]

In the two-hour tour of the museum through exhibitions on Potosí colonial art with detailed panels dedicated to the colonial life of the city and an intricate explanation of the coin production process, the colonial and modern history of Indigenous and African labor was curiously absent from the museum narrative. When pausing in front of the famous anonymous eighteenth-century painting *Virgin Cerro Rico* for a long explanation of its metaphoric content, there was little reference to the colonial condition that produced the rendering. In the painting, Cerro Rico Mountain is symbolized as a syncretized Virgin Mary, with a depiction of Diego Hualpa folded into the deity's mountain skirt. The Aymara discoverer of silver lights his way through the cavernous spaces of the deep mine. Even while the dense symbols of this painting were thoughtfully interpreted by our guide, what he did not address were the enslaved eight million Indigenous and the thirty thousand African peoples who labored within Cerro Rico. Or was there any mention of the one million whose remains are still buried within it. Finally, the gender, sexed, and racialized meaning of the Cerro Rico Mountain, as a mestiza Virgin Mary, was also not commented upon.

How can we understand the disappearance and silencing of Indigenous and African labor within the museum narrative of primitive accumulation that jump-started the global economy? Where were the displays that attended to the memories of the slavelike conditions of the *mita* (forced labor) system that lasted from the sixteenth to the late eighteenth century? As I moved from one cold thick-walled adobe room to another, the museum continued to forestall an answer. Overcome by these thoughts, I could not find warmth within the vault-like spaces.

As the museum tour came to a close, I looked up in the courtyard and hanging several feet above me was a large brown mask with a smile on its face and a thick bandana over the forehead. This "red face" mask hung over the courtyard entrance, a cartooned and racist presence that reminded the visitor of the conspicuous disappearance of Indigeneity elsewhere.[2] Finding a slice of warm sun on the patio, I ditched my tour guide and instead made room for a groundskeeper who was also in need of sunlight. As we looked out onto the pale orange Cerro Potosí in the distance, we noted how from our two-kilometer vantage point we could not see the sinkhole on the top of the mountain that had been created by five hundred years of overextraction.

As a majority Aymara Indigenous space and the site of primitive accumulation since the sixteenth century, Cerro Rico represents a highly symbolic geography of Spanish colonialism and early extractive capitalism. It is also a dense site of heteropatriarchy because of the mining industry's tendency to absent Indigenous gendered labor from national and local narratives.[3] My tour through the amnesiac corridors of the Casa del Museo de la Moneda led me to study intersectional critique and histories replete with the memory of collective and embodied resistance as found in the genealogies of Indigenous anarcho-feminisms.

My analysis in this chapter attends to the complex of anticolonial and anticapitalist genealogies that are also linked to Indigenous anarcho-feminisms. As Silvia Rivera Cusicanqui has critically conceptualized, Indigenous anarcho-feminisms simultaneously defy the capitalist global economy and find routes of escape from the reinscription of Andean patriarchy.[4] Thus, the specific connections I develop in this chapter move through genealogies of contestation that presence enactments of feminist, queer, anarchist, and Indigenous resistance that refuse and contend with institutions of foreign control, the *criollo* (European elite) state, sex normalcy, and forms of Andean and colonial patriarchy.[5] More specifically, I examine Indigenous anarcho-feminisms as decolonial gestures, or political enactments that articulate the complexity of overlapping forms of subjugation from within the extractive zone.

Anarcho-Indigenous feminisms represent a form of living otherwise that opposes, critiques, makes visible, and remakes the extractive zone. What lessons can be learned from anarcho-Indigenous feminism, which is both rooted within and disidentified from coloniality and Andean "tradition"? How does this form of social affiliation and long-standing intersectional critique provide a model for moving beyond the colonial divide and the extractive zone?

Since the 1980s, Mujeres Creando has been an important nexus of activity for anarcho-Indigenous feminisms. The group uses the principle of embodied and autonomous critique as a source for knowledge production. It draws upon historical models of horizontal organizing endemic to Indigenous Andean societies and anarchist praxis, articulating a mode of critical living that is not satisfied with the erasure of gender/sex embodiment. Rather than a land-based episteme, it is an intellectual and vernacular formation that begins with modes of being, thinking, doing, and relating otherwise, that are experienced through the body and in relation to each other.

Mujeres Creando represents two different paths of anarcho-feminism, both of which are rooted in antiracist work and within decolonial expressive praxis.[6] I address early Mujeres Creando performances and the later instantiations that include Julieta Paredes's work with feminist cultural center Café Carcajada as well as her writings, and María Galindo's activities at the cultural house in La Paz, also called Mujeres Creando. I also analyze one of the most important expressions of current anarcho-Indigenous feminisms, the rewriting of Evo Morales's Plurinational Constitution (2011) as "The Feminist Constitution."

It is impossible to understand a formation such as Indigenous anarcho-feminism and the important work it does to lift decolonial perspectives without thinking about the extractive zone that is silver and tin mining. In the first part of the chapter, I complicate the parameters of radical history within the Andes to rewrite the narrative of colonial dissent through anarcho-Indigenous feminist critique. These early sections allow me to show how Mujeres Creando and Mujeres Creando Comunidad, two different, if imbricated, formations, have inherited this genealogy, activating anarcho-Indigenous-feminist politics, aesthetics, and communal modes of decoloniality from within the extractive zone.

### The Potosí Zone

Whether resisting the forced labor of the *mita* system or by creating forms of local trade, horizontal living, or land-based economies that parallel the colonial order, the sheer number of revolutionary social movements and alternative models in the region lead me to describe the particular extractive zone of silver and tin mining as one of permanent insurrection.[7] Like the Black radical tradition born from inquiry into racialized subjugation and disidentification with the death project of transatlantic slavery, the Andean radical tradition emerged during the sixteenth century to critique, contend with, and seek routes out of colonial subjugation and violence. Indeed, this intellectual and grounded genealogy of struggle presences the Indigenous laborer and resistance in the extractive zone, in spaces such as Cerro Rico, throughout the mining economies of Bolivia, and later within the urban peripheries of La Paz.

To move toward an anarcho-Indigenous feminist critique of the extractive zone, several points are key. First, as Glen Coulthard, Sarita See, and many others have pointed out, Marx's concept of primitive accumulation incompletely theorized that capitalism was historically predicated upon Indigenous dispossession.[8] Second, because Indigenous peoples and their territories have long figured as a shadow global labor force, whose territories fuel the global capitalist system, critical Indigenous theory becomes a major, rather than minor, analytical frame in relation to the topic of extractivism. And third, like the *maquila* (assembly factory) industry along the US border, and the garment industry that depends upon Asian and Latina/Latin American working-class labor, mining extracts from and profits upon gendered and sexed bodies to literally power global capitalism.[9] Thus, using the lens of Indigenous feminisms, an analytic that does not conform to European gender and sex systems, allows us to see deeper into the workings of the mining industry, its demand for racialized and gendered labor within the extractive zone, and genealogies of resistance.

As a gendered enterprise, mining plays a major economic, political, and cultural role within Andean societies,[10] often to the exclusion of its female laborers. For instance, since the nationalization of natural resources in 1952, mining cooperatives such as the Corporación Minera de Bolivia continue to retain a highly visible, powerful, and much celebrated culture of mining organized through masculine work and survival. Within mining, female Indigenous workers have often been relegated to a secondary status, and within studies of revolutionary activity, female organizing has been even less visible, overshadowed by a masculinist narrative of revolutionary heroism. The lesser-known story of mining is its dependence on the labor of women and children, a fact that is often hidden from archives of anticapitalist and anticolonial struggle. In particular, women and children provide labor to the extractive zone by supporting the heterosexual "mining family" at home, while also working within the slag waste piles that lie just to the south of Cerro Rico, the million-ton heap of the mining sector's wasted materials. Over the course of five centuries, hundreds of thousands of women and children have labored as porters, recycling mining extraction's toxic materials.[11]

In her study *Nos/Otras en democracia: Mineras, cholas, y feministas, 1976–1994* (Us Feminists: Miners, Cholas, and Feminists), Lourdes Zabala details how extreme exploitation within the mining industry could take place only by normalizing patriarchy, a condition that was later refuted by female anarchists who organized among working-class women. In the context of labor's increasing radicalization during the 1920s, female laborers worked alongside their male counterparts to achieve the eight-hour workday. Furthermore, through hunger strikes and other embodied means of protest, they also successfully liberated political prisoners and improved wages, developing an antistate and profeminist agenda.[12] Thus, Indigenous and working-class women often articulated their dissent through multiple viewpoints and perspectives, opening the hemisphere's horizon of radical politics beyond that of a heteronormative and masculinist vision.

In *We Eat the Mines and the Mines Eat Us*, June Nash famously interviewed Aymara leader and organizer Domitila Chúngara about the hunger strike led by Indigenous women in 1962 to protest a labor union lockout in the tin mine industry. In the interview, Chúngara describes how the "housewives organized themselves because they did not pay their salaries on time. The army came and imprisoned the union leaders. Then all the workers declared a strike. Those women whose husbands were in jail . . . went to get their husbands' liberty, but failed. They decided to unite and make a solid front to ask for their liberty."[13] Though female organizing began as an expression of solidarity for male union leader mistreatment, it soon unfolded into a force of its own that grew in both size and consequence.

Moreover, as a response to the lack of remuneration, female leaders structured their protests through collective bodily dissent, namely through the public activity of self-starving. As Chúngara describes it, "The committee went to La Paz and declared a hunger strike. Radio 'Pio XII' censured the act because it was immoral—they said a person could not declare a hunger strike because it was against God's law . . . but the hunger strike was successful because they brought in the food and pay and also their husbands. At first there were only seventeen women in the strike, but it grew."[14] As news of the hunger strike traveled, more joined, to the point that self-starving bodies became a critical nexus for antistate, anticapitalist resistance within structurally impossible conditions.[15] Chúngara and the Comité de Amas de Casa (Housewives' Committee) worked to rearticulate their positions within the mining economy, challenging the extractive gaze that made their unremunerated work invisible. By engaging in hunger strikes and mining organizing efforts, they showed how their labor was not menial to but rather a mainstay of the global economy, and thus demanded visibility for their embodied labor. Given that mining firms routinely withheld payment to their employees and systematically imprisoned those suspected of labor organizing, mining has been the hotspot of Bolivian labor discontent and organizing activities, with female organizers leading slowdowns, strikes, marches, and other activities of dissent.

Another group of workers that have been rendered invisible within the extractive zone are the poorly paid *pailliris*, or slag pile workers, who opened up new spaces of visibility and a discursive terrain of struggle in otherwise masculine radical narratives and geographies of gender occlusion. During the late 1960s and 1970s, when the Lozada authoritarian regime was in power, the authoritarian state extracted gendered Indigenous labor through a military and police apparatus that was deployed to control "dissidents." In this period, the slag pile workers and female counterparts to male miners emerged as main protagonists, organizing against the increasing tide of state violence. Radicalized by their experience and successes, Indigenous female workers within the mining industry challenged and endured some of the most brutal conditions, and police patrols controlled their labor. Collective resistance by *pailliris*, then, has been essential to a genealogy of anarco-Indigenous feminist critique within mining economies.

Given that extractive economies depend on Indigenous and female reproductive labor as part of its primitive accumulation, anticapitalist organizing must necessarily take place at the interstices of the peripheral and global economies. By opposing the heteropatriarchal structures embedded within the industry, Indigenous female anarchistic resistance placed duress upon extractive capitalism's uneven distribution. As I show in the next section, as colonial capitalism historically expanded and gave rise to an uneven process of modernity, the field of opposition also increased such that the social ecologies produced out of struggle also rose to the surface. In other words, new articulations of Indigenous feminist politics and sex managed to slip through the tight grip of the extractive zone.

### The *Chola*'s Submerged Activities

Writing on the interstices of resistance within the extractive zone, Silvia Rivera Cusicanqui and Julieta Paredes both cite the *chola* market woman as a key figure of Indigenous anarcho-feminism. In this section, I analyze how *cholas*, or Indigenous women in the local market spaces of La Paz, historically organized and represent an important genealogy to present forms of anarcho-feminism. Unlike the slag-pile workers, the *chola* operated through new market circuits, linking her activities to traditional ways while disidentifying from the dominant European heterosexual order and from Andean patriarchy. In this way, *chola* market women posed an alternative to bourgeois and racialized norms of femininity while also challenging the hegemony of global capitalism. Even as their decolonial acts were often hidden, *cholas* radicalized the local, national, and international political sphere by linking anarchism, Indigeneity, and feminism in ways that produced new publics for themselves and their communities.

Let me elaborate. Early in the twentieth century, anarchism and Indigeneity found similitude in ways that proved fruitful to intersectional challenges to capitalism and heteropatriarchy. Given the exploitative legacies of coloniality, within modernity new forms of radicalism passed through anarcho-syndicalism in which female subjects were vitally present.[16] Lacking access to elite privileges, working-class and Indigenous women found new avenues of visibility through anarcho-syndicalism, such as the groups Sindicato de Minos de Oficios Varios and Federación Obrera Femenina, which included the participation of such female anarchist activists as Catalina Mendoza, Petronila Infantes, and Susana Radar.[17]

There were important resonances between Indigenous formations and anarcho-syndicalism. For Aymara peoples, the main social and economic formation was the *ayullu*, or horizontal bartering and exchange system, which functioned as a flexible and nonhierarchical social structure. Similarly, during modernization, anarchist principles challenged hierarchies by seeking alternatives outside of the capitalist system. Bartering, horizontal decision making, and nonhierarchical forms of living were central to daily life in Bolivia. In this way, the rise of anarcho-syndicalism found resonance within Indigenous communities, presenting social alternatives and models of political organizing that addressed the inequalities of the "winner take all" approach of extractive industries.

As Indigenous women entered the labor market in vast numbers during twentieth-century industrialization, they found themselves within an increasingly complex matrix of coloniality. With capitalism expanding into the hinterlands, rural to urban migration dramatically altered the social fabric, intensifying racial and cross-class contact and enhancing the uneven conditions of a gendered public sphere. In this context, Bolivian middle-class women fought for suffrage rights within organizations such as El Ateneo Feminino. Meanwhile, Indigenous feminisms made visible the asymmetries within the labor market, while also drawing attention to the racialized and moralizing exclusions within gender-equality campaigns.

As touchstone figures within a rising and defiant anarchist feminist political culture, *cholas* actively worked against the normative structures of gender and sexuality. Zabala documents how *cholas* challenged middle-class and upper-class feminists by raising such issues as "couple violence, and the need for a new morality, the defense of free love, absolute divorce, and the rejection of civil marriage," and incorporating such principles into a radical new feminist agenda.[18] The radical proposals by *cholas* paid close attention to sex and gender in ways that challenged moral discourses while also addressing the dramatic changes wrought by Bolivian modernity. For instance, they challenged the presumption of bourgeois marriage, and the idea that sex had to be tied to one partner within a normative European or *criollo* family structure.

Over the course of the twentieth century, *cholas* gained considerable power through their commercial success that came from selling, buying, and bartering goods in the regional marketplace, creating a network of female Indigenous activists that pushed beyond the constraints of a masculine public sphere. As Julieta Paredes told me, according to her grandmother, who was an Aymara market woman, the *chola* was not someone to be messed with: she had the confidence and skill that made her dominant within a supposedly male economic sphere.[19] *Cholas* organized, sold, and bartered within complex marketplace economies using the *ayullu* system as a system of commercial exchange that was not legible to the rules and structures of capitalism; they also created new social systems and extended kinship networks, thereby growing the spaces of influence for Andean cultural forms. Thus, local market spaces run by *chola* women represented a submerged network of economic and cultural activity within the wider global structure of the extractive mining economy. And within urban spaces that were in close contact with the rural sector, *chola* market women were powerful and visible brokers of alternative commercial exchange.

However, *cholas*' newfound visibility functioned in contradictory ways, as they were often met with hostility by a racialized and gendered system of coloniality that sought to circumscribe Indigenous and mestiza women's roles within society. While *cholas* continued to mediate the marketplace, retaining authority in alternative economic circuits, they increasingly faced workplace discrimination for wearing Indigenous clothing, such as *polleras* (Indigenous skirts and petticoats) and the bowler hat that was popular from the 1920s on. In short, because of their rising economic and political position, *cholas* often contended with ever-changing forms of racism and sexism that reproduced their invisibility within masculine spheres even as their highly visible image was appropriated by national culture.[20]

In addition to *criollo* society's contradictory discourses, which often scrutinized the "less than moral" behaviors of *cholas*, masculinist political movements also occluded the presence of Indigenous feminisms, specifically in relation to anarchism. Silvia Rivera Cusicanqui threads together how the history of anarchism in Bolivia and throughout the Américas has been contained and obscured by leftist Marxist hegemony.[21] She shows how revolutionary forces increasingly consolidated around a growing Marxist hegemony that culminated in taking state power, forcing feminist anarchist leaders to pull back in subsequent decades. Although the rise in 1954 of the Movimiento Nacional Revolucionario (MNR) nationalized the substantial wealth that came from Bolivia's resources, for instance, it did not register significant levels of female membership during its reign. What happened in Bolivia, as Rivera Cusicanqui explains, is that "there have been two official histories: The official history written by the [Revolutionary] Nationalist Party—MNR—that basically denies all the agency of both workers and peasants and indigenous peoples; and the official history of the Left that forgets about anything that was not Marxist, thus eclipsing or distorting the autonomous history of anarchist unions. It's the links between the anarchists and the indigenous people that gave them another nuance, because their communities are self-sustained entities and they basically are places where anti-authoritarian type of organization can take roots."[22] Rivera Cusicanqui analyzes how the MNR tended to write out non-Marxist lineages from Bolivia's history, specifically marginalizing anarchism from radical history. She later addresses the eradication of female protagonists as another significant omission. Then, as now, anarchist feminist Indigenous critique offers other models of anticolonial struggle often imperceptible to the official Marxist political narrative.

By giving primacy to the social, cultural, economic, and political role of *cholas* and *pailliris* within the modern capitalist global economy, an Indigenous feminist genealogy of radicalism emerges. Piecing together these histories, as Rivera Cusicanqui reminds us, *cholas* reshape masculine revolutionary narratives "because the *chola* figure, the women, the female fighter, the female organizer are all part of Bolivian daily life."[23] Engaging Indigenous anarcho-feminist critique by centering on the *chola* offers a powerful decolonial femme perspective that peers into the hidden but parallel economies of the global capitalist system. At the same time that Indigenous anarcho-feminisms enliven the social ecologies that organize to survive within the extractive zone, they also lift the hidden transcripts of non-normative sexualities.

## Decolonial Gestures

Over the next several decades, the afterlives of authoritarianism, the rise of neoliberalism, and the ravages of a debt economy demanded new spaces of anarcho-feminist intervention. As in many nations of the Global South, and especially within South America, the 1980s represented a period of hyperinflation, with devastating outcomes for the middle and working classes. Bolivia, in particular, was in the middle of a US austerity experiment and an uneven transition to liberal democracy.[24] As Julieta Paredes, cofounder of Mujeres Creando, explained, "Feminist communalisms offered economic and social alternatives, as well as a critical stance during the failure of the Washington Consensus."[25] Thus, the Mujeres Creando network was created at a time of acute capitalist crisis, a time when Bolivia was undergoing intense political and economic change within an expulsive and debt driven global economy.

A series of video performances from this decade, produced by Mujeres Creando and housed with the Hemispheric Institute for Performance and Politics, shows how anarcho-Indigenous feminisms addressed sexuality, desire, and the invisibility of homoerotic intimacy amid this bleak economic backdrop. In one performance, an Aymara woman stands in the middle of a tin container filled with water and washes her feet. The cityscape of La Paz stretches behind her, as she pauses, looks into the camera, and directly states, "I am a *chola*."[26] In this direct address, she affirms her Indigenous feminist positionality. In the next scene, the same member of Mujeres Creando addresses her sexual preference by saying, "It has been very lovely to be in the company of other women." She then declares herself heterosexual, recounting that it has taken her a very long time to make such a decision. Posed defiantly as she unbraids and then combs through her hair, she tells the story of how she met and decided upon being with her current partner. As she says, "He needed to know that *soy una chola diferente, soy una chola libre*" (I am a different kind of chola, a free chola), and "you will have to accept that."[27]

The Mujeres Creando video archive represents a composite consideration of the intertwining of race and gender within the stratified public sphere, and a confrontation to expectations about traditionalism. It also articulates local vernaculars with respect to sexuality. As Paredes describes it, this work emerged in a time of neoliberal transition when anarcho-feminist performances symbolically blocked the reach of US Empire by moving away from imported discourses about gay liberation toward the declaration, "I am a different *chola*, a free *chola*." Linking this difference back to the history of coloniality, Indigenous embodiment has long been inscribed within Spanish conduct codes and outside of the bourgeois paradigm of heterosexual female normalcy. While these constructions produce few actual spaces of sexual autonomy, the performance videos archive the importance of *chola*'s free expression in whatever form it takes.

An instance of this emerges in another performance video, in which a large bed is framed within an open public square in an unidentified part of La Paz. On the bed, two female lovers lie provocatively and openly. While this may seem like a simple act of visibility, the political implications of the work are profound, especially given that at the time lesbianism and female sexuality were themes that were hardly publicly addressed. Thus, the performance extends the site of homoerotic desire and political aesthetics from the bedroom to—in this case, quite literally—the public square.

Public expressions by the Indigenous and mestiza women of Mujeres Creando have often taken an even more confrontational approach, making the colonial hierarchies of the extractive zone visible through a range of interruptions. For instance, dressed in *polleras* and with their hair in long braids, Mujeres Creando would enter high-end restaurants of La Paz and wait to be served. If denied service, members of Mujeres Creando would decry differential treatment by the restaurant owners and its patrons, denouncing such spaces as exclusionary. The objective of such actions was not solely to contest the vernacular condition of racism or to recenter a politics of recognition through the figure of the *chola*. By visibly performing the *chola* identity in spaces of economic and cultural exclusion, members of Mujeres Creando also were not "playing Indian" or putting on "redface." Indeed, given that the members of Mujeres Creando were mostly Aymara and mestiza with intimate connections to *chola* cultural forms, such interruptions instead presenced the gender and racial nonnormativity of *cholas* within the Bolivian public sphere.

Perhaps the best-known work by Mujeres Creando is their graffiti, signature slogans with distinctive cursive writing that found their way first onto city walls and later into the exhibition hall of the Reina Sofía museum. The tag line, "Ser indígena es tán bonito como ser lesbiana o ser maricon" (To be Indigenous is as beautiful as being a Lesbian or a fag), spoke to the late 1990s political moment in the context of Indigenous uprising and the increasing visibility of lesbian, gay, bisexual and transgender rights. In fact, these graffiti expressed symbolic interpolations of the self/other as an alternative form of knowledge production and dissemination, writing anarco-feminist Indigenous histories through condensed and public formats. When the street graffiti were translated into the museum site of the Reina Sofía in Madrid, the critique addressed Spain's historical debt with the Américas.[28]

A memorable graffiti I encountered in the public sphere of La Paz was "Ní Dios, ní amo, ní marido, ní partido, Mujeres Creando" (Not God, nor boss, nor husband, nor Party, Women Creating), with the sign for "woman" crossed through with an A for "Anarchy" at its closure. This graffiti strikes through the cityscape with its triple-threat refusal of heteronormativity, Indigenous nationalism, and national party politics, while offering the proposal of "Mujeres Creando" (Women Creating) as an open invitation to its viewer.

In contrast to the normalizing visions of urban development and gentrification, graffiti served as a form of visual disobedience, perforating La Paz with moments of anarchic feminist rupture. Graffiti by Mujeres Creando marked out their political terrain not through capitalist transaction, as with real estate speculation or the building of new infrastructure, but instead through the somato-political improvisations of the written word. Furthermore, the expressive formats of Mujeres Creando dialogued with the street to interrupt the association of the public as inherently and primarily a space of male privilege.

### Mujeres Creando: A Closer Look

Founded in 1985 by Julieta Paredes, María Galindo, and Monica Mendoza, Mujeres Creando is an important locus of anarcho-feminist critique and of the creation of intentional horizontal networks, or feminist communalisms.[29] From its inception, the group was composed of mostly female-bodied members, representing a range of genders, sexualities, and races—though mostly mestiza and Aymara—some of whom openly identified as lesbian, bisexual, or transgender.

Since its inception, Mujeres Creando saw itself as the inheritor of an anarcho-feminist Indigenous lineage. Therefore, it is not surprising that one of its founders would analyze social problems by linking gender and sex to the coloniality of neoliberalism and state politics. As Paredes writes in the opening chapter of *Hilando Fino: Desde el feminismo comunitario* (recently published in its third edition),

> Con los cuerpos marcados por el colonialismo, las mujeres hemos recorrido la historia, relacionándonos unas con otras y relacionándonos como mujeres con los varones, también. Estas relaciones, que se han dado en el contexto de un colonialismo interno, tienen por resultado un comportamiento colonial en el erotismo, el deseo, la sexualidad, el placer y el amor, por supuesto.
>
> Sín duda las mujeres de clases medias y altas se beneficiaron en la época neoliberal y se siguen beneficiando del trabajo manual y doméstico de las mujeres jóvenes indígenas.

> Given that our bodies are marked by colonialism, women have moved through history in relation to each other, such as women have also been in relation with men. These relationships have taken place within a context of internal colonialism that has, of course, resulted in colonial behaviors within erotics, desire, sexuality, pleasure, and love.
>
> Without doubt, middle- and upper-class women benefited during the neoliberal period and they continue to benefit from the manual and domestic labor of young indigenous women.[30]

In these lines, Paredes yokes the neoliberal and extractive condition to a specific critique of the gender/race/class order that neoliberalism intensifies. As Paredes defines it, internal colonialism resonates with an anarcho-Indigenous feminist critical lens that begins to disentangle the overwrought colonial histories of feminized and racialized embodiment.

The theory and praxis of anarcho-feminism often blend through vernacular experience. As Victoria Aldunate Morales analyzes, what it means to do the daily work of anarchist feminism exceeds the ability to theorize and find a language for it.[31] As a member of Mujeres Creando Comunidad,

Morales describes how the group "works through collective experiences, reasoning through the body, and elaborating a never-ending flow of ideas, concepts, categories, proposals, images, that gives a new vision to feminists and other women." Such close attention to embodiment, collectivity, and new forms of being requires what Aldunate Morales calls "opening one's eyes in ways that cannot be closed again, either from oneself or in relation to the female eye."[32] From specific positions, the notion of a "female eye" could be read as liberal, essentialist, and as possessing an exclusionary definition of gender. However, I read Aldunate Morales's "female eye" perspective here as a mode of seeing that is embodied, non-essentialist and that multiple genders have access to. The decolonial female eye, with an emphasis placed on decolonizing the female within a binary gender system, articulates intersectional consciousness visually, or in this case, defines an anarchist feminist perspective that subverts and exceeds the colonial sight of the normative. In this way, the multiple perspectives of the female eye perceives in opposition to the extractive gaze, the singular, patriarchal, and hierarchical organizing vision of gendered capitalist economies. Rather than an essentialist move, the term "the female eye" expresses a standpoint that moves beyond the cycloptic colonial view, envisioning theories, activities, and solidarities that the state cannot reduce, or that extractive capitalist economies cannot fully capture.

In the broader work of Mujeres Creando, Paredes asserts feminist pedagogies, including exchange with the other's life history as a source of political insight. Paredes also advocates that nonindigenous feminists might see differently through an Aymara worldview, and that mestizas might find a new source of relationality through what she refers to as "communal feminisms" as a way to link back to the *ayullu* principle by specifically invoking anticapitalist ideas. Paredes's project also queers the idea of Indigenous tradition by analyzing *chachawarmi*, or gender complementarity, as a Western projection of Indigeneity that operates within Andean societies without change. As I described in chapter 2, the notion that "men" and "women" have distinct but equal spheres of influence within Indigenous societies is a static concept of Indigenous tradition, yet it is one that continues to circulate within dominant renderings of Andean Indigeneity.[33] Native feminisms counters this normative idea of gender complementarity by analyzing how a liberal feminist vision of gender equality functions as its own episteme.[34]

Paredes and Mujeres Creando trouble the epistemological certainty of gender and sex by rethinking tradition-bound conventions. More specifically, Paredes believes that *chachawarmi*, or the model of Andean complementarity, often reproduces forms of patriarchal authority that reinscribe national and masculinist forms of power. Rather than fixate on a timeless gender system and the presumed durability of extended kin relations, Paredes seems to theorize and put into practice an emergent and alternative structure of affiliations. By producing critical bonds through new circuits of intimacies, Mujeres Creando enlivens new, and future-oriented, horizontal networks. In such instances, Paredes reaches for a theory of multivalent criticalities that asks anarchic feminisms to challenge Indigenous traditions while asserting how Indigenous cosmopolitics help decolonize and rearrange the meaning of liberal feminism. In other words, anarcho-Indigenous feminisms create new transfeminist models that are appropriate to local and regional conditions, linking back to a genealogy of radical dissent, but reaching toward utopic potential.

In early July 2013, I visited Paredes at her La Paz home, a split-level brick house perched high above the center of the city, at the same altitude as white floating clouds. The house was filled with the books that she and Galindo had published together during the 1990s, including texts on sex education, the meaning of lesbian love, the principles of anarchism, and the graffiti of Mujeres Creando Comunidad. During Evo Morales's control of the Bolivian state (2005–present), issues of gender and sex have been overshadowed by a state decolonization discourse that has continued through *caudillismo*, or the charisma of male leadership.[35] When the Plurinational Constitution was institutionalized by Morales's Movimiento al Socialismo (Movement for Socialism, MAS) government in 2011, abortion rights, same-sex marriage legislation, and even the right to divorce were either overshadowed by religious morality regimes or underplayed in favor of anti-imperial and wealth redistribution concerns, even as the state continued to invest in an extractive economy. Even within its own rubric that emphasizes Indigenous subjects, languages, and cultures as central to the new government's project, Morales's government has not met its own benchmark of decolonization.[36] In contrast, Paredes and Galindo also consider sex/gender politics as an important pathway to the complex situating of decolonization, a counterpoint to the official version.

I was invited to present my research to Mujeres Creando Comunidad at the feminist cultural center Café Carcajada. Tucked off a small side street near the center of La Paz, the space attracts a racially diverse group of differently gendered students, activists, and artists who have collaborated together for anywhere from a few months to up to fifteen years. Julieta Paredes and her partner, Adriana, run the cultural center and continue to make anarchist feminist Indigenous politics the center of their expressive agenda, publishing columns in local newspapers, producing lectures and cultural events, and making and selling their arts, crafts, and books.

During my talk, I made historical connections to the hunger strikes in mining by at one point characterizing the practice of Indigenous female hunger striking as a performative act that literally, as Patrick Anderson calls it, "wastes away" before the public view.[37] While some of the participants appreciated this theoretical point, one member in particular found the idea of equating hunger striking to a performative act to be a decidedly North American colonizing gesture that misappropriated the painful reality of hunger striking to propagate US performance theory. Though I hold on to the analysis and interpretation that hunger striking is performative, as well as often an intentionally visible political enactment, I also understand how the participant at the event questioned the way local vernaculars of struggle are run through the machine of North American theories, abstracting from local conditions of possibility and constraints. The contradiction, of course, in the member's thoughtful opinion was that Mujeres Creando Comunidad had, in fact, used performative gesture as one of its emblematic modes of dissent. While the participant's point about overly theoretical language was a necessary question to the proliferation of academic texts coalescing around the term "decolonial"—and the ever-capacious understanding of the term "performance" for that matter—what stuck with me most was not this often-stated critique of theory. Instead, I wondered how the conceptual language I named might indeed have emerged from my own vantage point that conditioned regional experience through the mill of US theory.

This kind of critique seemed central to the anti-imperial decolonial gesture in the new incarnation of Mujeres Creando Comunidad. As Paredes states, "Political activity does not only happen in political parties or in organized groups; it happens as soon as you are conscious of your actions and your decisions—an intuitive kind of feminism. . . . Through feminism, women come to know themselves and each other, with all our potential, our strengths, our weaknesses, and we discover a freedom that we keep on developing."[38] While what constitutes the category "women" in this quote might certainly be troubled, and could be widened to a perspective of trans-feminisms that is inclusive of genders not assigned female at birth, the idea of freedom as an operation of political activity that keeps on developing is an unusual and prescient way to define feminist and anarchic potential. Whether referring to the *chola*, the female slag-pile worker, or the hunger striker, together these figures produce a counterhistory of anarchist Indigenous feminisms that cannot be reduced to the heteropatriarchal confines of the extractive zone.

## The Feminist Constitution

My second visit to Mujeres Creando occurred in September 2014, this time to the site of María Galindo's radio program, which has a restaurant café on its premises and is managed by local Aymara Indigenous women. When I first walked into the crowded two-story colonial house, where lunch patrons were tucked in eating steaming bowls of Andean potato quinoa soup, I was visually overwhelmed by an enormous, gorgeous photograph of an Indigenous woman plastered onto the adobe wall. Written below the photograph was the question, "What does racism look like to you?" This was the first time I had seen racism so visibly acknowledged and questioned anywhere within South America. Given that racism is often occluded within the public sphere, these direct and visible instances of race/class analysis within the feminist project of anarchism show the importance of Mujeres Creando's stance and its intervention.

María Galindo's radio shows, video work, performances, and ongoing writing on decolonization carry a decidedly direct critique of Andean patriarchy, Catholic morality, Morales's extractivist politics and neoliberal agenda, and what I can only describe as a punk anarchist attitude. Galindo's book, *No se puede descolonizar sin despatriarcalizar: teoría y propuesta de la despatriarcalización* (It is impossible to decolonize without destroying patriarchy: Theory and proposals for destroying patriarchy), opens with a dedication to "la india solitaria," "la puta fiera," "la lesbiana indomable," "y a todas las mujeres rebeldes" (the solitary Indigenous woman, the fierce sex worker, the indomitable lesbian, and to all rebel women).[39] When I

Nicole Hayward, "To think is highly feminine,"
María Galindo (*left*) with author Macarena Gómez-Barris, 2014.
Photo courtesy of Nicole Hayward.

asked Galindo if this included trans-women, she responded, "trans-women also disobey gender norms." In an earlier period, perhaps such a direct and forceful response would not have come from Mujeres Creando, but the LGBT rainbow tide in Latin America has certainly made trans-awareness more widespread and central to its future oriented project.[40]

Unlike my interviews at that time with Julieta Paredes, which were somewhat more tempered in their analysis of Morales's path to decolonization, Galindo was decidedly more critical, calling his politics paternalistic and regressive, and showing visible contempt for the "Aymara path to Andean socialism" rhetoric as mere liberal multiculturalism.[41] In this regard, Galindo's efforts, alongside those of Mujeres Creando, include drafting the Feminist Constitution, an important critique of the 2011 Plurinational Constitution that Morales passed through a series of regional and then national assemblies. While the Plurinational Constitution made important gains, the Feminist Constitution functioned as a polemic against it, producing the single most important document of anarchist feminist Indigenous critique in the contemporary period.[42] Born of the assembly process initiated by Morales, yet reaching into the nexus of recent sex-positive rights discussions, while pushing back against the morality of colonial Catholicism and the rhetoric of tradition and family, the Feminist Constitution is a poetic, raging collaboration, and presents a parallel effort to its better-known counterpart. The Feminist Constitution's objective is not only to critique existing paradigms of state-centered decolonization but also to imagine concrete visions and proposals that extend Indigenous anarchic feminist projects.

I have discussed the many facets of the work of Mujeres Creando and Mujeres Creando Comunidad as two important collaborative efforts that use Indigenous feminist anarchist histories to build a present- and future-oriented imaginary of another kind of society. "The Feminist Political Constitution of the State: The Impossible Nation We Build as Women" is, in my mind, the pinnacle expression of this multidirectional articulation. Writing from the vernacular subjectivities and experience of Indigenous women, sex workers, and lesbians—those that "have been left out of the official constitution"—the document was drafted out of a collective sense of urgency. Because of its inclusion of perverse and amoral sexualities, feminist propositions, and queer locations, while also both building upon and inverting Morales's decolonization project, I engage this document as a transfeminist mode of theorizing and perceiving otherwise.

As Sayak Valencia explains, transfeminism has genealogies in global and local hemispheric sites, the postporn movement in Spain, and decolonial border activism and theorization. She states:

> Los sujetos del transfeminismo pueden entenderse como una suerte de *multitudes queer/cuir* que a través de la materialización performativa logran desarrollar agenciamientos g-locales. La tarea de estas *multitudes cuir* es la de seguir desarrollando categorías y ejecutando prácticas que logren un agenciamiento no estandarizado y decolonial—es decir que no busquen asimilarse a los sistemas de representación impuestos por la hegemonía capitalista del sistema heteropatriarcal/clasista y racista y que inventen otras formas de acción crítica—que pueda ser aplicado en distintos contextos de forma re-territorializada, reconfigurando la posición del sur como un posicionamiento crítico y no sólo como un emplazamiento geopolítico.[43]

Transfeminist subjects understand themselves within a nexus of queer/ *cuir* multitudes that through performative instances are able to develop local forms of agency. The task of this *cuir* multitude is to keep developing and executing different kinds of practices that do not lead to standardizations of the decolonial; that is, they do not work toward assimilation as systems of representation imposed by capitalist hegemony and heteropatriarchal, classist, and racist systems, but instead invent other forms of critical action that can be applied to distinct contexts as forms of reterritorializations, reconfiguring the position of the South as a critical positioning rather than a geopolitical restructuring.[44]

Using this model of transfeminism with a multidirectional attention to the issues of coloniality and Indigeneity, the Feminist Constitution analyzes MAS's decolonization project from the position of "political and social problems, pending and deferred . . . that stretch out into a remote and uncertain future."[45] The deferred future that María Galindo refers to in this quote is the decolonization process that gained political legitimacy by subsuming gender/sex difference into a homogeneous platform. Galindo's statement brings forward how the assembly constituent process that brought Evo Morales to power functioned as "a pact among men regarding their gazes, their parceling out of power." Reaching further back, it also emphasizes how the "ancient law of obligatory heterosexuality" has deferred equality for female subjects, extracting their labor to reproduce patriarchy even before capitalism.

Though Morales's road to the presidency included radical feminist proposals, once he was in office, these were put aside. Mujeres Creando articulated critical views of the nexus of forces that continued to absent radical female participation from the new configuration of state power:

> We make clear that the voices of women in the official constitution were mediated, brokered, censored, and measured by the political parties that legitimated only the liberal NGOs and the conservative voices of indigenous women who spoke for their men, for their sons, and for their churches and their dogmas of faith. Other women's voices have been left out, left out of the constitutional text, expelled from history once more, along with all of the political and social problems, pending and deferred, that our eyes see, that stretch out into a remote and uncertain future.[46]

The reference to the "pending and deferred, that our eyes see, that stretch out into a remote and uncertain future" is precisely the turn away from the extractive gaze and toward a submerged perspective that I have affirmed throughout this volume, and here takes a decided turn away from conservative formulations.

The Feminist Constitution is organized as a series of legislative, poetic, and sweeping proposals and gestures. Under the subsection "Forms of Government," Galindo states "no governments should exist," revealing the antistate ideology embedded within anarchic feminisms. In other sweeping and playful acts, the Feminist Constitution abolishes the armed forces, restricts religion to its spiritual function, makes art and artistic expression the universal language, dissolves the police apparatus, grants rights to animals, allows Indigenous peoples a future-oriented tense (rather than being fixed in the past), abolishes political parties, and considers the autonomy of the body a fundamental principle. Given the heated discussions regarding abortion and the conflicts within national governments throughout South American progressive governments, this last point about the female body's autonomous decision making reasserts transfeminist autonomy as central to multiple projects of liberation.

### Conclusion

The Feminist Constitution calls for the visibility of submerged perspectives and the networked potential of social ecologies. In the last line it states how "this constitution is a fabric that weaves the daily with the historic, the utopian with the immediate, forming a rainbow of struggles and dreams that we will continue building without sacrificing a single one of them." This transfeminist, Indigenous anarcho-perspective imaginatively sees and describes the impulse behind not only the arc of radical genealogies but also their potential future.

Like the extractive viewpoint that flattens heterogeneity, masculine revolutionary politics has written out smaller yet pivotal histories of radical Andean feminisms. My work in this chapter has been to thread together a genealogy of anarcho-Indigenous feminism that makes connections between multivalent forms of critique and dissent that address the complexities of the extractive zone. That is, an anarcho-Indigenous feminist perspective builds upon multidirectional opposition to the excesses of capitalism, the hierarchies of patriarchy, the normativity of heterosexuality, and the racism of colonialism in order to provide alternative models of sociality and perception.

We might consider the possibilities and limitations of hemispheric Indigenous feminist critique that would consider the principles of Mujeres Creando as part of a broader transfeminist and decolonial project. Again, the submerged perspective here is to challenge the idea of Indigenous tradition as static or pure, setting the stage for a more multivalent theory and actualization of critical praxis. As a method of perceiving and doing otherwise, this submerged form of organizing, critiquing, and living potentially makes visible the path toward undoing coloniality.

# The View from Below

I have addressed visual and embodied knowledges, intellectual genealogies, and trans-feminist, Indigenous, and networked formations that exceed, escape, mediate, and invert the extractive view. And I have discussed how the extractive view refers to state and corporate logics that map territories as commodities rather than perceive the proliferation of life and activities that make up the human and nonhuman planetary. The geographies we have explored emerge out of specific regions within the Américas, placing South American living social ecologies at my study's center. I have focused on majority Indigenous territories but have also referenced Afro-descended ontologies, for how they perceive otherwise and contain the capacity to erode the extractive gaze, even as the figure of the African slave within the *mita* system in the South American extractive zone is often disappeared, even from radical histories. These modes of seeing and critiquing urge a reconsideration of the submerged, and of the heterogeneity that resides within the matrix of coloniality.

Throughout the introduction and the volume's five chapters, I put into view other modes of perception that organize time, space, sociality, and the cosmos. These include Mapuche visuality, Andean phenomenology, anarchist-feminist Indigenous analysis, Yasuní cooperatives, and a fish-eye episteme. Such fecund sites and methods constitute inverted visualities, and reversals of power through vernacular practices that dynamically shift the meaning of Enlightenment and Western forms of thought, feeling, and being. What these proposals share is a decolonial, and anti-authoritarian vision; they project the potential of future planetary inhabitance, beyond the "rise of slime," as oceanographer Jeremy Jackson has coined impending ecological disaster.[1] As the diametric opposite of the "rise of slime" that is born from the homogenizing force of decimation, the muck that I refer to in the preface, and throughout my study, is animated by the intangibility of biodiverse life forms, the poiesis of difference, the untaming of the other, refusals and reversals that emerge out of the extractive zone.

I used the term "intangibility" to refer to the thickness and heterogeneity of life residing within global geographies that require careful practices of conservation against the acceleration of racialized and colonial capitalism. The multiplicity of life forms found within spaces of the extractive zone complicate the relation between self and other, nature and culture, human and the nonhuman, and exist beyond the grasp of the monocultural and extractive divide. Beneath the surface, where digital technology scans for earthly resources, and outside of the conversion of nature into monetary exchange, something else emerges. Namely, the dream of "another world" is not merely a future-oriented utopia but it is already in motion, teeming with the alternatives we desire. Seeing the muck, dwelling in it, and finding ways to make it visible become important antidotes as present-past ways to recognize and strengthen these alternatives.

Over the last decade, I have shared experiences with activists, communities, and scholars throughout South America, spending long days within regional geographies consumed by the histories and contradictions of coloniality. Being in relation to the spaces I study, living there off and on over a decade, and having the privilege of moving within them has been central to crafting a decolonial queer episteme and method, a porous form of knowledge production that listens to and takes in social worlds to write about them with a measure of epistemological freedom without having to make objective claims. Paying attention to sex/gender difference as its own source of enlivenment and dispossession is part of this perception. Given the dangers of reproducing coloniality, I recognize the ethical significance of treading lightly, but without situated site work, I would not have seen what emerges, grows, adapts within and refuses the extractive zone.

My viewpoint, I hope, has been capacious enough not to reify, fix, or fully describe or comprehend the myriad forms of life and potentialities I have encountered. Instead of emphasizing an analysis of equivalence that conventionally compares regions, or tracing disciplinary tracks of evidence, I have focused instead on the submerged perspectives and social ecologies that reside within the extractive zone, taking my cues from the blurring of an ecotone's boundaries, or from the fish that see below the river's surface, or from the memory of the *pehuen* trees that have witnessed the duration of colonial violence. Therefore, my standpoint does not aim to quell the histories of the violence upon Indigenous peoples and territories within the hemisphere, and the specific forms of objectification, commodification, and "transits of Empire," as Jodi Byrd terms it, that intercede and overcome the peoples and geographies that I have written about. Instead, I have attended to the complexities of inhabiting the extractive zone by finding new concepts and language that propel our understanding of how the leveling of capitalism is negotiated and resisted, refused, and forestalled. Perceiving through the extractive divide has changed me by allowing for dreams, imaginaries, and forms of living as forcefully and continually emergent.

In the process of researching and writing this book, my perspective on how to challenge extractive capitalism has shifted. Indigenous scholars focusing on the United States and Canada have analyzed the limitations of legal recognition, critiquing the law's liberal impulse, and the constrained ability to affect change through the highly codified system of representation that condones private property. As Joanne Barker and Glen Coulthard rightly argue, we must move beyond the recognition paradigm. We must also broaden our perspective on recognition beyond the law and nation-state, beyond liberal multiculturalism, and ultimately beyond the settler colonial and occupational state of extractive capitalism.[2] There are clear proposals here. Listening to and learning from the Andean world's phenomenological orientation, and Indigenous land-based cosmologies more broadly, we might recognize Pachamama as an important source of a collective future rather than a delimited regional worldview. In other words, we might perceive and enact how Pachamama does not just belong to Andean ways but can be somehow recognizable as our own Earth Being while not giving into the surface-level viewpoints of the New Age. The toxifying condition of commodity capitalism is precisely about the appropriative logics of Indigenous technologies, aesthetics, worldviews. Reckoning with Indigenous epistemes, whether land-based, through intellectual genealogies, the remembering of colonial histories, or through cultural production, we might move beyond coloniality and extinction. This submerged planetary perspective invites us into another realm of perception that leaves the extractive zone behind.

The promise of new "progressive" states in Latin America has unfortunately distracted us with their institutionalization of *buen vivir* politics. Extractive states crack down on Indigenous and ecological politics while denying the gravity of theft and contamination, as Indigenous and Afro-descendent communities acutely suffer through increased cancer rates, expanded dispossession, and life's reduction. This is not to say that progress has not been made on integrating Indigenous and African-based viewpoints into historically Eurocentric nation-states. However, as anarcho-Indigenous feminist critique presciently illuminates, the colonial state cannot be remade.

My analysis of conservation has also been radically altered by being in proximity to these locations. Against militarization and state intrusion, radical conservation is already being carried out by land defenders and through alternatives to late capitalism, but only alongside multidirectional social movements such as YASunidos in Ecuador and ASOQUIMBO and Rios Vivos in Colombia. These movements understand the web of interdependence rather than feed into the matrix of coloniality. Like these trans-regional and intersectional assemblages, we might repel the dominant capitalist logic that presumes that finite natural resources are already depleted. Such pessimism subsumes us even further into the clutches of accelerated capitalism's no future, facilitating extraction, waste, and the occlusion of differential pain within the extractive zone.

Yet, we can still choose to collectively shift our attention. We can lower our view to where the wild boars make their mushy homes, and watch the ant cutters on their path within the forest's cycles of entropy. Similarly, we can shift perspective by raising our view, and see from a bird's-eye view—or a satellite's view—all that reaches to perceive space and temporality with attention, precision, attunement. The artistic work of Francisco Huicha-queo and Carolina Caycedo has shown us this elsewhere, this other side of the colonial divide, this possibility of perceiving and sensing complexly.

In response to Ruth Wilson Gilmore's always present, provocative, and necessary question "What is to be done?,"[3] I have shown that in these extractive South American regions, there is already so much being done that what we require is a practice of listening to and then amplifying present-future analyses, responses, and proposals. As I mentioned in the introduction, we must also listen. For instance, the 2005 *¡Escucha Winka!* statement written by three Mapuche historians, José Millalén, Pablo Marimán, Rodrigo Levil, and the Mapuche sociologist, Sergio Caniuqueo, is a blueprint for autonomous Indigenous governance that dually frustrates assimilative state management and the exigencies of a capitalist growth model. Collectively, these authors find non-normative ways to sovereignly negotiate the thickets of neoliberal governmentality, the monocultural condition of extraction, and the prevalent extinction paradigm of international environmentalism. Specifically, the term *winka* refers to the Mapudungun word for a nonindigenous subject, a mestiza/o, potentially a gringa/o, and potentially you and me. *¡Escucha Winka!* literally translates to, "Listen up, white man!"

Mapuche writers hail non-Mapuche subjects with the command to *¡Escucha!* not as an insulting interpellation, or as a mere critique of present-past colonialism. Rather, the effort to speak directly to the *winka* is, most generatively, a patient call for a listening practice that hovers at the edge of capitalism's noise, a whispered suggestion to settlers that enables a louder message: "Listen, *winka*, because occupying Indigenous territories is not good for you, either." This kind of Indigenous autonomous thought sharpens the edge of the liberal endgame of multiculturalism and state recognition. Mapuche autonomous thinking rescrambles how we understand progress, and reassigns meaning away from the devaluing of life at the core of capitalism.

The authors of *¡Escucha Winka!* state that their formulations of collective autonomy "represents an aspiration to recover our 'suspended sovereignty.'" It is this condition of suspension that awaits us. In the epilogue of this text, autonomy is "a form of government, a way to exercise self-administration in our territories," not as a nostalgic glance back to earlier social and political collective formations but as a proposition for governance that works to guarantee autonomous decision making. The authors express the challenge of working "in a sovereign fashion about their political, social, economic and cultural futures as well as about the structure of government and form of participation they desire."[4] The use of "us" and "them" varies throughout the text, as the authors switch between referring to Indigenous peoples—the Mapuche/Pehuenche/Huilliche people of these territories—and calling out to the reader, and then reflexively situating the authorial collective, while also engaging *winka* settlers. This expo-

nentiation of subject positions as a mutable hailing, invitation, interpellation, and instruction provides the document with a multiplicity that moves
far beyond the flattened premise of the extractive zone.

The submerged perspective of Mapuche hailing and proposal that is in
motion within this text is the "consciousness about ourselves as a people
who have exercised the right to govern ourselves and to develop our own
institutionality."[5] A proposal for a nonstate state that centers a Mapuche
worldview imagines guaranteed rights and participation for "us" through
new/old ways of how to account for each other while acknowledging and
being in relation to Indigenous territories. *¡Escucha Winka!*, therefore, inverts the extractive view on territoriality, and ultimately makes a loud request for epistemological unmooring, for the settler to think differently
about our relations to social and ecological worlds as we peer into the muck
within the extractive zone. Perceiving these submerged perspectives opens
up the decolonial potential that already exists.

# NOTES

## Preface

1 Maurice Merleau-Ponty, *Phenomenology of Perception* (1945: 178). The other classic and obvious text to cite here is Jon Berger's *Ways of Seeing* who links seeing to meaning, knowledge and belief systems through art and image production (1972).

2 My methodology is informed by the decolonial turn and underpinned by a vast literature of interdisciplinary study that emphasizes coloniality, which includes Sylvia Wynter's oeuvre "Unsettling the Coloniality of Being/Power/Truth/Freedom" (2003) and, specifically on coloniality in the Américas, her "1492: A New World View" (1995); Walter Mignolo's *Local Histories/Global Designs*; Emma Pérez's *The Decolonial Imaginary* (1999); and Nelson Maldonado-Torres's *Against War: Views from the Underside of Modernity* (2008). In Mignolo's key bibliography, "Modernity and Coloniality," he cites many origin points for the decolonial turn, including the 1955 Bandung Conference, the intellectual production of Frantz Fanon (1952, 1961) and Anibal Quijano's classic essay "Coloniality of Power, Eurocentrism, and Latin America" (2001).

3 For work that troubles the colonial politics of mastery at the intersections of postcolonial thought, decolonial critique, and new theorizations of humanisms see Julietta Singh's *Unthinking Mastery: Dehumanism and Decolonial Entanglements*, 2017.

4 Since the 1980s the lack of national sovereignty that conditions these processes has been challenged by Left political anti-imperialist platforms. However, over the last decade Latin American nations have turned away from the Washington Consensus, the system that exports a US-centered hegemonic economic model, only to become entangled within the Beijing Consensus a few years later.

5 In Saskia Sassen's analysis, these expulsions are connected to complex systems of legality, policy and accounting that enable governments to acquire land in foreign territories (2016). Again, though she does not mention this, such geographies are often Indigenous territories that require the expulsion of Native and rural peoples through the complexity of coordination that is advanced extractive or expulsive capitalism.

6 Eduardo Galeano, *Open Veins of Latin America* (1971).

7 Racial capitalism expanded its reach through violent legislative and bureau-cratic arrangements that legitimated the rule of a European administration over African-descended and Indigenous populations. Through the produc-tion of racial hierarchies, scientific classification, colonial mapping, the tech-niques of the law, and the system of private property, a hemispheric colonial project split humans into categories differentiated from each other and from nonhuman life (Wynter, 2003, 2012).

8 Throughout the book I unpack the racial capitalist logics of new extractiv-isms, especially in relation to Indigenous territories. Even though my analy-sis is largely about how this unfolds in the post neoliberal era, Angelina Snodgrass-Godoy's "Converging on the Poles: Contemporary Punishment and Democracy in Hemispheric Perspective," describes similar convergence of political economic processes in relation to state criminal justice institu-tions and the increased rhetoric of crime and terrorism against peoples of color throughout the hemisphere (July 2005). Also see Quimantú, *Resistencias Mapuches al Extractivismo*, a book of collected articles published by Mapu-express (2016) for how this contexually operates on Mapuche territories. In *Represent and Destroy*, an important formulation of racial capitalism's logics, Jodi Melamed argues that liberal racial regimes have enabled and normalized new US state-capital formulations that perpetuate anti-Black violence (2011). Melamed investigates how liberal antiracist formations actually sustain racial injustice, delimiting the possibility for social and political transformation.

9 For a decolonial analysis of how the term queer is used and reworked in Latin America, see Diego Falconí Trávez, Santiago Castellanos, and María Amelia Viteri's, *Resentir lo queer en América Latina*, 2013.

10 In extraordinary work that extends the already significant scholarship on Native Studies, Indigenous Feminisms, and Native queer studies, see Joanne Barker's edited volume, *Critically Sovereign: Indigenous Gender, Sexuality and Feminist Studies*, 2017.

11 See Enrique Dussel, "Transmodernity and Interculturality: An Interpretation from the Perspective of Philosophy" (2003). Lynda Lange's important work on Dussel's philosophy articulates the subtlety of his approach and its radi-cal decentering of Eurocentric logics, as well as its anti-Indigenous racism analytics (2000). However, Lange argues that while Dussel best expressed the problem of the Enlightenment as a developmental fallacy, he also invested in the idea that human communities possess different levels of maturity (see Lange's article in Linda Alcoff and Eduardo Mendieta's, *Thinking from the Underside of History: Enrique Dussel's Philosophy of Liberation*).

12 Anibal Quijano, "Coloniality and Modernity/Rationality," April 2007.

13 For the quote and for an analysis of the justification of extractivism within progressive discourses, see "Latin America: New Governments, Old Econo-mies: The New Latin American 'Progresismo' and the Extractivism of the 21st

Century," by Carmelo Ruiz Marrero, February 17, 2011, http://lab.org.uk /latin-america-new-governments-old-economies. Eduardo Gudynas's works that have not been translated into English are extremely useful on questions of extractive capitalism and sustainable environments. His book *Ecología, economía, y etica el desarrollo sostenible* is an often-cited work for discussions on extractive capitalism (2002).

14  Jon Beasley-Murray's book *Posthegemony* is an example of this line of critique that works to obscure increased focus on indigenous critique by overgeneralizing certain strains of Latin American Cultural Studies (2010).

15  Mary Louise Pratt's term "contact zone," in *Imperial Eyes: Travel Writing and Transculturation*, invokes the imperial periods of European and American expansionism in South America through scientific, military, and tourist expeditions (1999). By using the term colonial contact zone, I similarly refer to the asymmetrical spaces of interaction that have dominated the region from the fifteenth century forward, emphasizing coloniality as a key analytic.

16  The term "ecocide" can also refer to the massive death of ecosystems by global climate change and extractive capitalism. Then Swedish prime minister Olaf Palme employed the term "ecocide" during the 1970s to discuss the use of Agent Orange by US forces in Vietnam. For a map that tracks recent shifts and the rise of murders of ecological activists, see "Deadly Environment," Global Witness, April 15, 2014, https://www.globalwitness.org/en/campaigns /environmental-activists/deadly-environment/.

17  For a discussion of the pipeline and Idle No More, see Glenn Coulthard's *Red Skin, White Masks: Rejecting the Colonial Politics of Recognition*, especially chapter 5 on indigenous emergence and forms of land defense in Canada. For extractivism upon Indigenous territories within Latin America, see Eduardo Gudynas, "El Nuevo Extractivismo Progresista," in *Nueva Crónica*, January 30, 2011, http://www.gudynas.com/periodismo/GudynasExtractivismoNva CronicaBolEne10.pdf; and Henry Veltmeyer and James Petras, *The New Extractivism: A Post-Neoliberal Development Model or Neoliberalism in the Twenty-First Century?* (2014).

18  This statement draws from fieldwork conducted between January and May 2015, and is also widely documented by the important movement, *Acción Ecológica* that has recently been threatened with forced closure by the Correa government. Despite the Rafael Correa government's early progressive gains, since 2012 activists describe an increasing climate of fear and repression, including alarming levels of surveillance of anti-extractivist organizing and visibility. Furthermore, as megaextractivist projects increase their purview and reach, so increases the criminalization of land defenders; concomitantly, as social contestation becomes more intense, digital repression expands. Global corporate imbrication with military states results in the killing of human and nonhuman life for extractivist ends, or ecocide, as well as an upswing in the surveillance and repression of land defense activism.

19 The attack upon Honduras Indigenous activists is truly alarming. Four
months after Berta Cáceres was killed March 3, 2016, Lesbia Janeth Urquía's
body was found abandoned in a dump within the municipality of Marcala.
Both Cacéres and Janeth Urquía aimed to stop the construction of multiple
hydroelectric projects in Western Honduras. At least fourteen Indigenous
activists have been found murdered in Honduras making it the deadliest place
in the world for ecological defense according to Global Witness.

20 See Audra Simpson, *Mohawk Interruptus: Political Life Across the Borders of
Settler States* (2014); and Jodi Byrd, *Transits of Empire* (2011); Glen Coulthard,
*Red Skin, White Masks*; Joanne Barker, *Native Acts: Law, Recognition and Cul-
tural Authenticity* (2011); Mishuana Goeman, *Mark My Words, Native Women
Mapping Our Nations* (2013).

21 In Alberto Moreiras's *The Exhaustion of Difference: The Politics of Latin American Cultural Studies* (2001), he moves to consider subalterity as a way to respond to epistemological homogenization. This volume expands the terms of
engagement that extend cultural theory through decolonial critique, arguing
that difference is indeed inexhaustible.

22 Ann Stoler's work *Along the Archival Grain: Epistemic Anxieties and Colonial
Common Sense* (2010) has informed my ability to think of decolonial methods
in tandem with a practice and perception of what she refers to as the confused
epistemic spaces of colonialism. In Stoler's ethnography of the state archive
she opens an analysis of the affective dimensions of colonial governance. I
have also been influenced by Lisa Lowe's stunning *The Intimacies of Four Continents* (2015) that addresses modern liberal subjectivity by connecting it to
the rise of European coloniality to confront "the often obscure connections
between the emergence of European liberalism, settler colonialism in the
Americas, the transatlantic slave trade, and the East Indies and China trades
in the late eighteenth and early nineteenth century" (1). Both works are essential to sociological inquiry that have limited their sights to modernity rather
than inquired into the foundational condition of colonialism.

### Introduction

1 See Eve Tuck and K. Wayne Yang's "Decolonization is Not a Metaphor," in
*Decolonization: Indigeneity, Education & Society* for a specific critique of the
problem of overusing the term decolonization when not in relation to the re-
patriation of Indigenous territory and life (2012).

2 By "multiperceptual cosmologies" I am referring to Brazilian anthropological insights. See the foundational work of Eduardo Viveiros de Castro, for
instance, "Cosmological Perspectivism in Amazonia and Elsewhere," accessible in English as four Cambridge lectures, February–March 1988. Vivieros
de Castro's work signals a shift in Brazilian anthropology that has been widely

influential for its epistemological undoing of colonial perspectives and re-
defining the terrain of alterity.

3 My use of Édouard Glissant here with respects to other Américas is to bring
forward the grounded theory of the Caribbean Afro-diaspora as producing
the kinds of sensibilities and orientations that opens up the theorization for
other regional spaces of this study. Recognizing the particular transcultural
histories of First peoples and Afro-diasporic populations within the Caribbean and Glissant's fluidity with European, especially French traditions is part
of the layered meaning systems that shape Glissant's work.

4 See Glissant's *Poetics of Relation* (1997) whose elusive poetics, rich language,
and complex circularities impede reduction of the work to a singular thesis or
argument. Also see Manthia Diawara, "Édouard Glissant's Worldmentality"
(2014). In this short, beautiful piece Diawara refers to the process of making
his film, *Édouard Glissant: One World in Relation*, K'a Yéléma Productions
(2009) and Glissant's search out of transparency over complexity, reason
against poetry, and the traps of monolingualism.

5 I refer here to Fred Moten and Stefano Harney's *The Undercommons: Fugitive
Planning and Black Study*, whose elaboration of social poiesis by extending the
genealogy of the Black Radical Tradition also contributes to decolonial theory
and methods (2014). This text is generative for the historical legacies of mar-
ronage and communal autonomy by former African slaves in the Américas.
I am particularly in dialogue with its rich theoretical language for producing
new modes of study. Also see Alvin O. Thompson, *Maroons in the Americas*
(2006).

6 See Arturo Escobar's *Territories of Difference* (2008), where an important discussion on territoriality as the locus of self-governance is elaborated in relation to *Proceso de Comunidades Negras* (PCN) within Colombia's Pacific region
and in relation to palm oil monocultural production.

7 To elaborate the concept of the emergent within extractive capitalism, I build
upon Stuart Hall's notion of "vernacular modernities" originally developed
as a theory about the after-condition of enslavement, and particularly in relation to Afro-Caribbean histories. "Vernacular modernities" refer to how
local identities and cultures can never be wholly articulated or captured by
the onset of capitalism. As Hall puts it, this is a "new kind of localism that is
not self-sufficiently particular, but *which arises within*, without being simply a
simulacrum of, the global" (my emphasis). See Stuart Hall, "Conclusion: The
Multicultural Question," in *Un/Settled Multiculturalisms, Diasporas, Entanglements, Transruptions* (2000), 261. Also see Hall's seminal essay, "Negotiating
Caribbean Identities" (1995).

8 My point is to not collapse African-descended peoples and the history of
trans-Atlantic slavery with the colonization of Indigenous peoples, even
as the work of John Brown Childs and Guillermo Delgado-P, among many

others, have shown their long and complex imbrications in the Américas (2012). Throughout the chapters, I contend with the different colonial and racial formations of each geography I discuss, underscoring what Eduardo Galeano, Lewis Gordon, Sylvia Wynter, and many others have defined as the complex space of colonial convergence that emerges from colonial afterlives.

9   The work of Viveiros de Castro investigates the Yawalapíti and other Indigenous groups of the Amazonian Brazilian basin, undoing Claude Lévi-Strauss's structuralist anthropology based on Indigenous groups within Central Brazil. Viveiros de Castro writes against the grain of structural and ethnocentric strains of anthropology by conceptualizing a "multinaturalist perspectivism," or a non-anthroprocentric virtuality of the idea of species. Again, see Viveiros de Castro, "Cosmological Perspectivism in Amazonia and Elswhere."

10  Walter Mignolo's classic text *Darker Side of the Renaissance* (1995) acknowledges the importance of theories of race and racism and Africana philosophy in shifting Eurocentric knowledge towards decolonial critique. About the work of Lewis Gordon on *existentia Africana*, Mignolo states that "geographical and bio-graphical genealogies of thought are at the very inception of decolonial thinking" (Mignolo, *Darker Side*, xxiii).

11  In this introduction, for the sake of not confusing genealogies of thought, I try to stay a course by using the term "decolonial," even while anticolonial thinkers from the Caribbean, the Américas, and the Global South more broadly are also cited as important to the decolonial turn. What these thinkers share is a commitment to analyze from coloniality rather than modernity, what Sylvia Wynter terms the "paradigm of discovery" that sees modern analysis as new rather than as ensconced within longer processes of war, colonization, violence, slavery, and capitalism (2003, 2012). For an excellent overview of decoloniality, see Nelson Maldonado-Torres's introduction to a special issue of *Transmodernity* 1, issue 2 (Fall 2011): 1–15.

12  See the broad literature here on Global South ecological activisms and theorizations that center feminist perspectives, including Nobel Peace Laureate Wangari Maathai's work as the founder of the Greenbelt Movement in Kenya. Her book addresses the challenges of the movement and the importance of replenishing the Earth during a period of extended crisis (2003). Also see Anrudathi Roy's work on dams and *Capitalism: A Ghost Story* (2014). Also, see chapters three and four for decolonial femme perspectives and inversions on land and water.

13  Lee Edelman's critique of reproductive futures through the figure of the child is the most obvious text to cite here on a theory of "no future" (2014), but I am more specifically referring to the recent spate of popular literature, such as Elizabeth Kolbert's *The Sixth Extinction: An Unnatural History* (2014) and other models that give primacy to the excesses of the Anthropocene. With the exception of Naomi Klein's *This Changes Everything*, the "no future" paradigm often does not explicitly name capitalism as the dominant culprit. Further-

more, within Indigenous spaces in the Américas, a critique of reproductive futures has to be balanced against the historical weight project of eugenics, anti-Indigenous policies, and the state-centered project of *mestizaje*. For an astute recent discussion of *mestizaje* in relation to anti-Indigenous violence see Nicole Guidoletti-Hernandez's *Unspeakable Violence: Remapping US and Mexican National Imaginaries* (2011).

14  Vandana Shiva's work continues to be a defining study of the implications of biotechnology on the Global South; see *Monocultures of the Mind* (2003). New eco-feminisms also build upon and engage Shiva's discussions of earlier articulations of eco-feminism that may have not fully considered gender nonconformity or the unilinearity of the biological category of "woman." See chapters 1 and 5 for more instances.

15  For an exceptional account of global racism see Denise Ferreira da Silva's *Toward a Global Idea of Race* (2007).

16  See Anibal Quijano, "Coloniality and Modernity/Rationality" (2007), 178.

17  For a rich discussion of some of the absences of women of color scholarship within the body of work and citational practice that is decolonial theory see Laura Pérez, "Enrique Dussel's *Etica de la liberación*, US Women of Color Decolonizing Practices, and Coalitionary Politics amidst Difference" (Spring/Summer 2010).

18  Cedric Robinson's foundational *Black Marxism: The Making of the Black Radical Tradition* (1983) carefully catalogues the rise of capitalism's long and imbricated history with racialized violence, which hierarchized difference by establishing a political economy that drew surplus from Black and Brown bodies.

19  Michel Foucault, *Discipline and Punishment* (1978).

20  Gilles Deleuze, "Postscripts on Societies of Control" (1992).

21  By narrating a counterhistory of visuality, Nicholas Mirzoeff links the authority of colonial actors to the naturalization of the right to look. Countervisuality finds forms to see otherwise within and through a self-authorizing system of power (see especially the introduction, "The Right to Look or How to Think With and Against Visuality," 1–34).

22  See James Scott's important work *Seeing Like a State: How Certain Schemes to Improve the Human Condition Have Failed* (1998) for a grounded theoretical treatise on the utopian schemes of development. Scott argues for a turn to local knowledge sources to counter the epistemic and material violence of authoritarian state decision-making.

23  For instance, in its global war on terror, the United States utilized satellite images not only for war in Iraq and Afghanistan but also for what Lisa Parks refers to as the production of "digital real estate," or intellectual property owned by the US government and its corporate surveillance apparatuses, where remote sensing literally absorbs "territories into a global digital economy." See Lisa Parks and James Schwoch, eds., *Down to Earth: Satellite Technologies, Industries, and Cultures* (2012).

24 See Parks and Schwoch, *Down to Earth*.

25 In their book *Remote Sensing of Natural Resources*, Guangxing Wang and Qui-hao Weng describe the sampling applications and image-based algorithms that can be used for scientific researchers as easily as it can be used by corporate.

26 Maurice Merleau-Ponty's *Phenomenology of Perception* is the classic citation here, an important critique of the Cartesian split between mind and body by establishing the body as a site of perception. My reference here is to the lesser-known but equally prescient work of Maturana and Varela that foregrounds epistemologies of perception based on neurobiology, including the important concept of "autopoiesis," which refers to the autonomous dynamic within complex recursive and self-referential living systems. Maturana and Varela, *El árbol del conocimiento* (1984), *The Tree of Knowledge*. Also see Ira Livingston's *Between Science and Literature* (2006) that thinks through autopoetics as open social and discursive knowledge formations in relation to the sciences.

27 This is part of Humberto Maturana's response to Morris Berman's critique of *The Tree of Knowledge*, which Maturana analyzes as Berman not fully understanding. See "Response to Berman's Critique of the Tree of Knowledge" (1981).

28 Considering the current importance and acuteness of racialized politics of knowledge production, I would like to make explicit my entry into the extractive condition. I am not Indigenous, and do not pretend to speak for nor fully understand the realities of the spaces I have lived in, researched, and analyzed, but instead offer my partial and situated relational view as a South American mestiza, and Latina queer femme.

29 Here, I am invoking and citing a range of work that could broadly be situated as queer of color critique, including José Muñoz's *Disidentifications: Queers of Color and the Performance of Politics* (1999), Roderick Ferguson's *Aberrations in Black: Toward a Queer of Color Critique*; and Gayatri Gopinath's *Impossible Desires: Queer Diasporas and South Asian Public Cultures* (2005), which names postcolonial diasporic queer critique. Queer femininity is addressed especially in Gopinath's work and in Juana Rodriguez's *Sexual Futures, Queer Gestures, and Other Latina Longings* (2014). Putting this conversation in connection with decolonial literature and extending both into the field of multiplying difference against the monocultural view is my point here.

30 José Muñoz's *Cruising Utopia: The Then and There of Queer Futurity* (2009) is an important model of theorizing world-shaping activities as future-oriented endeavors. See also Jack Halberstam's *In a Queer Time and Place: Transgender Bodies, Subcultural Lives* (2005), especially his analysis of the subcultural and queer temporality as non-normative modes of study, creative production, and being.

31 See the queer decolonial text *Phenomenology of Chicana Experience and Identity: Communication and Transformation in Practice* (2000). In it, Jacque-

line M. Martinez references *Phenomenology of Communication: Merleau-Ponty's Thematics in Communicology and Semiology* (1988) by Richard L. Lanigan as a source of inspiration for her theory building. Also see Martinez's more recent *Communicative Sexualities: A Communicology of Sexual Experience* (2011) for how to address the pedagogy of theory and praxis in relation to queer orientation. See Sara Ahmed, *Queer Phenomenology: Orientations, Objects, Others* (2006), though my notion of femme positionality slightly differs from Ahmed's formulation early in the book. Rather than being connected to butch masculinity as the pull and orientation for a relational understanding of self, the decolonial queer method considers nonnormative femininity as a mode of perceiving the world, an autonomous format that is dialogically formed by queer relations and perspectives beyond the extractive view.

32 Linda Tuhwai Smith's game changing book, *Decolonizing Methodologies: Research and Indigenous Peoples* (1999) discusses the importance of sovereign forms of Indigenous knowledge production as central to transforming the activity of research. By focusing on Indigenous and mestizx cultural production and critically examining power relations within the extractive zone, I work to delink from the traps of Western knowledge that condition Indigenous knowledge as "Other."

33 See my edited volume with Herman Gray, *Toward a Sociology of a Trace* where we seek to reframe the problematic of disciplinary social inquiry, a frame that I have expanded here to include a rethinking of the ongoing working of coloniality. Avery Gordon's *Ghostly Matters: Haunting and the Sociological Imagination* (1998) is a key text for our elaboration of a sociology of a trace. Given that sociology is predicated upon observation, and the disciplines of the university self-affirm visibility as the key site of social analysis, methods that formulate quantitative and descriptive knowledge projects formulate the evidentiary in terms of the literal ability to see to know. While I critique empiricism, I retain a place for the importance of grounded research that learns from vernacular knowledges on the same plane of valuation as official knowledge.

34 In *The Reorder of Things: The University and Its Pedagogy of Minority Difference* (2012), Roderick Ferguson describes an interdisciplinary rather than disciplinary frame for his institutional critique, namely how the interdisciplines do not fundamentally break with the expansion of neoliberalism in the university. Liberal multiculturalism finds support through the university mandate of diversity.

35 Having worked as an academic sociologist at a US research institution over the past ten years, though also situated within a comparative ethnic studies department, I have been faced with the epistemic assumptions of the disciplinary very directly in my knowledge production. These include problems of reproducing the elevated status of evidence, or too easily rendering social life as fractured, dependent, and impoverished. As the domain of observable behavior, sociology—and "American" sociology in particular—reproduces

through and invests in truth-value that can be seen and therefore recorded. It is, moreover, a modern discipline that deploys and gives meaning to the colonial European scientific method, and defers questioning either the epistemology of its narrowed perspective, or the geopolitical locus of enunciation that frames its inquiry.

36 Gurminder K. Bhambra's *Connected Sociologies* addresses how classical sociology continues to narrativize history and modernity without reference to coloniality, reproducing European origin stories of world history (2014). Her work recognizes a broader plurality of theoretical positions, constructs, and interpretations than modern and Eurocentric Sociology.

37 See Ricardo D. Salvatore's *Disciplinary Conquest: US Scholars in South America, 1900–1945* for an analysis of the period prior to the consolidation of Area Studies (2016).

38 Roman de la Campa's classic book *Latin Americanism* contains a synthetic discussion on the imperial trouble with area studies (1999).

39 W. E. B. Du Bois famously attributed "double consciousness" with piercing the veil of racism by making the subjectification of Blackness visible (*Souls of Black Folk*, 1903). In Du Bois's rewriting of the Civil War in *Black Reconstruction in America* (1935), a decolonized perspective allows a dual critique, one that renarrates American history as a racial and nationalist project, while also writing from the standpoint of Black workers.

40 I refer here to a construction of violence as ensconced within and against Indigenous (and African) being at the very core of the colonial definition of the human and human progress. See Anibal Quijano's "Coloniality of Power, Eurocentrism, and Latin America" (2000) and the introduction to Katherine McKittrick's *Sylvia Wynter: On Being Human as Praxis* (2015).

41 Salvatore Eugenio Pappalardo, Massimo de Marchi, Francesco Ferrares, "Uncontacted Waorini in the Yasuní Biosphere Reserve," June 19, 2013, PLOS Journal, http://journals.plos.org/plosone/article?id=10.1371/journal.pone.0066293. Also see Matt Finer et al., "La frontera extractiva avanza en el Parque Yasuní," November 12, 2013 (http://www.geoyasuni.org/?p=1283) for a history of the intangible zone's legal protection, an important rendering of the legal loopholes that facilitate state and corporate extraction.

42 I am referring here to Phillip De Loria's *Playing Indian* (1998).

43 See Patrick Wolfe's discussion of the elimination of the Native in relation to Australian settler colonialism (2006). While this article has been critiqued for being applied too widely outside of the specific settler condition of Australia, in the context of Chilean ideology in relation to Mapuche, Huilliche, Pehuenche, Fuegan, and other Indigenous peoples the terminology "elimination of the Native" can be aptly used in relation to the discourses and practices of the colonial and modern state since the sixteenth century.

44 Elsewhere I have written a feminist decolonial discussion of Mapuche hunger strikes. See "Mapuche Hunger Acts: Epistemology of the Decolonial" (2012).

45  For a discussion of utopic visions centered within the state's capture of power see Nancy Postero's "Andean Utopias in Evo Morales's Bolivia" (2007).

## Chapter 1. The Intangibility of the Yasuní

1   Bruno La Tour, "Circulating Reference: Sampling the Soil in the Amazon Forest" (1999).

2   William Sacher, personal communication with the author, May 18, 2015.

3   In a reconsideration of the epistemes of ethnographic method, Eduardo Kohn places the human within a web of complexity that is based upon fieldwork in Ecuador's upper Amazonian region (2017). Though my work differently situates the threat of extractive capitalism, my thinking in this chapter is influenced by this rich study and theorization of the Ecuadoran Amazon.

4   See Gilles Deleuze and Félix Guattari, *A Thousand Plateaus: Capitalism and Schizophrenia* (1980).

5   In *Autopoiesis and Cognition*, Humberto Maturana and Francisco Varela explore cognition as a biological matter at the basis of all living systems and as self-referential systems that operate outside of the logics of observer and observed (1980). This is the epistemological foundation for how I am using the term social ecologies of intangibility in this chapter. Also see Ira Livingston's concept of autopoetics that expands these ideas (2006).

6   Werner Herzog's *Fitzcarraldo* (1982) is the cinematic expression of colonial madness that is at the center of director Les Blank's documentary *Burden of Dreams* (1982).

7   In her work on the overdetermined representations of the natural world, *Entangled Edens: Visions of the Amazon* (2001), Candace Slater attends to the hegemonic representation of the Amazon as a diversity of flora and fauna that functions to absent Native inhabitants within the rain forest. Slater's book disentangles how the Amazon functions as an idealized icon rather than the complex set of competing visions that it is.

8   The Tagaeri and Taromenane must also be named here, the tribes who broke off from the Huaorani, rejecting colonization to live deeper in the forest as a "no contact" group. While many Indigenous groups have also put pressure on the Amazon with hunting practices and an expanding population, the balance I am referring to here is about the level of engagement with the outside world.

9   This is quoted in Esperanza Martínez's important and speedy account of these events that unfolded from 2009 to 2014, with continuing processes and effects unfolding around the Yasuní today. See Esperanza Martínez, *Yasuní, el turtuoso camino de Kioto a Quito* (2013).

10  Martínez, *Yasuní, el turtuoso camindo de Kioto a Quito* (2013), 15.

11  As cited in the *Guardian* report that revealed these agreements, the document, titled "China Development Bank Credit Proposal," bears the name of Ecuador's Ministry of Economic Policy Coordination on every page. Under

the heading "Results of the 1st Negotiating Round: Preliminary Agreements," which took place between May 13 and May 23, 2009, it states, "Last minute clause: The Ecuadorian party has said it will do all it can to help Petro-China and Andes Petroleum explore ITT and Block 31." David Hill, "Ecuador Pursued China Oil Deal While Pledging to Protect Yasuní, Papers Show," *The Guardian*, February 19, 2014.

12  Freddy Javier Álvarez Gonzaléz, "El Buen Vivir, Un Paradigma Anti-Capitalista," *Pacarina del Sur: Revista de Pensameinto Crítico Latinoamericano*, November 2016.

13  In terms of Afro-descended peoples along the Caribbean coast, Arturo Escobar elaborates upon local models of nature that he does not term *el buen vivir*, perhaps due to the date of publication as preceding these public debates, which took place in 2000. The communities he describes certainly practice what might now be labeled by the principles of *el buen vivir*. For instance, Escobar notes how the central principle of Black communal knowledge is that of transformation prevalent in nature as much as in human interaction. "It is because plants mediate between the natural, the human, and the supernatural—between life and death, masculine and feminine, past and present—that the model enacts a logic of multiplicity and fragmentation" (Escobar, *Territories of Difference*, 116).

14  Eduardo Gudynas and Alberto Acosta, "El buen vivir," 71–81.

15  Atawallpa Oviedo Freire, *Buen vivir vs. Sumak Kawsay*, 45.

16  Atawallpa Oviedo Freire, *Bifurcación del buen vivir y el Sumak Kawsay*. In his preface to the same volume, Oviedo Freire pushes this comparison further, engaging not only the Indigenous practices of "rightful living," but also the way that Afro-based cultural formations enable a particular set of ethical behaviors in relation to the natural world.

17  Salvador Schavelzon, *Plurinacionalidad y vivir bien*, my translation.

18  Michel Foucault's notion of governmentality refers to how the state exercises control and governs the populace and is theorized throughout his College de France lectures. Extractive capitalism requires a particular form of governmentality that is corporate, seizes upon Indigenous territories, and subsumes the complex logic of social ecologies to expand its representational and material control over human and inhuman life. See especially Foucault's *Security, Territory, Population (1977–1978)* and *The Birth of Politics (1978–1979)*.

19  Pablo Piedra, personal communication with the author, April 8, 2015.

20  Rafael Correa, "El Buen Vivir: Plan Nacional, 2013–2017." Accessed October 5, 2016. http://www.buenvivir.gob.ec.

21  Correa, "El Buen Vivir," 313, my translation.

22  Amazon Watch is in the process of publishing papers on the high polluters of the oil industry in Ecuador and of the top ten, five are Ecuadoran companies.

23  Translated from Spanish into English on Political Database of the Americas. Accessed May 21, 2015. http://pdba.georgetown.edu/Constitutions/Ecuador

/english08.html. To view the entire Ecuadoran Constitution, see http://www
.asambleanacional.gov.ec/documentos/constitucion_de_bolsillo.pdf.

24 "Rights of Nature Articles in Ecuador's Constitution." Accessed February 14,
2015. http://therightsofnature.org/wp-content/uploads/pdfs/Rights-for
-Nature-Articles-in-Ecuadors-Constitution.pdf, my translation.

25 Acosta A., Gudynas E., Martínez E., Vogel J. (2009). "Leaving the Oil in the
Ground: A Political, Economic, and Ecological Initiative in the Ecuadorian
Amazon," Washington, DC: Center for International Policy, April 17, 2011.
Accessed May 1, 2017. http://americas.irc-online.org/am/6345.

26 Diana Coryat, "Extractive Politics."

27 See YASunidos. Accessed March 9, 2017. http://sitio.yasunidos.org/en/, my
translation.

28 For an account and theorization of how intersectional coalitions emerge out
of intimate connections, see Claudia Sofia Garriga-López on the Ecuadoran
context of transfeminism that roots itself within broader feminist movements
and praxis (2017).

29 Acción Ecológica, in addition to a number of alternative journalistic efforts,
has worked to document the criminalization of Indigenous peoples and ecological allies. Despite the Ecuadoran Constitution's legal protections of land
defenders, surveillance has expanded, as discussed in the introduction. See
"Criminalización de defensores de la naturaleza," Acción Ecológica. Accessed
June 10, 2015. http://www.accionecologica.org/criminalizados.ac.

30 Coryat, "Extractive Politics," 8.

31 "Ecuador: The Tagaeri Taromenane Intangible Zone in Yasuní Park," World
Rainforest Movement. Accessed October 17, 2016. http://wrm.org.uy/articles
-from-the-wrm-bulletin/section1/ecuador-the-tagaeri-taromenane-intangible
-zone-in-yasuni-park/.

## Chapter 2. Andean Phenomenology

1 Marisol de la Cadena's important book *Earth Beings* (2015) considers the
multiple ecologies that can be found across the Andes and through the entanglements between Indigenous and nonindigenous worlds. These ecologies
include the practices of communication across incommensurate differences
where Indigenous political strategies reach beyond binary logics towards
other ways of thinking, being and inhabiting.

2 In the Pisac marketplace of the Sacred Valley, there is a mix of local handi-
crafts made by Indigenous cooperatives and imported crafts both from the
national Peruvian industry, but increasingly also from the industrial crafts
market in China and other locations outside of Peru. The perception of souvenir authenticity is a reoccurring theme within the broader context of tourism and tourism studies. See the recent article by Pooneh and Susan M. Arai
(2013) for an analysis of "handmade" crafts and the tiers of authenticity that

circulate within tourist economies. On the political economies of handmade objects more broadly see Julia Bryan-Wilson's forthcoming book *Fray* (2017), especially the chapter "Threads of Protest," which considers the complex dimensions of handmade objects, art, and authenticity in relation to the work of installation artist Cecilia Vicuña.

3   See Lisa Aldred's classic essay on the topic, "Plastic Shamans and Astroturf Sun Dances: New Age Commercialization of Native American Spirituality," (2000), 331.

4   Cheryl Harris, "Whiteness as Property."

5   Edward Said, *Orientalism*.

6   For a thoughtful examination of the making of matter into insensate and immobile categories, especially in relation to racialized histories and representations, see Mel Y. Chen's *Animacies*.

7   Sylvia Wynter, "1492: A New World View."

8   Nelson Maldonado-Torres, *Against War*.

9   Here, I am referring to colonial legacies of racial inheritances that continue to impress themselves upon the daily negotiations of mestizx and Indigenous lives. For an in-depth analysis of the modern histories of race and Indigeneity in Peru, see Marisol de la Cadena, *Indigenous Mestizos: The Politics of Race and Culture in Cuzco, Peru* (1919–1991) (2011).

10  For an analysis of these fictions in relation to colonial Mexico and the caste system, see Maria Elena Martinez's *Genealogical Fictions: Limpieza de Sangre, Religions, and Gender in Colonial Mexico* (2008).

11  Rolena Adorno, *Guaman Poma*.

12  Kathryn Burns, *Colonial Habits*.

13  Michael Taussig, *Shamanism*.

14  Taussig, *Shamanism*, 100.

15  See Daniel Serrano, *El cazador de gringos* [The gringo hunter] (2007). This popular book of short stories puts into circulation the term *brichero* to describe a straight male mestizx figure of the tourist economy that traffics in sex and mysticism in search of a US green card by "hunting gringas." This heterosexual economy, like its counterpart in spiritual tourism, constructs and mediates forms of Indigenous embodiment through the consumer desire for authenticity.

16  Taussig, *Shamanism*.

17  Josef Estermann, "Ecosofia Andina."

18  Estermann, "Ecosofia Andina," 77.

19  For a Fanonian analysis that rethinks the presuppositions of Marxism from Indigenous modes of thinking and being see Glen Coulthard, *Red Skin, White Masks: Rejecting the Colonial Politics of Recognition* (2014).

20  Jane Bennett, *Vibrant Matter* (2012).

21  Rosie Braidotti, *Nomadic Theory* (2012)

22  Enrique Dussel, *Ethics of Liberation* (2013).

23  Walter Mignolo, *Local Histories/Global Designs* (2000). See also Gloria Anzaldúa's *Borderlands: The New Mestiza* (1987).

24  For a now classic essay on the topic of decolonization in relation to Indigenous land dispossession, see Eve Tuck and K. Wayne Yang's "Decolonization Is Not a Metaphor" (2012). Rebekah Garrison's dissertation on settler responsibility and island epistemology invokes the methodology of settler responsibility through a comparison of Hawai'an, Guam, and Vieques struggles against militarization and settler coloniality. Garrison's notion of settler responsibility informs my understanding here. For a more extended discussion, also see Sarah Fong, Rebekah Garrison, Macarena Gómez-Barris, and Ho'esta Mo'e'hahne's "Decolonizing Horizons" in *Amerasia Journal* (2016).

25  These migrations from the North to the South by American ex-pats can also be referred to as "lifestyle migrations," such as those that Maria Amelia Viterbi has written about, albeit in the context of Cotacachi, Ecuador (2015).

26  See Diane Dunn, introduction to *Cusco: The Gateway to Inner Wisdom: A Journey to the Energetic Center of the World* (2007). Accessed March 22, 2017. http://pazyluzperu.com/wp/books-articles/dianes-books/gateway/gateway-introduction/.

27  Diane Dunn, *Cusco*.

28  For an important treatment of new age as a particular religious identity that arises with the advent of neoliberalism see Paul Heelas, *The New Age Movement: The Celebration of the Self and the Sacralization of Modernity* (1996).

29  Diane Dunn, *Cusco*.

30  Diane Dunn, *Cusco*, 129–31.

31  Diane Dunn, *Cusco*.

32  Lorenzo Veracini, *Settler Colonialism* (2010).

33  Joanna Drzewieniecki, "Indigenous People, Law and Politics in Peru," paper given at the Washington D.C. Latin American Studies Conference, 1996.

34  José María Arguedas, *Formación de una cultura nacional indoamericana* (1981), 25.

35  Diane Dunn, personal communication with the author, May 17, 1011.

36  Diane Dunn, personal communication with the author, April 11, 2011.

37  Michael Hill, "Contesting Patrimony."

38  Taussig, *Shamanism*.

39  Gail Valaskakis, *Indian Country*; Phillip Jenkins, *Dream Catchers*; Lisa Aldred, "Plastic Shamans"; Cynthia Snavely, "Native American Spirituality: Its Uses and Abuse by Anglo-Americans."

40  Phillip De Loria, *Playing Indian*, 7.

41  Jodi Byrd, *Transits of Empire*, 54.

42  Dunn, *Cusco*.

43  Ricardo Valderrama Fernández and Carmen Escalante Gutiérrez, *Andean Lives*.

44  See Paul H. Hellas and Gabriela Martinez Escobar, trans., introduction, *Andean Lives*, 13.

45  Gelles and Martinez Escobar, *Andean Lives*, 11.

46  Chicana feminists have been writing about the sacred toward a model of decolonization for some time, even while citational practices often reduce this literature only to the work of Gloria Anzaldúa. Emma Perez's *The Decolonial Imaginary: Writing Chicanas into History* (1999) and, more recently, Clara Román-Odio's study, *Sacred Iconographies in Chicana Cultural Production* (2013) are inspired books in this direction. Also see the theoretically important example of epistemic disturbance in Laura E. Pérez's *Chicana Art: The Politics of Spiritual and Aesthetic Altarities* (2007).

47  Don Francisco, personal communication with the author, August 6, 2008.

48  Don Francisco, personal communication with the author, August 6, 2008.

## Chapter 3. An Archive for the Future

1  See *Mencer: Ni Pewma* (2011), experimental documentary, directed by Francisco Huichaqueo. Accessed May 16, 2017. http://huichaqueo.cl/2011/02/01/mencer-ni-pewma/.

2  Francisco Huichaqueo, personal communication with the author, July 6, 2016.

3  Francisco Huichaqueo, personal communication with the author, May 22, 2015.

4  See Pamela Wilson and Michelle Stewart, eds., *Global Indigenous Media: Cultures, Poetics and Politics* (2008).

5  See Glen Coulthard, *Red Skin, White Masks* (2014).

6  It could also be situated more broadly within a growing discussion of Indigenous film, documentaries, and representations. For an important analysis of Hollywood films that centers Indigenous actors, directors and spectators, see Michelle Raheja's *Reservation Realism: Redfacing, Visual Sovereignty, and Representations of Native Americans in Film* (2011). For a decolonial focus on Ecuadoran documentary film made by Indigenous directors see Christian Manuel León Mantilla's *Reinventando al Otro: El Documental Indigenista en el Ecuador* (2010).

7  See Ximena Troncoso's essay on the topic, "Mariluán: Lautaro en la encrucijada," in *Anales de Literatura Chilena* 4 (2003).

8  Patricia Richards, "Of Indians and Terrorists," 62.

9  The instances of this are numerous in mainstream press, but also within right-wing and military discourses, where "Mapuche anarchism" is seen as the justification for an increased militarized presence. See for instance, "Diez carabineros lesionados deja enfrentamiento con mapuches en la Araucanía." Accessed October 8, 2014. http://www.defensa.pe/forums/showthread.php/3556-Problematica-Mapuche-y-el-Anarquismo.

10  Joanna Crowe, *The Mapuche in Modern Chile* (2012).

11 Charles Hale, *Más que un indio* (2006). Blest Gana's novel romantically depicts Lautaro as a national hero whose identity has been conveniently whitened.

12 For an astute discussion of primitive accumulation on Indigenous territories see Jimena Pichinao Huenchuleo's "La Mercantilizacón del Mapuche Mapu: Hacia le expoliación absoluta," in *Awükan ka kuxankan zugu wajmapu mew: Violencias coloniales en Wajmapu,* 2015. The entire bilingual Spanish/Mapudungun volume represents an Indigenous episteme that decolonizes knowledge production through collective editorial and study of the southern territories through Indigenous research.

13 See Luis Campos Muñoz's article, "Chile's Mapuche: Not Yet Pacified," that references the long struggle against state encroachment and the "Pacification" wars of the nineteenth century, https://nacla.org/article/chiles-mapuche-not -yet-pacified. Accessed May 16, 2017.

14 Thomas Klubock, *La Frontera,* 218.

15 Like the repeal of Article 27 in the Mexican Constitution, Pinochet's legal architecture reformulated the legal concept of territories facilitating privatization, as I soon discuss in more detail.

16 Timothy Clark, "Putting the Market in Its Place," 160.

17 See Scott Morgenson, "The Biopolitics of Settler Colonialism" (2011). Morgenson's rewriting of the figure of the homo sacer by working through the biopolitics of settler colonialism is essential to understanding the politics of elimination that are at the troubling center of the settler nation. Here, I continue to work with the figure of the homo sacer to understand the production of bare life as the starvation practices of the Chilean settler state in relation to Mapuche activism and struggles that have been criminalized. For a thoroughgoing critique of the discourses of bare life and biopolitics in relation to how profoundly the idea of the human is shaped by race and racial discourse see Alexander Weheliye, *Habeas Viscus* (2014).

18 Giorgio Agamben, *Homo Sacer,* 62.

19 Gil Hochberg, *Visual Occupations* (2015).

20 Aucán Huilcamán, interview with the author, San José, Costa Rica, March 15, 2004.

21 Though there have been recent discussions of the lack of ability to use the "elimination of the Native" idea beyond the settler colonial practices of Australia, the techniques of the colonial state in Chile parallel many of those described by Patrick Wolfe in "Settler Colonialism" (2006).

22 Jennifer Doyle, *Hold It Against Me* (2013).

23 Fred Moten's "Black Mo'nin" attends to the close relationship between "mourning" and "moaning," where "moaning" becomes the "sonic augmentation" of "mourning." Moten's analysis of the photograph of Emmett Till is to note the sonic substance that is a trace within the visual domain, as a kind of "difference semiotics" and challenge to theory (63). My point in citing this

work here is not to compare these specific histories of racial violence, but to suggest the repetition of ancestral moaning with Mapuche mourning that Huichaqueo returns to as central to the audiotrack of the film.

24 For a beautiful historical treatment of the machi in relation to feminism, see the work of Ana Mariella Bacigalupo, "Rethinking Identity and Feminism," an analysis I take up elsewhere. See Gómez-Barris, "Mapuche Mnemonics" (2016).

25 In a major contribution on Hochunk representation that speaks back to the legacies of colonial photography, see Jones et al., *People of the Big Voice: Photographs of Hochunk Families by Charles Van Shaick, 1879–1942*. Northern Native peoples are depicted through family portraits that engage a deeper sensibility of Indigenous communities and daily lives, dress, roles, and ceremonies, even within the space of the studio (*People of the Big Voice*).

26 Zurita quoted in Piña (1990), 195–233. The text accompanying the image on the back cover reads, "Ahora Zurita, que rapado y quemado, te hace el arte / Santiago de Chile 1979" (Now Zurita, shaved and burned, art makes you / Santiago de Chile 1979).

27 See Nelly Richard's classic work *Margins and Institutions* (1986), 66, 68. See also Richard's book, *Critica de la memoria* (2010), 185. For an astute analysis of Zurita's performance see Matías Ayala's essay, "Bolaño, Zurita, Vidal: Vanguardia, violencia, sacrificio" (2015).

28 Dawn Ades, Rita Elder, and Graciela Speranza, *Surrealism in Latin America* (2012).

29 Stephen Amend and Thora Amend, eds., *National Parks without People*, 13.

30 Some German settlers later had ties to the Nazi party that had continuous influence through the Pinochet regime. See "Nazis y Movimiento Nazi en Chile, 1931–45." Accessed May 16, 2017. http://www.archivochile.com/Poder _Dominante/doc_gen/PDdocgen0007.pdf. For a source that tracks this in English see Graeme S. Mount's *Chile and the Nazis: From Hitler to Pinochet* (2001).

31 For another critical perspective on Donald Tompkins's conservation schemes, see Frank Zeller, "Buy Now and Save! Preserving South American Wildness by Buying It Up," Worldwatch, July/August 2005. Accessed November 12, 2014. http://www.worldwatch.org/system/files/EP184C.pdf.

32 See chapter 1 for an analysis of postdevelopmental representation by Indigenous communities, and also on Ecuadoran international imaginaries and the role of Rainforest Action Network as well as International Rivers Network as providing a different international approach to the hitherto dominant relationships among conservation, extractivism, and Indigenous peoples.

33 Daniel Gutierrez-Vilches, "Chilean Legislation on National Parks," 177.

34 Martin Berger, *Sight Unseen*.

35 See Zeller, "Buy Now and Save!"

36 Gutierrez-Vilches, "Chilean Legislation on National Parks," 176–77.

37 See Fred Moten and Stepfano Harney, *The Undercommons* (2014).

38 Francisco Huichaqueo interview with the author, Santiago, Chile, July 11, 2016.

39 Francisco Huichaqueo interview with the author, Santiago, Chile, July 13, 2016.

## Chapter 4. A Fish-Eye Episteme

1 This work by Carolina Caycedo was first presented in DAAD Gallery in Berlin in 2012.

2 I am referring here to the important book by Patrick McCully, *Silenced Rivers: The Ecology and Politics of Large Dams* (2001), a careful study of the controversial technology and impacts of large dams. In the new edition, McCully suggests that the growing anti-dam movement is one way to counter the planetary spread of dam construction. Rather than focus on anti-dam movements exclusively, my analysis reaches across extractive regions to understand the wider intersectional and coalition work that takes place within social ecologies against development and mega-development.

3 Some might argue that Potosí and Cerro Rico silver extraction is the colonial megaproject precedent, as is Italupo River damming in Brazil. While I agree with this analysis, my point here is that megaprojects are now seen as reproducible and as a supposedly "new" extractivist model of hyperdevelopment and expansion.

4 In hydroelectric power, dammed water drives generators whose energy is measured by the proportional difference between the source and the water's outflow, yet, as studies have documented, such energy production is ultimately unsustainable (Bermann, "Impasses e controvérsias"). These projects decrease water quality, transmit disease through backwater formations, emit greenhouse gases, deforest and remove vegetation, reduce ecological biodiversity, and eliminate the functionality of other kinds of sustainable activities.

5 There are currently four dams in the world that are larger than 10GW, including the Three Gorges Dam (the first mega dam), the Xiloudu Dam, the Itaipu Dam across the Brazil-Paraguay border, and the Guri Dam in Venezuela. While the scale of dams ranges from small to large, and the cost of hydroelectricity is presumably cheap, wide-scale costs include displacement and ecological destruction.

6 The master plan for the Magdalena River can be seen at https://drive.google.com/file/d/0ByrzVKn6lnmSOVg4TkYwemhLMUE/view?usp=sharing. Accessed March 17, 2017.

7 "Colombia: Struggle against Quimbo Dam Reaches Critical Point," *Upside Down World*, July 17, 2015. Accessed April 15, 2017. http://upsidedownworld.org/main/news-briefs-archives-68/5397-colombia-struggle-against-quimbo-dam-reaches-critical-point.

8 My translation. The original reads, "El 14 de marzo de 2015 iniciaremos la gran

movilización por la defensa del Río Magdalena, los Territorios y la Vida. Recorreremos el país desde el Macizo Colombiano hasta Bocas de Ceniza, en rechazo al Plan Maestro de Aprovechamiento del Río Magdalena recuperando la memoria, la identidad y la cultura de todo un país que ha construido su vida, su territorio y su historia alrededor del río"; ASOQUIMBO, Movilización El Río de la Vida. Accessed March 19, 2017. http://www.quimbo.com.co/p /movilizacion.html.

9 See Carolina Caycedo's blog and site "Be Dammed." Accessed January, 25, 2017. https://carolinacaycedo.wordpress.com/2015/10/28/be-dammed -ongoing-project/.

10 Nicholas Mirzoeff, *Right to Look* (2011), xv.

11 See Caycedo's blog and site "Be Dammed." Accessed January, 25, 2017. https:// carolinacaycedo.wordpress.com/2015/10/28/be-dammed-ongoing-project/.

12 Boaventura de Sousa Santos, *Epistemologies of the South* (2014).

13 de Sousa Santos makes similar interventions into the main discipline of Sociology as Herman Gray and my arguments in our edited volume *Toward a Sociology of a Trace*. De Sousa Santos's and our approach to sociology draw from interdisciplinary methods and attend to the importance of social theory and the cultural sphere not as a separate realm of analysis but as integral to theories and studies of political spaces, colonialism, nationalism, economic change, and a history from below that is critical of the flattening tendencies of empiricism.

14 Outside of the United States, Eduardo Viveiros de Castro is increasingly taken up by US scholars who are perhaps more familiar with Nietzsche's philosophy on perspectivism that detracts from the idea that there is any one epistemological truth.

15 Viveiros de Castro, "Cosmological Perspectivism" (2012).

16 Following Lévi-Strauss's work on myth, yet against the separation of nature and culture that it, in the end reproduced, in "Exchanging Perspectives: The Transformation of Objects into Subjects in Amerindian Ontologies," Viveiros de Castro describes how "myths are filled with beings whose form, name, and behavior inextricably mix human and animal attributes in a common context of intercommunicability, identical to that which defines the present-day intra-human world" (464).

17 Viveiros de Castro, "Cosmological Perspectivism" (2012).

18 Bennett, *Vibrant Matter* (2012).

19 Diana Coole and Samantha Frost, *New Materialisms* (2010), 6.

20 Carolina Caycedo, *Yuma: Land of Friends* (2014).

21 Caycedo, *Yuma: Land of Friends* (2014).

22 Caycedo, *Yuma: Land of Friends* (2014).

23 Caycedo, *Yuma: Land of Friends* (2014).

## Chapter 5. Decolonial Gestures

1  For a historical analysis of colonial race relations in the broader Andean region, see Rachel Sarah O'Toole's *Bound Lives: Africans, Indians, and the Making of Race in Colonial Peru* (2012). O'Toole's book counteracts stereotypes about colonial Indigenous and African relations and shows the entanglements of everyday life within the matrix of violence that was Andean enslavement.

2  For a cultural and social approach to the violent vernacular of Indigenous representation see Ho'esta Mo'ehahne's chapter, "Corporeal Consumption and the Everyday Violence of Indigenous Signification: 'Uncle Yu Indian Theme Restaurant,'" Phd Dissertation, University of Southern California, June 2017.

3  Histories of African enslaved labor is decidedly missing from these colonial histories, and from the representation of the extractive global economy. There is little scholarship on this topic, yet over the past several decades the emergence of Afro-Bolivian identity and organizations has increased the visibility of this minority population within Bolivia, a population that is spread between La Yungas province, La Paz, Santa Cruz, and Cochabamba. During the 1990s, a resurgence of Afro-Bolivian identity emerged through new social movements, and there have been repeated cultural, intellectual and political efforts to raise the visibility of these histories and so to be counted within the national census.

4  The work of Sylvia Rivera Cusicanqui is essential to this chapter as it names Indigenous anarcho-feminisms as an intersectional formation from the Andean region. See especially *Chi'ixinakax utxiwa: una reflexión sobre practices y discursos descolonizadores* (2010), "Ser mujer Indígena, chola o birlocha" (1996), and "the Notion of 'Rights'" (2010).

5  The *criollo* state here refers to the legacies of the colonial Spanish caste system established in Latin American colonies from the sixteenth century onward. It placed *peninsulares*, Spanish-born elites, at the apex of the social triangle, and next were the *criollos*, those of Spanish genealogy and mixed descent that also occupied high status in the franchise colony but with lower status than *peninsulares*. See also Maria Elena Martinez's *Genealogical Fictions: Limpieza de Sangre, Religion, and Gender in the Colonial System* (2008) for a critical study of the racial ideologies and historical legacies of the caste system based on blood fictions in Mexico. During the nation-building period of the eighteenth and nineteenth centuries, Latin American nations took on specific characteristics of racialized gender that were reflected in a *criollo* state.

6  Since 2002, the cofounders María Galindo and Julieta Paredes went separate ways, and Mujeres Creando therefore split into two different feminist formations. Mujeres Creando is now represented by Galindo, and Mujeres Creando Comunidad is currently convened by Paredes.

7   See Sylvia Rivera Cusicanqui's *Chi'ixinakax utxiwa: una reflexión sobre prac-tices y discursos descolonizadores* (2010). Also see Steve J. Stern's book *Resis-tance, Rebellion, and Consciousness in the Andean Peasant World, 18th to 20th Centuries* (1987).

8   See Sarita See's important analysis of primitive accumulation in relation to Rosa Luxembourg's rethinking of Marx, specifically about the colonial dy-namics of global capitalism. "Accumulating the Primitive" (2014). Glen Coul-thard also analyzes Marx's thesis of primitive accumulation to discuss the essential dynamic of Indigenous dispossession for colonial capitalism as a "persistent role that unconcealed, violent dispossession continues to play in the reproduction of colonial and capitalist social relations to both the domes-tic and global contexts" (*Red Skin, White Masks*, 9). An important debate within Indigenous studies and within Marxist thought centers on the degree to which Marx focused his attention on the capitalist development of West-ern Europe rather than the rest of the world, and his undertheorized thesis of primitive accumulation in relation to Indigenous peoples and territories. See Coulthard, *Red Skin, White Masks*, especially 6–15, for an exceptional analysis of the primitive accumulation thesis in relation to Indigeneity and Indigenous studies.

9   Looking more broadly within the hemisphere, Josephina Saldaña-Portillo documents how revolutionary masculinity operates to occlude gendered nar-ratives within agrarian cultures and the twentieth-century revolutions within Latin America (*Revolutionary Imagination*). I make a similar argument here about how male heroism within mining culture has historically occluded the centrality of female resistance within extractive geographies.

10  Even as the sector technically constitutes only one-third of Bolivia's economic sector, and during the 1985 crisis constituted as little as 4 percent of the GDP, it has fundamentally shaped global, national, and local economies, where places such as Huanuni in the Oruro region annually produced almost 500,000 tons of silver.

11  As reports have highlighted, mining is also highly extractive of water re-sources, and given that the Cerro Rico is located at the top of major head-waters of the Rio Pilcomayo, mining has had extensive negative effects upon the watershed and underground water supplies (Strosnider, "Acid Mine Drainage"). Thus, in addition to being extractive of female Indigenous bodies, mining is a highly toxic and wasteful condition that negatively affects daily living.

12  Zabala, *Nos/Otras*, 29.

13  Nash, *We Eat the Mines*, 114.

14  Nash, *We Eat the Mines*, 114.

15  Elsewhere I have written about the role that female hunger strikers play within the extractive wars that criminalize Indigenous land defenders; see *Mapuche Hunger Acts* (2012). My point here is to suggest that hunger strikes throughout

the Américas have been an embodied response to territorial wars and labor conditions, especially as organized by female subjects in the public sphere. For an account of how settler sovereignty plays out in relation to the hunger striking practice of Attawaspikat Chief Therese Spence, see Audra Simpson's "The State Is a Man: Therese Spence, Loretta Saunders, and the Gender of Settler Sovereignty" (2016).

16  Lehm and Rivera Cusicanqui, *Los artesansos libertarios*.

17  Webber, *Red October*.

18  Zabala, *Nos/Otras*, 29.

19  Julieta Paredes, personal communication with the author, August 9, 2013.

20  Within an expanding mestizx urban society, the *chola* mediated Aymara cultural traditions by occupying a pivotal role as a Bolivian national icon (Poole, *Vision, Race, and Modernity*). However, she was also targeted by bourgeois society through negative stereotypes within discriminatory public spheres, such as the media.

21  Silvia Rivera Cusicanqui, "Ser mujer Indígena, chola o birlocha" (1996).

22  "Indigenous Anarchism in Bolivia: An Interview with Silvia Rivera Cusicanqui." Accessed June 15, 2016. http://theanarchistlibrary.org/library/silvia -rivera-cusicanqui-andalusia-knoll-indigenous-anarchism-in-bolivia.

23  Rivera Cusicanqui, "Ser mujer Indígena, chola o birlocha," 1996.

24  Bolivia experienced a series of false democratic transitions in the late 1970s and early 1980s that resulted in a military dictatorship (1980–82) and culminated in the second Hernán Siles Zuazo presidency. This tumultuous time of hyperinflation, increased urban and rural labor radicalization, and state violence made the formation of Mujeres Creando that much more necessary.

25  Julieta Paredes, interview with the author, La Paz, Bolivia, August 9, 2013.

26  This performance is currently available at the Hemispheric Institute of Performance and Politics archive, http://hidvl.nyu.edu/video/003888408.html, May 26, 2015, in the Mujeres Creando Collection, Mujeres Creando, *Acción* 6.

27  See Mujeres Creando, *Acción* 6, Hemispheric Institute for Performance and Politics.

28  For an analysis of this exhibition and its impact within Madrid cultural circuits, see "Mujeres Creando. Ten cuidado con el presente que constuyes, debe paracerse al future que sueñas." Accessed March 18, 2017. http://www.museo reinasofia.es/exposiciones/mujeres-creando-ten-cuidado-presente-que -construyes-debe-parecerse-al-futuro-que-suenas.

29  The focus on *mujeres* has been a constant nomenclature, which has led to tensions with transgender political and subject formations. Though its history in relation to transgender rights is complex, to be fair, Mujeres Creando has not organized exclusively around "women's issues" and has often included an analysis of multiple genders and sexual identifications.

30  Paredes, *Hilando Filo*, 3.

31  Commentary on *Hilando Filo* blog, Mujeres Creando Comunidad blog site.

Accessed January 12, 2015. http://memoriafeminista.blogspot.com/2010/04/3
-edicion-del-libro-hilando-fino-desde.html.

32  See the first book in the independent series by Victoria Aldunate and Julieta
Paredes, *Constuyendo Movimientos* (2009).

33  In what I find to be a somewhat troubling analysis of the politics of *chachawarmi* in the gender-equality debates in Bolivia, Anders Burman analyzes the
issues of Aymara silence as an oft-found trait of Indigenous women (Burman,
"*Chachawarmi*"). While his line of questioning is not dissimilar to my own
concerns around coloniality, tradition, and decolonization, we come to different conclusions with respect to our observations about feminist radical histories in Bolivia. In part, this difference lies in Burman's overreliance on political narratives and ethnographic observation that positions Aymara feminisms
within and against a frame of Western feminisms, which is not that useful for
discerning what I identify as a utopic horizon. Feminist-indigenous-anarchic
critique has its own regional genealogies that need not be compared to other
forms of gender analysis but must be seen as challenging stagnant ideas about
indigeneity, including the overdetermination of Indigenous female silence.

34  See Mishuana Goeman and Jennifer Nez Denetdale's "Native Feminisms"
(2009). Also see Joanne Barker's important recent edited volume, *Critically
Sovereign* (2017) that addresses autonomous embodiment and theorizations
within a North American Indigenous context.

35  For a longer discussion of this, see Green and Lackowski, "Bolivian Radical
Feminist."

36  Nancy Postero, "Andean Utopias" (2007).

37  See Patrick Anderson's brilliant book on the politics of hunger and self-
starvation, *So Much Wasted* (2010).

38  See Julieta Paredes in the interview "Disobedience Is Happiness: The Art of
Mujeres Creando," with "Notes from Everywhere." Accessed April 3, 2017.
http://artactivism.members.gn.apc.org/allpdfs/256-Disobedience%20Is
%20Happiness.pdf.

39  María Galindo, *No se puede descolonizar* (2013).

40  For a quick overview of the rise of gay marriage rights and trans-rights processes throughout the Américas see Chris Lewis, "Rainbow Tide Rising: How
Latin America became a Gay Rights Haven," Alternet, February 13, 2014. Accessed March 19, 2017. http://www.alternet.org/world/how-latin-america
-became-haven-gay-rights. See also my forthcoming *The Rainbow Tide: Beyond Politics as Usual* (2018).

41  María Galindo interview with the author, La Paz, Bolivia, August 12, 2014.

42  Because of its importance, we translated Mujeres Creando and María
Galindo's "Constitución política feminista del estado" from Spanish into
English.

43  Sayek Valencia, "Interferencias transfeministas." Accessed April 14, 2017.

http://hemisphericinstitute.org/hemi/es/e-misferica-111-gesto-decolonial
/valencia.

44 Valencia, "Interferencias transfeministas," my translation.

45 Galindo, "Constitución política feminista del estado," "No se puede descolonizar," 2013. The English version is accessible at http://hemisphericinstitute
.org/hemi/en/emisferica-111-decolonial-gesture/galindo. Accessed March 22,
2017.

46 Galindo, "Constitución política feminista del estado," "No se puede descolonizar," 2013. The English version is accessible at http://hemisphericinstitute
.org/hemi/en/emisferica-111-decolonial-gesture/galindo. Accessed March 22,
2017.

## Conclusion

1 See "Ecological Extinction and Evolution in the Brave New Ocean," by Jeremy
B. C. Jackson, Proceedings of the National Academy of Sciences, 2008.

2 Barker, *Native Acts*; Coulthard, *Red Skin, White Masks*.

3 Ruth Wilson Gilmore, "What Is to Be Done?" American Studies Association,
Presidential Address, June 2011.

4 Millalén et al., *Escucha Winka!*. Accessed April 4, 2017. http://hemispheric
institute.org/hemi/en/emisferica-111-decolonial-gesture/carcamo.

5 Millalén et al., *Escucha Winka!*. Accessed April 4, 2017. http://hemispheric
institute.org/hemi/en/emisferica-111-decolonial-gesture/carcamo.

# BIBLIOGRAPHY

Ades, Dawn, Rita Eder, and Graciela Speranza, eds. *Surrealism in Latin America: Vivísmo Muerto*. Los Angeles: The Getty Research Institute, 2012.

Adorno, Rolena. *Guaman Poma: Writing and Resistance in Colonial Peru*. Austin: University of Texas Press, 2000.

Agamben, Giorgio. *Homo Sacer: Sovereign Power and Bare Life*. Stanford, CA: Stanford University Press, 1998.

Ahmed, Sara. *Queer Phenomenology: Orientations, Objects, Others*. Durham, NC: Duke University Press, 2006.

Alcoff, Martín Linda. "The Construction of Indigenous Peoples." In *Thinking from the Underside of History: Enrique Dussel's Philosophy of Liberation*, edited by Linda Martín Alcoff and Eduardo Mendieta. Oxford: Rowman and Littlefield, 2000.

Aldred, Lisa. "Plastic Shamans, Astroturf Sun Dances: New Age Commercialization of Native American Spirituality." *American Indian Quarterly* 24, no. 3 (2000): 329–53.

Aldunate, Victoria, and Julieta Paredes. *Constuyendo Movimientos*. La Paz: Hilvanando, 2009.

Alexander, Jacqui M. *Pedagogies of Crossing: Meditations on Feminism, Sexual Politics, and the Sacred*. Durham, NC: Duke University Press, 2006.

Alfaro, Raquel. "Mujeres creando comunidad: Feminización de la comunidad." *Bolivian Studies Journal, Revista de Estudios Bolivianos*, issues 15–18 (2010): 211–36.

Alsina, Miguel Rodrigo. "Elementos para una comunicación intercultural." *Revista CIDOB* 36 (1997): 11–21.

Álvarez Gonzaléz, Freddy Javier. "El Buen Vivir, Un Paradigma Anti-Capitalista," *Pacarina del Sur: Revista de Pensameinto Crítico Latinoamericano*, November 2016.

Alvarez, Sonia E., Evelyn Dagnino, and Arturo Escrobar, eds. *Cultures of Politics and Politics of Culture: Revisioning Latin American Social Movements*. Durham, NC: Duke University Press, 1998.

Amend, Stephan, and Thora Amend, eds. *National Parks without People? The South American Experience*. Cambridge: World Conservation Union, 1995.

Anderson, Patrick. *So Much Wasted: Hunger, Performance, and the Morbidity of Resistance*. Durham, NC: Duke University Press, 2010.

Antileo Baeza, Luis Cárcamo-Huechante, Margarita Calfío Montalva, and Herson Huinca-Piutrin, eds. *Awükan ka kuxankan zugu wajmapu mew: Violencias Coloniales en Wajmapu*. Bilbao: Ediciones Comunidad de Historia Mapuche, 2015.

Anzaldúa, Gloria, *Borderlands: The New Mestiza*. San Francisco: Aunt Lute Books, 1987.

Arguedas, José María. *Formación de una cultura nacional indoamericana*. 2nd ed. Mexico City: Siglo Vienteuno Editores, 1997.

Bacigalupo, Ana Mariella. "Rethinking Identity and Feminism: Contribution of Mapuche Women and Machi from Southern Chile." *Hypatia* 18, no. 2 (2003): 32–57.

Barker, Joanne. *Native Acts: Law, Recognition, and Cultural Authenticity*. Durham, NC: Duke University Press, 2011.

Barker, Joanne, ed. *Critically Sovereign: Indigenous Gender, Sexuality and Feminist Studies*. Durham, NC: Duke University Press, 2017.

Barrios Chúngara, Domitila, Victoria Ortiz, and Moema Viezzer. *Let Me Speak! Testimony of Domítila: A Woman of the Bolivian Mines*. New York: Monthly Review Press, 1978.

Bass, Margot S., Matt Finer, Clinton N. Jenkins, Holger Kreft, Diego F. Cisneros-Heredia, Shawn F. McCraken, Nigel C. A. Pitman, Pether H. English, Kelly Swing, Gorky Villa, Anthony Di Fiore, Christian C. Voigt, and Thomas H. Kunz. "Global Conservation Significance of Ecuador's Yasuní National Park." *PLOS One Journal*. January 19, 2010. http://www.plosone.org/.

Beasley-Murray, Jon. *Posthegemony*. Minneapolis: University of Minnesota Press, 2010.

Bennett, Jane. *Vibrant Matter: A Political Ecology of Things*. Durham, NC: Duke University Press, 2012.

Berger, John. *Ways of Seeing*. New York: Penguin, 1972.

Berger, Martin. *Sight Unseen: Whiteness and American Visual Culture*. Berkeley: University of California Press, 2006.

Bermann, Célio. "Impasses e controvérsias da hidreletricidade." *Estudos Avancados* 21, no. 59 (2007): 139–53.

Bhambra, Gurminder K. *Connected Sociologies*. London: Bloomsbury, 2014.

Braidotti, Rosi. *Nomadic Theory*. Columbia Press: New York, 2012.

Bretón de Solo de Zaldívar. "Etnicidad, desarrollo y 'buen vivir': Reflexiones críticas en perspectiva histórica." *European Review of Latin American and Caribbean Studies/Revista Europea de Estudios Latinoamericanos y del Caribe*, no. 95 (October 2013): 71–95. www.erlacs.org.

Burman, Anders. "*Chachawarmi*: Silence and Rival Voices on Decolonization and Gender Politics in Andean Bolivia." *Journal of Latin American Studies*, 43 (1) 65–91, February 2011.

Burns, Kathryn. *Colonial Habits: Convents and the Spiritual Economy of Cuzco, Peru*. Durham, NC: Duke University Press, 1999.

Byrd, Jodi. *The Transits of Empire: Indigenous Critiques of Colonialism*. Minneapolis: University of Minnesota Press, 2011.

Carcamo-Huechante, Luis. "Indigenous Interference: Mapuche Use of Radio in Times of Acoustic Colonialism." Special issue, *Latin American Research Review* 48 (2013): 50–68.

Chen, Mel Y. *Animacies: Biopolitics, Racial Mattering and Queer Affect*. Durham: Duke University Press, 2012.

Childs, John Brown, and Guillermo Delgado-P. *Indigeneity: Collected Essays*. New Pacific Press, 2012.

Clark, Timothy David. "Putting the Market in Its Place: Food Security in Three Mapuche Communities in Southern Chile." *Latin American Research Review* 46, no. 2 (2011): 154–79, 267, 269.

Clastres, Pierre. *Society against the State: Essays in Political Anthropology*. New York: Zone Books, 1989.

Comunidad de Historia Mapuche. *Ta iñ fijke xipa rakizuameluwün, Historia, colonialismo y resistencia desde el país Mapuche*. Temuco: Ediciones Comunidad de Historia Mapuche, 2012.

Coole, Diana, and Samantha Frost, eds. *New Materialisms: Ontology, Agency, and Politics*. Durham, NC: Duke University Press, 2010.

Coryat, Diana. "Extractive Politics, Media Power, and New Waves of Resistance against Oil Drilling in the Ecuadoran Amazon: The Case of Yasunidos." *Journal of International Studies* 9 (2015): 3741–60.

Coulthard, Glen. *Red Skin, White Masks: Rejecting the Colonial Politics of Recognition*. Minneapolis: University of Minnesota Press, 2014.

Crowe, Joanna. *The Mapuche in Modern Chile: A Cultural History*. Gainsville: University Press of Florida, 2013.

———. "Mapuche Poetry in Post-Dictatorship Chile: Confronting the Dilemmas of Neoliberal Multiculturalism." *Journal of Latin American Cultural Studies* 17, no. 2 (August 2008): 221–40.

de la Cadena, Marisol. *Indigenous Mestizos: The Politics of Race and Culture in Cuzco, Peru, 1919–1991*. Durham, NC: Duke University Press, 2000.

De la Campo, Román. *Latin Americanism*. Minneapolis: University of Minnesota Press, 1999.

Deleuze, Gilles. "Postscript on the Societies of Control." *October* 59 (Winter 1992): 3–7.

De Loria, Phillip J. *Playing Indian*. New Haven: Yale University Press, 1998.

Delsing, Riet. *Articulating Rapa Nui: Polynesian Cultural Politics in Latin American Nation-State*. Honolulu: University of Hawai'i Press, 2015.

De Marchi, Massimo, Salvatore Eugenio Pappalardo, and Francesco Ferrarese. "Zona Intangible Tagaeri Taromenane (ZITT): Delimitación cartogramfica, análisis geográfico y pueblos indígenas aislados en el camaleónico sistema territorial del Yasuni." Quito, Ecuador: Independently published, 2013.

Den Berghe, Van, Pierre L. and Jorge Flores Ochoa. "Tourism and Nativistic Ideology in Cuzco, Peru." *Annals of Tourism Research* 27, no. 1 (2000): 7–26.

de Sousa Santos, Boaventura. *Epistemologies of the South: Justice against Epistemicide*. Boulder, CO: Paradigm, 2014.

Diawara, Manthia. "Édouard Glissant's Worldmentality: An Introduction to *One World in Relation*." Accessed February 13, 2017. http://www.documenta14.de/en/south/34_douard_glissant_s_worldmentality_an_introduction_to_one_world_in_relation.

Doyle, Jennifer. *Hold It Against Me: Difficulty and Emotion in Contemporary Art*. Durham: Duke University Press, 2013.

Drzewieniecki, Joanna. "Indigenous People, Law, and Politics." Paper presented at Latin American Studies Association, September 28–30, 1995, Washington D.C.

Du Bois, W. E. B. *Black Reconstruction in America*. New York: Harcourt, Brace, and Company, 1935.

———. *The Souls of Black Folk*. Chicago, IL: A. C. McClurg, 1903.

Dussel, Enrique. *Ethics of Liberation: In the Age of Globalization and Exclusion*, 1973. Durham, NC: Duke University Press, 2013.

———. "Europe, Modernity, and Eurocentrism." *Nepantla: Views from South* 1, no. 3 (2000): 465–78.

———. "Transmodernity and Interculturality: An Interpretation from the Perspective of Philosophy," *Journal of Peripheral Cultural Production of the Luso-Hispanic World* (Spring 2012): 28–58.

———. *The Underside of Modernity, Apel, Ricoeur, Rorty, Taylor, and the Philosophy of Liberation*. New York: Prometheus Books, 1998.

Edelman, Lee. *No Future: Queer Theory and the Death Drive*. Durham: Duke University Press, 2004.

Escobar, Arturo. *Territories of Difference: Place, Movements, Life, Redes*. Durham, NC: Duke University Press, 2008.

Estermann, Josef. "Ecosofia Andina." In *Bifurcación del buen vivir y el Sumak Kawsay*, edited by Eduardo Gudynes, Josef Estermann, Freddy Alvarez, Javier Medina, and Atawallpa Oviedo Freire. Quito, Ecuador: Ediciones Sumak, 2014.

Falconi Trávez, Diego, Santiago Castellano, and María Amelia Viterbi, eds. *Resentir lo queer en América Latina: Dialogos desde/con el sur*. Barcelona and Madrid: Eguales, 2013.

Fanon, Frantz. *Black Skin, White Masks*, New York: Grove Press, 1952.

———. *The Wretched of the Earth*. New York: Grove Press, 1963.

Ferguson, Roderick. *Aberrations in Black: Toward a Queer of Color Critique*. Minneapolis: University of Minnesota Press, 2003.

———. *The Reorder of Things: The University and Its Pedagogies of Minority Difference*. Minneapolis: University of Minnesota, 2012.

Ferreira da Silva, Denise. *Toward a Global Idea of Race*. Minneapolis: University of Minnesota Press, 2007.

Finer, Matt, Varsha Vijay, Salvatore, Eugenio Pappalardo, and Massimo de Marchi. "La frontera extractiva avanza en el Parque Nacional Yasuní." Geoyasuni. November 12, 2013. http://www.geoyasuni.org/?p=1283.

Fong, Sarah, Rebekah Garrison, Macarena Gómez-Barris, and Ho'esta Mo'e'hahne. "Decolonizing Horizons" in *Amerasia Journal* 42, no. 3 (2016): 129–41.

Foucault, Michel. *The Birth of Politics: Lectures at the Collège de France, 1978–1979.* New York: Picador, 2004.

———. *Discipline and Punish: The Birth of the Prison.* New York: Vintage Books, 1995. First published in 1975.

———. *Security, Territory, Population: Lectures at the Collège de France, 1977–1978.* New York: Picador, 2010.

———. *Society Must Be Defended: Lectures at the Collège de France, 1975–1976.* New York: Picador, 2003.

Galeano, Eduardo. *Open Veins of Latin America: Five Centuries of the Pillage of a Continent.* New York: Monthly Review Press, 1973.

Galindo, María. "Constitución política feminista del estado: El país imposible que construmos las mujeres / Political Feminist State Constitution: The Nation We Impossibly Build as Women." In "Decolonial Gesture," edited by Macarena Gómez-Barris, Marcial Godoy-Anativia, and Jill Lane, special issue, *E-misférica* 11, no. 1 (July 2014). Accessed March 18, 2017. http://hemispheric institute.org/hemi/es/e-misferica-111-gesto-decolonial/galindo.

———. *No se puede descolonizar sin despatriarchalizar: Teoría y propuesta de la despatriarcalización.* La Paz: Mujeres Creando, 2013.

García Barrera, Mabel. "El discurso poético Mapuche y su vinculación con los 'temas de Resistencia cultural.'" *Revista Chilena de Literatura*, no. 68 (April 2006): 169–97.

Garriga-López, Claudia Sofia. "Transfeminist Crossroads: Reimagining the Ecuadorian State," *Transgender Studies Quarterly* 3, no. 1–2 (2017): 104–19.

Gelles, Paul H. "Introduction." In *Andean Lives: Gregorio Condori Mamani and Asunta Quispe Huamán.* Austin: University of Texas Press, 1986.

Gilmore, Ruth Wilson. *Golden Gulag: Prisons, Surplus, and Opposition in Globalizing California.* Berkeley: University of California, 2005.

———. "What Is to Be Done?" American Studies Association, Presidential Address. *American Quarterly* 63, no. 2 (June 2011): 245–65.

Glissant, Édouard. *Poetics of Relation*, trans. Betsy Wing. Ann Arbor: University of Michigan Press, 1997.

Goeman, Mishuana R. and Jennifer Nez Denetdale. "Native Feminisms: Legacies, Interventions, and Indigenous Sovereignties." *Wicazo Sa Review* 24, no. 2 (Fall 2009): 9–13.

Gómez-Barris, Macarena. "Andean Translations: New Age Tourism and Cultural Exchange in the Sacred Valley." Special issue, *Latin American Perspectives* (August 6, 2012): 68–78.

———. "Mapuche Hunger Acts: Epistemology of the Decolonial." *Transmodernity: Journal of Peripheral Cultural Production of the Luso-Hispanic World* 1, no. 3 (2012): 1–13.

———. "Mapuche Mnemonics: Reversing the Colonial Gaze through New Visualities of Extractive Capitalism." *Radical History Review*, vol. 2016, no. 124: 1, 90–101.

———. "Mnemonic Visuality: Mapuche Cultural Memory." Special issue, *Memory Studies Journal*, 90–101.

———. *Where Memory Dwells: Culture and State Violence in Chile*. Berkeley: University of California Press, 2009.

Gómez-Barris, Macarena, and Clara Irazábal. "Transnational Meanings of *La Virgen de Guadalupe*: Religiosity, Space and Culture at Plaza Mexico." *Culture and Religion* 10, no. 3 (2007): 339–57. http://www.informaworld.com/smpp/content~content=a916553642~db=all~jumptype=rss.

Gómez-Barris, Macarena, and Herman Gray. *Toward a Sociology of a Trace*. Minneapolis: University of Minnesota Press, 2010.

Gómez-Barris, Macarena, Marcial Godoy-Anativia, and Jill Lane, eds. "Decolonial Gesture." Special issue, *E-misférica* 11, no. 1 (2014). Accessed May 14, 2017. http://hemisphericinstitute.org/hemi/en/e-misferica/1834-111-the-decolonial-gesture.

Gopinath, Gayatri. *Impossible Desires: Queer Diasporas and South Asian Public Cultures*. Durham: Duke University Press, 2005.

Gordon, Avery. *Ghostly Matters: Haunting and the Sociological Imagination*. Minneapolis: Minnesota, 1997.

Green, Sharyl, and Peter Lackowski. "Bolivian Radical Feminist Maria Galindo on Evo Morales, Sex-Ed, and Rebellion in the Universe of Women." *Upside Down World*. April 2, 2010. http://upsidedownworld.org/main/bolivia-archives-31/3549—bolivian-radical-feminist-maria-galindo-on-evo-morales-sex-ed-and-rebellion-in-the-universe-of-women.

Groesfoguel, Ramon. "The Epistemic Decolonial Turn: Beyond Political Economy Paradigms, *Journal of Cultural Studies*, volume 21 (2007): 211–23.

Gudynas, Eduardo. *Ecología, economía, y etica el desarrollo sostenible*. Montevideo, Uruguay: CLAES, 2002. http://www.ecologiapolitica.net/gudynas/GudynasDS5.pdf.

Gudynas, Eduardo, and Alberto Acosta. "El buen vivir mas allá del desarrollo." *Que Hacer* (2011): 71–81.

Guha, Ranajit, ed. *A Subaltern Studies Reader, 1986–1995*. Minneapolis: University of Minnesota Press, 1997.

Guidotti-Hernández, Nicole. *Unspeakable Violence: Remapping US and Mexican National Imaginaries*. Durham: Duke University Press, 2011.

Gutiérrez Vilches, Daniel. "Chilean Legislation on National Parks: Use of Natural Resources." In *National Parks without People? The South American Experience*, edited by Stephan Amend and Thora Amend, Cambridge: World Conservation Union, 1995.

Halberstam, J. Jack. *In a Queer Time and Place: Transgender Bodies, Subcultural Lives*. New York: NYU Press, 2005.

Hale, Charles. *Más que un indio: Racial Ambivalence and Neoliberal Multiculturalism in Guatemala*. Santa Fe, NM: School of American Research Press, 2006.

Hall, Stuart. "Conclusion: The Multicultural Question," in *Un/Settled Multiculturalisms, Diasporas, Entanglements, Transruptions*. Edited by Barnor Hesse. New York: Zed Books, 2000.

———. "Negotiating Carribean Identities." *New Left Review* I /209, January-February 1995.

Harris, Cheryl. "Whiteness as Property." *Harvard Law Review* 106, no. 8 (June 1993), 1709–91.

Heelas, Paul. *The New Age Movement: The Celebration of the Self and the Sacralization of Modernity*. New York: Blackwell Publishers, 1996.

Hill, David. "Ecuador Pursued China Oil Deal while Pledging to Protect Yasuni, Papers Show." *Guardian*, February 19, 2014.

Hill, Michael D. "Contesting Patrimony: Cusco's Mystical Tourist Industry and the Politics of *Incanismo*." *Ethnos* 72, no. 4 (December 2007): 433–60.

———. "Inca of the Blood, Inca of the Soul: Embodiment, Emotion, and Racialization of the Peruvian Mystical Tourist Industry." *Journal of the American Academy of Religion* 76, no. 2 (June 2008): 251–79.

Hochberg, Gil Z. *Visual Occupations: Violence and Visibility in a Conflict Zone*. Durham, NC: Duke University Press, 2015.

Huenchuleo, Jimena Pichinao. "La Mercantilizacón del Mapuche Mapu: Hacia la expoliación absoluta," in *Awükan ka kuxankan zugu wajmapu mew: Violencias Coloniales en Wajmapu*. Edited by Enrique Antileo Baeza, Luis Cárcamo-Huechante, Margarita Calfío Montalva, Herson Huinca-Piutrin. Bilbao: Ediciones Comunidad de Historia Mapuche, 2015.

Huinao, Gabriela. *Desde el fogón de una casa de putas Williche/From the Hearth within a House of Williche Prostitutes*. Independently published. Santiago, Chile, 2012.

Ingold, Tom. *The Perception of the Environment: Essays on Livelihood, Dwelling, and Skill*. New York: Psychology Press, 2000.

Jenkins, Phillip. *Dream Catchers: How Mainstream America Discovered Native Spirituality*. Oxford: Oxford University Press, 2004.

Jones, Tom, Michael Schmudiach, Matthew Daniel Mason, Amy Lonetree, and George A. Greendeer. *People of the Big Voice: Photographs of Ho-Chunk Families by Charles Van Schaick, 1879–1942*. Madison: Wisconsin Historical Society, 2011.

Kauanui, J. Kēhaulani. *Hawaiian Blood: Colonialism and the Politics of Sovereignty and Indigeneity*. Durham: Duke University Press.

Klein, Naomi. *This Changes Everything: Capitalism vs. the Climate*. New York: Simon & Schuster, 2014.

Klubock, Thomas M. *La Frontera: Forests and Ecological Conflict in Chile's Frontier*. Durham, NC: Duke University Press, 2014.

Kohn, Eduardo. *How Forests Think: Toward an Anthropology beyond the Human*. Berkeley: University of California Press, 2013.

Kolbert, Elizabeth. *The Sixth Extinction: An Unnatural History*. New York: Henry Holt and Company, 2014.

Kuecker, Glen. "Fighting for the Forests: Grassroots Resistance to Mining in Northern Ecuador." *Latin American Perspectives*, 34, no. 2 (March 2007): 94–107.

Lanigan, Richard L. *Speaking and Semiology*. Berlin: De Gruyter Mouton, 1991.

Lehm, Zulema, and Silvia Rivera Cusicanqui. *Los artesansos libertarios y la ética del trabajo*. La Paz, Bolivia: Taller de Historia Oral Andina, 1988.

León Mantilla, Christian Manuel. *Reinventando al Otro: El Documental Indigenista en el Ecuador*, 2010.

Leuthold, Steven. *Indigenous Aesthetics: Native Art, Media, and Identity*. Durham, NC: Duke University Press, 1998.

Lipsitz, George. *The Possessive Investment in Whiteness: How White People Profit from Identity Politics*. Philadelphia, PA: Temple University Press, 1999.

Livingston, Ira. *Between Science and Literature: An Introduction to Autopoetics*. Champaign: University of Illinois Press, 2006.

Lowe, Lisa. *The Intimacies of Four Continents*. Durham, NC: Duke University Press, 2015.

Lowry, Michael, and Robert Sayre. *Romanticism against the Tide of Modernity*. Durham, NC: Duke University Press, 1983.

Maathai, Wangari. *The Green Belt Movement: Sharing the Approach and the Experience*. New York: Lantern Books, 2003.

Maldonado-Torres, Nelson. *Against War: Views from the Underside of Modernity*. Durham, NC: Duke University Press, 2008.

———. "Thinking through the Decolonial Turn: Post-Continental Interventions in Theory, Philosophy, and Critique—An Introduction." *Trans-Modernity: Journal of Peripheral Cultural Production of the Luso-Hispanic World* 1, issue 2 (Fall 2011): 1–15.

Mallon, Florencia E. *La sangre del copihue: La comunidad mapuche de Nicolás Ailío y el Estado Chileno, 1906–2001*. Santiago, Chile: Lom Ediciones, 2005.

Martinez, Elizabeth. *Yasuní: El tortuoso camino de Kitoto a Quito*. Quito, Ecuador: Abya-Yala, 2009.

Martínez, Esperanza and Alberto Acosta. *La Naturaleza con derechos: de la filosofía a la política*. Quito, Ecuador: Ediciones Abya-Yala, 2011.

Martinez, Jacqueline. *Phenomenology of Chicana Experience and Identity: Communication and Transformation in Practice*. Rowman & Littlefield Publishers, 2000.

Maturana, Humberto. "Response to Berman's Critique of the Tree of Knowledge." *Journal of Humanistic Psychology* 31, no. 2 (1991).

Maturana, Humberto, and Francisco Varela. *El árbol del conocimiento: Las bases biológicas del entendimiento humano*. Santiago, Chile, Editorial Universitaria, 1984.

McKittrick, Katherine. *Sylvia Wynter: On Being Human as Praxis*. Durham, NC: Duke University Press, 2014.

Melamed, Jodi. *Represent and Destroy: Rationalizing Violence in the New Racial Capitalism*. Minneapolis: University of Minnesota Press, 2011.

Mendoza, Zoila. "From Folklore to Exotica: Yma Sumac and the Performance of Inca Identity." *Appendix, Out Loud*, August 29, 2013. Accessed March 19, 2017. http://theappendix.net/issues/2013/7/from-folklore-to-exotica-yma-sumac-and-inca-identity.

Merleau-Ponty, Maurice. *Phenomenology of Perception*. New York: Routledge, 1965. First published in 1945.

Mignolo, Walter D. *The Darker Side of Western Modernity: Global Futures, Decolonial Options*. Durham: Duke University Press, 2011.

———. *Local Histories/Global Designs: Coloniality, Subaltern Knowledges, and Border Thinking*. Durham: Duke University Press, 2000.

———. "Modernity and Decoloniality." October 2011. Accessed March 13, 2017. http://www.oxfordbibliographies.com/view/document/obo-9780199766581/obo-9780199766581-0017.xml.

Millalén, José, Pablo Marimán, Rodrigo Levil, and Sergio Caniuqueo. *Escucha Winka!* Santiago, Chile: Lom Ediciones, 2005.

Mirzoeff, Nicholas. *The Right to Look: A Counterhistory of Visuality*. Durham: Duke University Press, 2011.

Mo'e'hahne, Ho'esta. "Spaces of Violence: Indigenous Figuration and Los Angeles Colonial Culture." PhD dissertation, University of Southern California, 2017.

Moreiras, Alberto. *The Exhaustion of Difference: The Politics of Latin American Cultural Studies*. Durham: Duke Unversity Press, 2001.

Morgenson, Scott. "The Biopolitics of Settler Colonialism: Right Here, Right Now." *Settler Colonial Studies* 1, no. 1 (2011): 52–76.

Moten, Fred. In *In the Break: The Aesthetics of the Black Radical Tradition*. Minneapolis: University of Minnesota, 2003.

Moten, Fred, and Stefano Harney. *The Undercommons: Fugitive Planning and Study*. New York: Minor Compositions, 2014.

Motta, Roberto. "Ethnicity, Purity, the Market, and Syncretism in Afro-Brazilian Cults." In *Reinventing Religions: Syncretism and Transformation in Africa and the Americas*, edited by Sidney Greenfield and Droogers Andre, 71–85. New York: Rowman and Littlefield, 2001.

Muñoz, Jose. *Cruising Utopia, The Then and There of Queer Futurity*. New York: NYU Press, 2009.

————. *Disidentifications: Queers of Color and the Performance of Politics*. Minneapolis: University of Minnesota Press, 1999.

Nash, June. *We Eat the Mines and the Mines Eat Us*. New York: Columbia University Press, 1993.

"Nazis y Movimiento Nazi en Chile, 1931–45, Centro de Estudios Miguel Enriquez (EME)," Archivo Chile: Historia Politico Social, Movimiento Popular. Accessed May 16, 2017. http://www.archivochile.com/Poder_Dominante/doc_gen/PDdocgen0007.pdf.

Ochoa, Marcia. *Queen for a Day: Transformistas, Beauty Queens, and the Performance of Femininity in Venezuela*. Durham, NC: Duke University Press, 2014.

O'Toole, Rachel. *Bound Lives: Africans, Indians, and the Making of Race in Colonial Peru*. Pittsburgh: University of Pittsburgh Press, 2012.

Oviedo Freire, Atawallpa. *Bifurcación del buen vivir y el Sumak Kawsay*. Quito, Ecuador: Multiversidad Yachay Wasi, 2014.

————. *Buen vivir vs. Sumak Kawsay: Reforma capitalista y revolución alternativa: Una propuesta desde los Andes para salir de la crisis global*. Quito, Ecuador: Ediciones, CICCUS, 2013.

Paredes, Julieta. *Hilando Fino: Desde el feminismo comunitario*. La Paz, Bolivia: El Rebozo Collective, 2008.

Parks, Lisa, and James Schwoch, eds. *Down to Earth: Satellite Technologies, Industries, and Cultures*. New Brunswick, NJ: Rutgers University Press, 2012.

Perez, Emma. *Decolonial Imaginary: Writing Chicanas into History*. Bloomington: Indiana University Press, 1999.

Pérez, Laura. *Chicana Art: The Politics of Spiritual and Aesthetic Altarities*. Durham: Duke University Press, 2007.

————. "Enrique Dussel's *Etica de la liberación*, US Women of Color Decolonizing Practices, and Coalitionary Politics amidst Difference." *Qui Parle: Critical Humanities and Social Sciences* 18, no. 2 (Summer 2010): 121–46.

Piña, Juan Andrés, ed. *Conversaciones con la poesía chilena: Nicanor Parra, Eduardo Anguita, Gonzalo Rojas, Enrique Lihn, Oscar Hahn, Raúl Zurita*. Santiago, Chile: Pehén, 1990.

Pinho, Osmundo. Preface to Portuguese translation of *The Undercommons*. In "Decolonial Gesture," edited by Macarena Gómez-Barris, Marcial Godoy-Anativia, and Jill Lane, special issue, *E-misférica* (2014). Accessed March 20, 2017. http://hemisphericinstitute.org/hemi/emisferica-111-decolonial-gesture/harney#.

Pinto, Jorge. *La Formación del estado y la nación, y el pueblo mapuche: De la inclusión a la exclusión*. Santiago, Chile: Dibam, Centro de Investigaciones Diego Barros Arana, 2003.

Pinto, Maria. "Feminist Constitution." Republished in "Decolonial Gesture," edited by Macarena Gómez-Barris, Marcial Godoy-Anativia, and Jill Lane, special issue, *E-misférica* (2014). Accessed March 20, 2017. http://hemisphericinstitute.org/hemi/en/emisferica-111-decolonial-gesture/galindo.

Poole, Deborah. *Vision, Race, and Modernity: A Visual Economy of the Andean Image World*. Durham, NC: Duke University Press, 1997.

Postero, Nancy Grey. "Andean Utopias in Evo Morales's Bolivia." *Latin American and Caribbean Ethnic Studies* 2, no. 1 (2007): 1–27.

———. *Now We Are Citizens: Indigenous Politics in Postmulticultural Bolivia*. Stanford, CA: Stanford University Press, 2007.

Pratt, Mary Louise. "Arts of the Contact Zone," ed. David Bartholomae and Anthony Petrosky, *Ways of Reading*. New York: Bedford/St. Martin, 1999.

———. *Imperial Eyes: Travel Writing and Transculturation*. London: Routledge, 1992.

Quijano, Anibal. "Coloniality and Modernity/Rationality." *Cultural Studies: The Decolonial Option* 21, issue 2–3 (April 2007): 168–78.

———. "Coloniality of Power, Eurocentrism, and Latin America." *Nepantla: Views from the South* 1, no. 3 (2000): 533–80.

Quimantú. *A Mapuche Collective, Resistencias Mapuche al Extractivismo*. Santiago: Mapuexpress, 2017.

Raheja, Michell. *Reservation Realism: Redfacing, Visual Sovereignty, and Representations of Native Americans in Film*. Lincoln, NE: University of Nebraska, 2011.

Richard, Nelly. *Margins and Institutions: Art in Chile since 1973, Art and Text*. Special issue, vol. 21, 1986.

Richards, Patricia. "Of Indians and Terrorists: How the State and Local Elites Construct the Mapuche in Neoliberal Multicultural Chile." *Journal of Latin American Studies* 42, no. 1 (2010): 59–90.

Richter, Gerhard, ed. *Benjamin's Ghosts: Interventions in Contemporary Literary and Cultural Theory*. Palo Alto, Stanford University Press: 2002.

Rivera Cusicanqui, Sylvia. "The Notion of 'Rights' and the Paradoxes of Postcolonial Modernity: Indigenous Peoples and Women in Bolivia." *Qui Parle: Critical Humanities and Social Sciences*, 18, no. 2 (2010): 29–54.

———. "Ser mujer indígena, chola o birlocha en la Bolivia postcolonial de los años 90," La Paz: Ministerio de Desarrollo Humano, Secretaría Nacional de Asuntos étnicos, de Género y Generacionales, 1996.

Robbins, Nicholas. *Mercury, Mining, and Empire: The Human and Ecological Cost of Colonial Silver Mining in the Andes*. Bloomington: Indiana University Press, 2011.

Robinson, Cedric. *Black Marxism: The Making of the Black Radical Tradition*. Chapel Hill: University of North Carolina Press, 1983.

Rodriguez, Juana. *Sexual Futures, Queer Gestures, and Other Latina Longings*. Durham: Duke University Press, 2014.

Róman-Odio, Clara. *Sacred Iconographies in Chicana Cultural Production*. New York: Palgrave McMillan, 2013.

Roy, Anrudhati. *Capitalism: A Ghost Story*. New York: Verso Books, 2014.

Said, Edward. *Orientalism*. New York: Vintage Books, 1978.

Saldaña-Portillo, María Josefina. *Revolutionary Imagination in the Americas and the Age of Development*. Durham, NC: Duke University Press, 2004.

Salvatore, Ricardo D. *Disciplinary Conquest: U.S. Scholars in South America 1900–1945*. Durham: Duke University Press, 2016.

Sanjines, Javier. *Mestizaje Upside Down: Aesthetic Politics in Modern Bolivia*. Pittsburgh, PA: University of Pittsburgh Press, 2004.

Saskia, Sassen. *Expulsion: Brutality and Complexity in the Global Economy*. Cambridge: Belknap Press, 2014.

Schavelzon, Salvador. *Plurinacionalidad y vivir bien/Buen vivir: Dos conceptos leídos desde Bolivia y Ecuador post-constituyentes*. Quito, Ecuador: Abya Yala, 2015.

Scott, James C. *Seeing Like a State: How Certain Schemes to Improve the Human Condition Have Failed*. New Haven, CT: Yale University Press, 1998.

See, Sarita. "Accumulating the Primitive." *Settler Colonial Studies* 6, no. 2 (2016): 164–73.

Shaeffer-Gabriel, Felicity. "Technologies of Subjectivity and Mobility across the Americas." *American Quarterly* 58, no. 3 (September 2006): 891–914.

Simpson, Audra. "The State Is a Man: Theresa Spence, Loretta Saunders and the Gender of Settler Sovereignty." *Theory & Event* 19, no. 4 (2016).

Singh, Julietta. *Unthinking Mastery: Dehumanism and Decolonial Entanglements*. Durham, NC: Duke University Press, 2017.

Slater, Candace. *Entangled Edens: Visions of the Amazon*. Berkeley: University of California, 2002.

Snavely, Cynthia A. "Native American Spirituality: Its Use and Abuse by Anglo-Americans." *Journal of Religious and Theological Information*, Volume 4, Issue 1 (2001): 91–103.

Snodgrass-Godoy, Angelina. "Converging on the Poles: Law and Inquiry." *Journal of the Amerian Bar Foundation* 30, no. 3 (July 2005).

Spedding, Allison. *De cuando en cuando Saturnina*. La Paz, Bolivia: Editorial Mama Huachaco, 2005.

Stern, Steve. *Resistance, Rebellion, and Consciousness in the Andean Peasant World, 18th to 20th Centuries*. Madison: University of Wisconsin Press, 1987.

Stoler, Ann. *Along the Archival Grain: Epistemic Anxieties and Colonial Common Sense*. Princeton, NJ: Princeton University Press, 2010.

Strosnider, William H. J. "Acid Mine Drainage at Cerro Rico de Potosí II: Severe Degredation of the Upper Río Pilcomayo Watershed." *Environmental and Earth Sciences* 64, no. 4 (2011): 911–23.

Taussig, Michael. *Shamanism and the Wild Man: A Study in Terror and Healing*. Chicago, IL: University of Chicago Press, 1989.

Theidon, Kimberley. *Intimate Enemies: Violence and Reconciliation in Peru*. Philadelphia: University of Pennsylvania Press, 2012.

Troncoso Araos, Ximena. "Mariluán: Lautaro en la encrucijada." *Anales de Literatura Chilena* 4, no. 4 (December 2003): 59–72.

Tuck, Eve and K. Wayne Yang. "Decolonization Is Not a Metaphor," in *Decoloniza-tion: Indigeneity, Education and Society* 1, no. 1 (2012): 1–40.

Tuhiwai Smith, Linda. *Decolonizing Methodologies: Research and Indigenous Peoples*. New York: Zed Books, 1999.

Urry, John. *The Tourist Gaze*. London: Sage Publications, 2002.

Valaskakis, Gail Guthrie. "Indian Country: Negotiating the Meaning of Land in Native America." In *Disciplinarity and Dissent in Cultural Studies*, edited by Cary Nelson and Dilip Parameshwar Gaonkar. New York: Routledge, 1997.

———. *Indian Country: Essays on Contemporary Native Culture*. Waterloo, Ontario: Wilfrid Laurier University Press, 2005.

Valderrama Fernández, Ricardo, and Carmen Escalante Gutiérrez. *Andean Lives: Gregorio Condori Mamani and Asunta Quispe Huamán*. Austin: University of Texas Press, 1996.

Valencia, Sayak. "Interferencias transfeministas y pospornográficas a la colonia-lidad del ver." In "Decolonial Gesture," edited by Macarena Gómez-Barris, Marcial Godoy-Anativia, and Jill Lane, special issue, *E-misférica* 11, no. 1 (2014). Accessed March 18, 2017. http://hemisphericinstitute.org/hemi/es/e-misferica-111-gesto-decolonial/valencia.

Veltmeyer, Henry, and James Petras. *The New Extractivism: A Post-Neoliberal De-velopment Model or Imperialism of the Twenty-First Century?* London: Zed Books, 2014.

Veracini, Lorenzo. *Settler Colonialism: A Theoretical Overview*. New York: Palgrave Macmillan, 2010.

Vich, Victor. "The 'Royal Tour' of Alejandro Toledo." *Journal of Latin American Cultural Studies* 16, no. 1 (March 2007): 1–10.

Viteri, María Amelia, Cultural Imaginaries in the Residential Migration to Cota-chachi, *Journal of Latin American Geography* 14, no. 1 (2015): 119–38.

Viveiros de Castro, Eduardo. "Cosmological Perspectivism in Amazonia and Else-where." Four Lectures Given in the Department of Social Anthropolgy, Uni-versity of Cambridge, February–March 1998. Accessed March 30, 2017. http://haubooks.org/cosmological-perspectivism-in-amazonia/.

———. "Exchanging Perspectives: The Transformation of Objects into Subjects in Amerindian Ontologies." *Common Knowledge* 10, no. 3 (Fall 2004): 463–84. Accessed May 16, 2017. https://muse.jhu.edu/article/171397.

———. "Perspectivismo y multinaturalismo en la América Indígena." In *Tierra adentro: Territorio indígena y percepción del entorno*, edited by Alexandre Surrallése and Pedro García Hierro, 37–80. Lima, Peru: International Work Group for Indigenous Affairs, 2004.

Wang, Guangxing, and Quihao Weng. *Remote Sensing of Natural Resources*. New York: CRC Press, 2013.

Webber, Jeffrey R. *Red October: Left-Indigenous Struggles in Modern Bolivia*. Lei-den, Germany: Brill, 2011.

Weheliye, Alexander. *Habeas Viscus: Racializing Assemblages, Biopolitics, and Black Feminist Theories of the Human*. Durham, NC: Duke University Press, 2014.

Wilson, Pamela, Michelle Stewart, and Amalia Córdova. *Global Indigenous Media: Cultures, Poetics, and Politics*. Durham, NC: Duke University Press, 2008.

Wolfe, Patrick. "Settler Colonialism and the Elimination of the Native," *Journal of Genocide Research* 8, no. 4 (December 2006): 387–409.

Wynter, Sylvia. "1492: A New World View." In *Race, Discourse, and the Origin of the Americas: A New World View*, edited by Vera Lawrence Hyatt and Rex Nettleford, 5–58. Washington, DC: Smithsonian Institution, 1995.

———. "Unsettling the Coloniality of Being/Power/Truth/Freedom: Towards the Human, After Man, Its Overrepresentation: An Argument." *New Centennial Review* 3, no. 3 (September 2003): 257–337.

Zabala, Lourdes. *Nos/Otras en democracia: Mineras, cholas, y feministas, 1976–1994*. La Paz, Bolivia: ILDIS, 1995.

Zurita, Raúl. "Raúl Zurita: Abrir los ojos, mirar hacia el cielo." In *Conversaciones con la poesía chilena: Nicanor Parra, Eduardo Anguita, Gonzalo Rojas, Enrique Lihn, Oscar Hahn, Raúl Zurita*, edited by Juan Andrés Piña, 195–233, 209. Santiago, Chile: Pehén, 1990.

# INDEX

Acción Ecológica (Ecological Action), 33, 141n18, 150n29

Ades, Dawn, 82

African diaspora, transcultural history and, 143n3, 143n8

Afro-Indigenous cultures: *el buen vivir* (good living) practices and, 23–25, 150n13; resistance to hydroelectricity and, 101–6; slave labor and, 159n3

Agamben, Giorgio, 75–76

agrarian reform, spiritual tourism and, 54–55

Aguilar, Laura, 107

Ahmed, Sara, 146n31

Aldred, Lisa, 42

Aldunate Morales, Victoria, 123–24

*Along the Archival Grain* (Stoler), 142n22

Álvarez Gonzalez, Freddy Javier, 22–23

Amazon, colonial representations of, 19–20

Amazon Watch, 150n22

anarchism, history in Bolivia of, 118–20

anarcho-Indigenous feminism: chola market women and, 116–20; mining industry and, 114–16; resistance and, 16, 112–32

Andean cultures: language and mediation of, 61–65; phenomenology in, new settler colonialism and, 39–65; spiritual tourism and, 13–14

Andeanism, spatial imaginaries of, 43

*Andean Lives* (Valderrama Fernández and Escalante Gutiérrez), 58–59

Anderson, Patrick, 126

Anthropocene: Andean phenomenology and, 49, 63–65; extractive capitalism and, 4–5

Anti-Terrorist Law (Chile), 71

Anzaldúa, Gloria, 49

Arauco-Malleco Coordinator (CAM), 73–74

Arguedas, José María, 54

Asociación de Afectados por el Proyecto Hidroelectrico El Quimbo (Association of Affected Peoples of the Quimbo Hydroelectric Power, ASOQUIMBO), 93–96, 109, 136

asymmetrical power relations, Andean phenomenology and, 41–65

Athualpa (Incan King), 44

authenticity: consumption and loss of, 42, 151n2; tourism and desire for, 56–57, 152n15

autopoiesis, 146n26; of biological systems, 18–19

Avilá, Jose, 94

ayahuasca (hallucinogenic plant), 50

Ayala, Matías, 79–80

Aymara Indigenous people, 110–13, 117; anarcho-feminism and, 124–27, 162n33

*ayullu* system, 117–20, 124–25

Barker, Joanne, 135

Beijing Consensus, 139n4

Benjamin, Walter, 77

Bennett, Jane, 100

Berger: Jon, 139n1; Martin, 84–87

Berman, Morris, 146n27

*Beyond Control* (Caycedo), 98

Bhambra, Gurminder K., 148n36

*Bifurcación del buen vivir y el Sumak Kawasay* (Oviedo Friere), 24

Bío Bío region: extractive capitalism in, 8–9, 14–15, 66, 74–77, 85–86, n95; Indigenous films on, 69–74

"The Biopolitics of Settler Colonialism" (Morgenson), 155n17

"Black Mo'Nin" (Moten), 155n23

Black Radical Tradition, 143n5

*Black Reconstruction in America* (Du Bois), 148n39

Blank, Les, 19–20, 149n6

Blest Gana, Alberto, 70, 155n11

Bolivia: anarchism in, 119–20; decolonization in, 120–22, 161n24; extractive capitalism in, xxvii

Braidotti, Rosi, 49

Brazilian Anthropology, 3

Bryan-Wilson, Julia, 151n2

*Burden of Dreams* (documentary), 19–20, 149n6

Burman, Anders, 162n33

Burns, Kathryn, 45–46

Byrd, Jodi, 56–57, 135

Cáceres, Berta, 142n19

cacophony, racial dynamics of, 56–57

Café Carcajada, 112, 126

Caniuqueo, Sergio, 137

Caribbean Afro-diaspora, transcultural history of, 143n3

Caribbean and Community Summit, 25

Casa del Museo de la Moneda (House of the Coin Museum), 110–32

Catholicism: anarcho-feminism and, 128–31; colonialism in Chile and, 73–74; convent system for Indigenous women and, 45–47; syncretism of, 26–27, 111–13

*caudillismo*, 125

Caycedo, Carolina, 15–16, 60, 91–109, 136

Cay Pacha, in Q'ero cosmology, 47–49

ceiba tree, sacred power of, 36–37

Centro Paz y Luz, 40, 50

Cerro Rico mountain, 110–13

*chachawarmi* (gender complementarity), 124–25, 162n33

Chen, Mel, 43

Chiapas conflict, 14–15

Chicana feminism, 9; Andean phenomenology and, 49; decolonization and, 153n46

Childs, John Brown, 143n8

Chile: British imperialist culture in, 82–83; extractive capitalism in, 66; immigration in, 84–87; Indigenous revolutionary struggle in, 69–74; land dispossession and territorial expansion in, 74–77, 84–87

*chola* market women, 11n20, 116–20

Chúngara, Domitila, 115

"Citizen's Revolution" (Ecuador), 27–28

Clark, Timothy, 75

cognition, ecologies of intangibility and, 149n5

cognitive injustice, 99

colonial contract zone, 141n15

*Colonial Habits* (Burns), 45–46

colonialism: Andean phenomenology and, 44–65; Eurocentric philosophy and, 144n10; extractive view of, 5–9; globalization and extension of, 25; in Indigenous films, 69–74; Indigenous perspectives on, 2–5; Indigenous women annd, 117–20; mita (forced labor) during, 111–13; silver extraction and, 157n3; submerged ecology and, xvi–xx; territorial expansion under, 74–77; violence in, 11–12, 148n40

Comité de Amas de Casa (Housewives' Committee), 115

Condori Mamani, Gregorio, 58–59

*The Confluence of Two Rivers* (Stevens), xiii

*Connected Sociologies* (Bhambra), 148n36

Consejo de Todas las Tierras, 74–77

conservation initiatives: Indigeneity as obstacle to, 84–87; land defense initiatives, 135–36

consumption, loss of authenticity and, 42

Coole, Diana, 100–101

Corporación Minera de Bolivia, 114

Corporación Nacional de Desrrollo Indígena (CONADI) (Chile), 75–76

Correa, Rafael, 20–23, 25–27, 30, 32–34

Coryat, Diana, 30, 33

cosmologies, Andean phenomenology and, 47–49

Coulthard, Glen, 113, 135, 160n8

countervisuality, 145n21

criminalization of Indigeneity, 70–74

criollo state, colonialism and, 112, 118–19, 159n5

Crowe, Joanna, 71

Cuenca, Lucio, 86–87

cultural mediation, language and, 58–65

cultural production, spiritual tourism and, 47–48

Cusco (Dunn), 50–51

Dammed Landscapes (Caycedo), 91

Darker Side of the Renaissance (Mignolo), 144n10

data mining, extractive capitalism and, 7–8

decolonial queer femme methodology, xvi–xx, 9–11, 134–38, 146nn28–31; anarcho-feminist intervention and, 120–32; chola market women and, 116–20; cultural mediation and, 63–65

decolonization: anarcho-feminist Indigenous critique of, 110–32; Andean phenomenology and, 49; in Bolivia, 120–22; embodied geographies, 106–8; land dispossession and, 49, 66–69, 153n24; multimedia representation and, 87–90; perceptions of colonialism and, 3–5, 144n11; submerged perspectives on, xiv–xv, 11–12

Decolonizing Methodologies (Smith), 147n32

Decree Law 2.568 (1979) (Chile), 75

de la Cadena, Marisol, 41, 151n1

de la Vega, Garcilaso, 57

Deleuze, Gilles, 6; ecological agency model of, 18–19; radical immanence of, 49

Delgado-P, Guillermo, 143n8

Deloria, Phil, 56–57

Descolonizando La Jagua, 94, 106–8

de Sousa Santos, Boaventura, 98–101, 158n13

despacho ceremony, 41

de Valdivia, Pedro, 73

developmental fallacy, xviii, 145n22; Yasuní-ITT treaty and, 22–23

diasporic knowledge formation, colonial history and, 3–5

digital colonization, surveillance technology and, 96–98

disciplinary conquest theory, 11

double consciousness, submerged perspectives and, 12, 148n39

Doyle, Jennifer, 77

Dreams of Machi Silvia Kallfüman (film), 89–90

Du Bois, W. E. B., 12, sociology 48n39

Dunn, Diane, 50–55, 57–58, 60–61

Dussel, Enrique, xviii, 3, 49, 140n11

Earth (2011) (Galindo), 107–8

Earth Beings (de la Cadena), 41–42, 151n1

ecocide, 141n16

eco-feminism, 3, 145n14, 150n28

ecological governance: Andean cosmology and, 48–49; increase visibility of, 24; law and, 27–29; Napo Wildlife Center and, 35–37

ecology, submerged viewpoint of, xiii–xx

ecophilanthropy movement, 84

ecotourism, Napo Wildlife Center and, 35–37

Ecuador: extractive capitalism in, xxvii, 24–27, 149n11; growing debt burden of, 25–27; Intangible zone, Yasuní culture in, 17–38; regime transition in, 24; Yasuní-ITT treaty and, 12–13

Ecuadorean Constitution of 2008, 21–23, 28–29

Edelman, Lee, 144n13

Eder, Rita, 82

El Ateneo Feminino, 117

"El Buen Vivir: Plan Nacional, 2013–2017" (Ecuador), 26–27

el buen vivir (good living) practices: Afro-Indigenous principles and, 23–25, 150n13; extraction capitalism and, 12–13, 19; institutionalization of, 135–36; socialist compromise of, 25–27

El Mercurio newspaper, 71

El Quimbo Hydroelectric Project, 91, 94–109

El velo de Berta (film), 69–74, 82–83

embodied critique, anarcho-Indigenous feminism and, 112–32

embodied geographies, decolonization, 106–8

Endesa company, 15–16, 80, 94–109

Entre Aguas, 102

Epistemologies of the South (de Sousa Santos), 98–101

Escalante Gutiérrez, Carmen, 58–59

Escobar, Arturo, 3, 143n6, 150n13

¡Escucha Winka! statement, 137–38

Estermann, Josef, 48

Eurocentric philosophy: Andean cosmology and, 48–49; colonialism and, 144n10; extractive capitalism and, 5–9; new materialism and, 100–101

extractive capitalism: Andean phenomenology and, 43–65; Anthropocene terminology and, 4–5; in Chile, 66–67; colonialism and, xvii–xx; colonialism perspective of, 5–9; el buen vivir and concessions to, 26–27; hydroeletricity and, 93–109; legal limitations and, 135–37; racial capitalism and, xxvii, 140nn7–8; religion and early forms of, 46–47; spiritual tourism and, 13, 53–57; surveillance of resources and, 97–98

extractive zones, submerged ecology and, xv–xx

fabulation, spiritual tourism and, 56–57

Fanon, Frantz, 71

fear, colonial legacy of, 44–45

Federación Obrera Femenina, 117

feminism. See also anarcho-Indigenous feminism

"The Feminist Political Constitution of the State," xxvii, 129–31

Ferguson, Roderick, 147n34

films: Indigeneity in Hollywood films, 154n6; by Indigenous filmmakers, 69–74

fire and burning, Indigenous film-makers use of, 75–77

fish-eye episteme: resistance to hydroelectricity and, 101–6; submerged perspectives and, 15–16, 135–37

Fitzcarraldo (film), 19–20, 149n6

"Five Eyes" states, surveillance by, 7–8

forest decimation, Indigenous evacuation and, 83–87

Forest Law of 1931 (La ley de Bosques), 85–86

The Formation of National Indo-American Culture (Arguedas), 54–55

Foucault, Michel, 24–25, 150n18; panopticon of, 6

Four Winds company, 57–58

Fray (Wilson), 151n2

Freudian theory, Andean phenomenology and, 40–41

Friends of the LA River, 106–8

Frost, Samantha, 100–101

Fujimori, Alberto, 54

Galeano, Eduardo, xvi–xvii, 143n8

Galindo: María, 112, 122, 125, 127–31, 159n6; Regina, 107

Garrison, Rebekah, 153n24

Gelles, Paul, 59

gender: anarcho-Indigenous feminism and, 116–20; mining labor and role of, 114–16; Mujeres Creando Comunidad and issues of, 122–27, 161n29

geo-choreographies, 106–8

Gershberg, Seti, 47

Ghostly Matters (Gordon), 147n32

Gilmore, Ruth Wilson, 136
Glissant, Édouard, 1, 8, 143n3
global mapping, extractive capitalism and, 7–8
Global North, Yasuní-ITT treaty and, 21
Global South: biodiversity investment in, 22; feminist perspective on, 144n12, 145n14; scholarly and cultural production in, 97–101
Global Witness, xix
Gordon: Avery, 147n33; Lewis, 3, 143n8, 144n10
governmentality: land management and, 86–87; use of *el buen vivir* by, 24–25, 150n18
Gray, Herman, 147n33, 158n13
Greenbelt Movement, 144n12
Grosfuguel, Ramón, 3
Guattari, Felix, 18–19
Gudynas, Eduardo, xviii, 140n13
Gutierrez-Vilches, Daniel, 86

Hale, Charles, 71, 155n11
Hall, Stuart, 143n7
*Hamlet* (Shakespeare), 80–81
Hanan Pacha, in Q'ero cosmology, 47–49
Harney, Stefano, 86–87, 143n5
Harris, Cheryl, 43
Hayward, Nicole, 128
*The Headlong Stream Is Termed Violent, but the Riverbed Hemming Is Termed Violence by No One* (Caycedo), 97–98
Hemispheric Institute for Performance and Politics, 120–22
Herzog, Werner, 19–20, 149n6
*Hilando Fino* (Paredes), 123
Hill, Michael, 55
historical overdetermination: early colonialism and, 46–47; spiritual tourism and, 44–45
Hochberg, Gil, 76
Hochunk culture, 156n25
*homo sacer* concept, 76–77
Honduras Indigenous activists, attacks on, 142n19

Huaorani culture, 20, 149n8
Huichaqueo, Francisco, xiv–xv, 15, 60, 66–74, 75, 77–83, 87–90, 136
Huilcamán Paillama, Aucán, 76
Huilliche culture, 14–15; Indigenous films of, 69–74; land conservation and, 86–87; water at center of, 80–83
hunger strikes: Mapuche resistance and, 14–15, 76; mining labor resistance and, 115, 126, 160n15
Hydrochina (People's Republic of China), 94
hydroelectricity: land dispossession and, 26–27, 91–109, 157n4; submerged perspectives on, 98–101

Incan Empire: colonial decimation of, 44–65; Indigenous links to, 55–57; sacred sites from, 50–55
Indigeneity: Andean relationality in, 41–65; colonization and, 2–5, 143n3, 143n8; consumption and appropriation of, 42–65; ecotourism and, 35–37; in Ecuadorean Intangible Zone, 17–38; feminist anarchist critique and, 16; forced labor and, 111–16; Indigenous filmmakers on, 69–74; invisibility in extractive capitalism of, xxvii, 6–7; knowledge production and transfer and, 62–65, 147n32, 155n12; media representations of, 71–74, 154n9; philosophical challenges in, 99–101; postdevelopmental representation and, 156n32; race and, 45, 152n9; settler colonialism and, 14–15; spiritual tourism and, 54–55; violent subjugation of, 46–47; white obsession with, 56–57; YASunidos movement and, 30; Yasuní-ITT treaty and, 12–13
Indigenous Law (1993) (Chile), 75–76
*indio permitido* stereotype, 71
industrial fishing, 26–27
Infantes, Petronila, 117
intangibility, Yasuní culture in Ecuador and, 17–38, 134

Inter-American Court of Human Rights, 34

International Monetary Fund (IMF), 25

International Rivers Network, 156n32

*The Intimacies of Four Continents* (Lowe), 142n22

Inti-Raymi festival, 57

Jackson, Jeremy, 134

Janeth Urquía, Lesbia, 142n19

Kallfüman, Silvia, 88–90

*Kalül Trawün—Reunión del Cuerpo* video (Huichaqueo), xv

Kantian philosophy, Andean phenomenology and, 40–41

Kichwa cultue, 20

Klubock, Thomas Miller, 74

knowledge production, racialized politics of, 146n28, 147n32

Kohn, Eduardo, 18, 149n3

*La Frontera* (Klubock), 74

land conservation, Indigenous presence in, 83–87

land dispossession: Chilean "mercy titles," 74–77; colonialism and, 49, 66–69, 153n24; hydroelectric dams and, 91–109; Indigenous struggles against, 70–74; Mapuche resistance to, 83–87

Lange, Lynda, 140n11

language, cultural mediation and, 58–65

Lanigan, Richard, 9

Latin American Center for Social Ecology, xviii

Latin American Observatory of Environmental Conflicts, 86–87

Lautaro (Mapuche warrior), 69–70, 155

*La vida plena Andina*, 48–49

law: criminalization of Indigeneity and, 70–74; ecological governance and, 27–29

Law of Selective Immigration (1845), 84–87

Levil, Rodrigo, 137

Lévi-Strauss, Claude, 144n9

"lifestyle migrations," spiritual tourism and, 50–55, 153n25

*Lonely Planet* travel books, 54–55

*longko* (Mapuche male figure), 79

Lowe, Lisa, 142n22

Lugones, Maria, 3

Luxembourg, Rosa, 160n8

Maathai, Wangari, 144n12

*machi* figure (Mapuche female healer), 78, 88–90

Machu Picchu, 50

Magdalena River, 91, 93–95, 101–6

Maldonado-Torres, Nelson, 3, 44

*manos pintados* ritual, 20–21

Mapuche people: extractive capitalism and, xiv, 14–15, 66–69; Indigenous filmmakers' portrayal of, 69–74; land conservation and, 86–87; self-governance and, 138; territorial resistance by, 74–77; water at center of culture of, 80–83

*Mapuches sospechos*, 71

*Mapuches terroristas*, 71

*maqulia* industry, 114

*Mariluán* (Blest Gana), 70

Marimán, Pablo, 137

Marin Headlands Center for the Arts, xiii

Martínez: Esperanza, 22, 149n9; Jacqueline M., 9–10

Martinez Escobar, Gabriela, 59

Marxism, 113, 119, 160n8

masculinity: anarcho-feminism and, 124–27, 160n9; criminalization of Indigenous masculinity, 71–74; mining and, 114

Maturana, Humberto, 8, 18–19, 146nn26–27, 149n5

Mayan culture, Chiapas conflict and, 14–15

McCully, Patrick, 157n2

media coverage, criminalization of Indigeneity in, 71–74, 154n9 mega-extractive projects: hydroelectric dams as, 94–109, 157n5; racial capitalism and, xviii

Melamed, Jodi, 140n8

*Mencer: Ni Pewma* (film), 66–74, 77–83, 88–90

Mendieta, Ana, 107

Mendoza: Catalina, 117; Monica, 122

Merleau-Ponty, Maurice, xiv, 146n26

*mestizaje*: eco-tourism and, 4, 144n13; spiritual tourism and, 56–57, 152n9, 152n15

Mignolo, Walter, 3, 49, 144n10

militarization: extractive capitalism's use of, 4, 96; of Indigenous territories, 69–70

Millais, John Everett, 80–81

Millalén, José, 137

mind-body dualism, 8, 146n26

mining: anarcho-Indigenous feminism, 114–16; colonial silver extraction, 110–13; in Ecuador, 26–27; environmental impact of, 160n11

Ministry of Economic Policy Coordination (Ecuador), 25, 149n11

Mirzoeff, Nicholas, 97, 145n21

*mita* (forced labor), 111–16, 133

Mitchell, W. J. T., 97

modernist developmental theory, extractive capitalism and, 6–7

Morales, Evo, 24, 113, 125, 130–31

Morgenson, Scott, 75–76, 155n17

Moten, Fred, 86–87, 143n5, 155n23

Movimiento al Socialismo (Ma), 125

Movimiento Nacional Revolucionary (MNR), 119

Mujeres Creando artists, 16, 112–13, 129–31, 159n6; graffiti by, 122; performances by, 120–21

Mujeres Creando Comunidad, 16, 112–32, 159n6; anarcho-feminist intervention and, 120–22; founding of, 122–27

multinaturalist perspectivism, 99–101, 144n9

multiperceptual cosmologies, 142n2

multirelationality, Andean phenomenology and, 40–41

multivalent criticality, anarcho-feminism and, 125

Munay-ki healing rights, 57–58

Musica confederation, 101

Napo Wildlife Center, 34–37

Nash, June, 115

National Authority of Environmental Licenses (Colombia), 94

*National Parks without People? The South American Experience*, 83–87

neocolonialism, submerged ecology and, xvi–xx

neoliberalism: Indigenous visibility and, 24; interdisciplinary approach to, 147nn34–35; nation-making and, 86–87; privatization of Indigenous territories and, 66–69; settler colonialism and, 54–55; spiritual tourism and, 13–14, 47–48; territorial expansion in Chile and, 75–77

new age fantasies: Andean phenomenology and, 42–44; decolonization and, 55–57; spiritual colonialism, 53–55, 57–65, 153n28

new materialism, posthumanism and, 100–101

"no contact" populations, intangibilty of, 20, 22

"no future" theory, 4, 144n13

non-Indigenous scholarship, extractive capitalism and, xix

*No se puede descolonizar sin despatriarcalizar* (Galindo), 127–31

*Nos/Otras en democracia* (Zabala), 114

oil industry, in Ecuador, 17–18, 25–27

oil refineries, Yasuní-Ishpingo-Tambooocha-Tipituni treaty and, 19–23

Orientalism, 43

O'Toole, Rachel Sarah, 159n1

Oviedo Freire, Atwallpa, 23–24, 150n16

Pachamama (deity), 63–65, 135; Andean phenomenology and, 39–42; Rights of Nature and, 28–29

Páez River, 91

Paillán, Jeanette, 69–74

*pailliris* (slag pile workers), 115–16

Paraguay, colonial *reducciones* (land enclosures) in, 7

Paredes, Julieta, 16, 112, 116–27, 159n6

Parks, Lisa, 7–8, 145n23

*pehuen* (Monkey Puzzle) ancestral tree, 135; sacredness of, 73–74, 77–78

Pehuenche culture, 14–15; Indigenous films of, 69–74; land conservation and, 86–87; water at center of, 80–83

*People of the Big Voice* (Jones), 156n25

People's Republic of China: hydroelectric projects in Latin America and, 94; Latin American investment by, 25, 149n11

Pérez: Emma, 3, 9–10; Laura, 3, 5

Pérez Bermúdez, Alfredo, 24

*perrimonton*, Mapuche concept of, xiv, 66–68, 89–90

Peru, agrarian reform in, 54–55

*Phenomenology of Perception* (Merleau-Ponty), 139n1, 146n26

Piedra, Pablo, 25

Pinochet, Augusto, 66, 72, 74–75, 155n15

Pizarro, Francisco, 44

Plurinational Constitution (2011), 113, 125, 128–31

*Poetics of Relation* (Glissant), 1–3, 143n4

posthumanism, new materialism and, 100–101

"Postscript on Societies of Control" (Deleuze), 6

Potosí, Bolivia, 110–13, 113–16

power: Andean asymmetrical relations of, 42–65; extractive capitalism's perspective of, 6; mapping of, 96

primitive accumulation, extractive capitalism and, 113–16, 160n8

private property, spiritual tourism and, 53–55

*Proceso de Comunidades Negras* (PCN), 143n6

*Purgatorio* (Zurita), 79

*Q'ero Mystics of Peru* (documentary), 47

Q'ero peoples, 14; Andean phenomenology and, 39–42; cosmology of, 47–49; Incan heritage of, 45–47, 55–57; spiritual tourism and, 57–65; women's role in culture of, 63–65

Qichua community, ecotourism and, 34–37

Quechua language, cultural mediation and, 58–65

*quemadas* (land burning), 76–77, 79

Quijano, Anibal, xviii, 5

Quimantú, 140n8

Quispe Huamán., Asunta, 58–59

race and racism: extractive capitalism and, xxvii, 140nn7–8; Indigeneity and, 45, 152n9; land conservation and, 84–87; new age countercultures and, 56–57; spiritual tourism and, 51–55

Radar, Susana, 117

Rainforest Action Network, 156n32

Ralco Dam project (1996), 80–83, 95

*Red Skin, White Masks* (Coulthard), 160n8

*reducciones* (land enclosures), Spanish colonialism and, 7, 67

relationality, Glissant's theory of, 1–3

religious-ethical justifications of Spanish colonialism, 44

*Reorder of Things* (Ferguson), 147n34

*represa* (river flow), 96

*Represa/Repression* (Caycedo), 98

*Represent and Destroy* (Melamed), 140n8

reproductive futures, 4, 144n13

*Resistencias Mapuches al Extractivismo* (Quimantú), 140n8

Richards, Patricia, 70, 80

Righs of Nature (Ecuador): concessions to extractive capitalism and, 28–29; Yasuní-Ishpingo-Tambooocha-Tipituni treaty and, 20–21

*The Right to Look* (Mirzoeff), 97
Rios Vivos (Rivers Alive Colombia), 94, 109, 136
Rivera-Cusicanqui, Sylvia, 3, 16, 112, 116–20
Robledo, Jorge, 104–5
rubber economy, violent subjugation of Indigenous cultures for, 46–47

Sacher, William, 18
Sacred Valley of Cuzco, 41–65; geographies of, 50–55
Said, Edward, 43
Saldaña-Portillo, Josephina, 169n9
Salvatore, Ricardo D., 11
Sandoval, Chela, 3
Sassen, Saskia, 139n5
satellite technology, 145n23; global mapping for surveillance and extraction, 7–8; landscape surveillance and, 91
Scott, James C., 6–7, 145n22
See, Sarita, 113, 160n8
self: Andean Indigenous relationality and, 41–65; Western concepts of, 40–41
Serrano, Daniel, 152n15
settler colonialism: Andean phenomenology and, 39–65; elimination of the Native in, 148n43; evacuation of Indigeneity and, 84–87; Indigenous land dispossession and, 14–15, 49, 153n24; new age forms of, 53–55
sexuality, anarcho-Indigenous feminism and, 116–32
Shakespeare, William, 80–81
shamanism, spiritual tourism and, 47–50, 57–58, 60–65, 152n15
Shiva, Vandana, 4, 145n4
Shuar culture, 20, 38
*Silenced Rivers* (McCully), 157n2
Siles Zuazo, Hernán, 161n24
silver extraction, 110–13; as colonial megaproject, 157n3; mita (forced labor) for, 113–16
Sindicato de Minos de Oficios Varios, 117

slave labor, by Afro-Indigenous peoples, 26–27, 111–13, 159n3
Smith, Linda Tuhiwai, 10–11, 147n32
Snodgrass-Godoy, Angelina, 140n8
social ecology, decolonial theory and, 5, 147n33
socialism, compromised of *el buen vivir* by, 25–27
sociology, decolonial theory and, 9–11, 147nn33–35, 148n36
souvenir authenticity, 42, 151n2
sovereignty: extractive captialism's impact on, 28–29; of Indigenous knowledge production, 147n32; Latin anti-imperialism and, 139n4
Speranza, Craciela, 82
spiritual tourism: Andean phenomenology and, 40–65; ayahuasca (hallucinogenic plant) and, 50–55; extractive capitalism and, 13; growth of, 50; heterosexual economy and, 152n15; "lifestyle migrations" and, 153n25; racial dynamics of, 55–57
Stevens, May, xiii, 60
Stoler, Ann, 142n22
Subercaseaux, Pedro, 69–74
submerged perspectives: Andean phenomenology as, 43–65; commodification of water and, 15–16; extractive capitalism and, 11–12; hydroelectric projects and, 98–101; YASunidos as emergence of, 33–34
surrealism: decolonialism and, 87–90; in Latin American art and film, 82–83
surveillance: extractive capitalism and, 7–8, 145n23; of natural resources, 96–98
sustainability, in Andean cosmology, 48–49
"symbolic reoccupation," Mapuche strategy of, 76–77

Tagaeri culture, 22, 38, 149n8
Taripay Pacha, 51
Taromename people, 22, 38, 149n8

Taussig, Michael, 46, 55
*terra nullius* perspective, 85; extractive capitalism and, xxvii, 6–7
*Territories of Difference* (Escobar), 143n6
Texaco Corporation, Yasuní-Ishpingo-Tambooocha-Tipituni treaty and, 19–23
Tompkins, Douglas, 84
*Toward a Sociology of a Trace* (Gray and Gomez), 147n32, 158n13
transfeminism, Indigeneity and, 129–31
trans-women, anarcho-feminism and, 128–31
Tuck, Eve, 49, 153n24
Turpio: Mariano, 41; Nazario, 41

Uku Pacha, in Q'ero cosmology, 47–49
*The Undercommons* (Moten and Harney), 143n5
UNESCO, world heritage sites of, 18
United States, disciplinary conquest theory in, 11
Uribe Vélez, Álvaro, 94

Valderrama Fernández, Ricardo, 58–59
Valencia, Sayak, 129–31
Varela, Francisco, 8, 18–19, 146n26, 149n5
Veracini, Lorenzo, 52
vernacular modernities, 143n7
violence: colonialism and, 11–12, 58–59, 148n40; Indigenous resistance to land dispossession and, 95–96
Viollda, Alberto, 57–58
*Virgen Cerro Rico* (anonymous painting), 110–11
visuality: extraction capitalism and, 5–9, 145n21; surveillance of resources and, 96–98
Viveiros de Castro, Eduardo, 3, 99–101, 144n9, 158n14

*Wallmapu* (film), 69–74
Walsh, Catherine, 3
Wang, Guangxing, 145n25
Washington Consensus, 25, 120, 139n4
water, in Indigenous culture, 80–83
*Ways of Seeing* (Berger), 139n1
*We Eat the Mines and the Mines Eat Us* (Nash), 115
Weheliye, Alexander, 75–76
Weng, Quihao, 145n25
whiteness as property, spiritual tourism and, 43
Wolfe, Patrick, 77, 148n43
women. *See also* anarcho-Indigenous feminism: Catholic colonial socialization of Indigenous women, 45–48; colonialism's impact on, 117–20; Indigenous resistance by, 14–15; in mining, 114–16; in Q'ero culture, 63–65
women of color feminism, 49; decolonial theory and, 5, 145n17
World Watch Institute, 85–86
Wynter, Sylvia, 3, 143n8, 144n11

Yang, K. Wayne, 49, 153n24
Yasuní Biosphere Reserve, 33
Yasuní culture, Ecuadorean Intangible Zone and, 17–38
YASunidos coalition, 12–13, 30–34, 37–38, 136
Yasuní-Ishpingo-Tambooocha-Tipituni (ITT) treaty, 12–13, 19–23; extractive capitalism and, 22–38; YASunidos movement and, 30–34
Yasuní National Park, 17–18
*Yuma: Land of Friends* (video) (Caycedo), 92, 101–6

Zabala, Lourdes, 114, 118
Zurita, Raul, 79–80